25

QUEENS
OF THE
UNDERWORLD

QUEENS
OF THE
UNDERWORLD

A JOURNEY INTO
THE LIVES OF
FEMALE CROOKS

CAITLIN
DAVIES

The
History
Press

To Maureen Gill, Queen of the Bargain.
And in memory of Bruce Gill, with love.

First published 2021

The History Press
97 St George's Place, Cheltenham,
Gloucestershire, GL50 3QB
www.thehistorypress.co.uk

British Library Cataloguing in Publication Data.
A catalogue record for this book is available from the British Library.

ISBN 978 0 7509 9317 3

Typesetting and origination by The History Press
Printed and bound in Great Britain by TJ Books Limited, Padstow, Cornwall.

Trees for LYfe

CONTENTS

PROLOGUE

BLONDE MICKIE

On the morning of Easter Monday 1960, a petite, grey-eyed woman called Zoe Progl set off for work. She was wearing her usual outfit, a sporty tweed suit, brown flat-heeled shoes and a pair of semi-rimless spectacles. Her dyed blonde hair was pulled back into a chic hair bun, and she carried a large black handbag. It was unseasonably warm that April, so instead of her usual leather gloves, she wore a fashionable white nylon pair. The 32-year-old passed quite unnoticed on the train from London to Brighton, just another harmless schoolmarm heading to the seaside, along with thousands of others. But Zoe Progl was a day-tripper with a difference.

Around two o'clock that afternoon, as holidaymakers thronged along the beach and promenade, Zoe made her way to a Regency house in one of the town's most exclusive squares. She knocked on the door of the ground-floor flat, and when no one answered she rang the bell. Zoe was an expert at 'drumming' – ensuring that no one was home when she called – and she knew how to blend into her surroundings as if she belonged.

This was no impulsive trip, the flat belonged to a wealthy wholesale tobacconist who was said to keep a few thousand 'readies' at home, and

Zoe had already spent several days casing the joint. Once she established that the flat was empty, she took a 'loid' from her handbag. It was the main tool of the housebreaker's trade, a narrow strip of celluloid, about 2in wide and sharpened to a fine point. She slipped the loid between the wedge of the door and the lip of the lock and let herself in.

Zoe Progl had been a professional crook for fifteen years; she'd once stolen £250,000 worth of furs in a single evening, and a few months earlier she'd been arrested in London after breaking into a block of flats in St John's Wood and stealing a fur stole, Tiffany jewellery and a fat wad of dollar notes. 'Blonde Mickie', as she was known by the press, was now on bail, but as far as she was concerned, this was simply a licence to go on grafting.

The Brighton flat was sumptuously furnished, but despite rifling through every room, all she found was £11 in cash. Disappointed but not deterred, Zoe headed to a different address and an hour later she was forcing open the door to a seaside mansion. Diamonds were a girl's best friend, she reasoned, and she wanted some new friends. In the master bedroom, she found some choice items of 'tom' – tomfoolery or jewellery – carelessly dropped on a dressing table: rings, bracelets and brooches worth thousands of pounds. Zoe could immediately tell if an item was genuine and she'd recently stolen a diamond ring from a Mayfair apartment worth around £650, the average annual wage for a woman in 1960.

She gathered up the jewellery on the dressing table and put it in her handbag. The woman who owned them wouldn't mind very much, she told herself – no one kept valuables like these without making sure they were well insured. She might keep a piece as a souvenir to attach to her own gold charm bracelet, which now had several pieces lifted from some of the stateliest homes in England, including a miniature gold Cadillac.

Zoe let herself out of the Sussex mansion and returned to London in a merry mood. But a few days later, the Flying Squad arrived at her Clapham flat, and Zoe Progl learned that she'd made a serious mistake. As she'd broken into the Regency flat, the strip of celluloid had torn the right index finger of her fashionable nylon glove. Zoe had left a fingerprint, and Scotland Yard had just caught Britain's No. 1 Woman Burglar red-handed.

She was convicted of housebreaking and sent to Holloway Prison, the most notorious female jail in the UK, to serve two and a half years. But if the authorities thought she would take her punishment, they were wrong. On 24 July 1960, Zoe Progl climbed over the 25ft perimeter wall in her prison-issue bloomers, in the most successful jailbreak in seventy-five years.

She went on the run for forty days, along with her 4-year-old daughter Tracy, and by the time she was recaptured, Zoe Progl was an underworld celebrity. But, back in Holloway once more, and now facing an additional eighteen months, she had the chance to think things over. As she sat alone in her prison cell, Zoe decided she'd had enough of crime. She no longer wanted to be Queen of the Underworld; instead she wanted to forget her criminal past. She would write her memoirs, to serve as a warning to others – crime was no way of life for a woman. 'I *am* deeply sorry,' she confessed. 'I now have the chance of living an ordinary, decent life and fitting into society; the very society which I have abused for so long.'

Zoe owed her three children comfort, security and love, and when the prison gates opened on the morning of her release, Britain's No. 1 Woman Burglar had retired. Her criminal days were over – from now on, she would devote herself to being a good wife and mother.

INTRODUCTION

WOMAN OF THE UNDERWORLD

I'm walking down a quiet residential street in south London on my way to visit Zoe Progl's daughter. It's the summer of 2018 and in my bag, I have a copy of her mother's autobiography, *Woman of the Underworld*, a thrilling tale of a life of crime and her escape from Holloway Prison. A few weeks ago, I posted a photo of Zoe on Twitter, on the anniversary of her jailbreak, and I had no idea her daughter was even alive, until she sent me a tweet, 'Hey, that's my mum!'

I unlatch a wooden gate, climb the steps to a Victorian maisonette, and ring the bell. I'm not sure who or what to expect, but I want to know what happened after Britain's No. 1 Woman Burglar went straight.

When a slim, dark-haired man about my age opens the front door, I hesitate. 'I've come to see Tracy,' I explain.

The man gestures me into the front room, the windows half open on this sunny Sunday morning. Tracy Bowman is sitting on the sofa, dressed in a red tartan shirt and black trousers. She's in her early sixties, blonde hair falling in ringlets around a delicate face, her make-up careful and precise. I'm not sure how to start the conversation, but Tracy exudes an air of total serenity.

'Mum was a burglar,' she says. 'It's nothing for me to hide. I talk about her all the time.' She points to a vase in the corner of the room, 'Those are her ashes right there.'

Tracy's partner, Andy, goes to the kitchen to make tea and I take out my copy of *Woman of the Underworld*. 'Did your mum really write this in her prison cell?' I ask, putting the book on the table.

Tracy nods, 'She wrote the original draft, but then a *News of the World* journalist changed it. He wanted more sex and drugs, and he tried to make everything juicier.'

'Oh,' I say, a little worriedly, because I've recently quoted from *Woman of the Underworld* in a history of Holloway Prison. I look at the book on the table, wondering which parts of the story the journalist changed. But first, I want to show Tracy some old newspaper clippings about her mother's famous jailbreak.

I take out a copy of the *Daily Mirror* from 25 July 1960; the headline is 'Blonde Breaks Out of Holloway'. It includes a blurry headshot of 'Blonde Mickie', as well as an annotated photograph of her escape route, the ladder still in place against the wall. The article begins with a phone call Zoe made to a friend two hours after the escape. 'I'm out ducks,' she told her, 'and I'm alright.'

Tracy reads the first paragraph and laughs, 'Mum wouldn't have said that, she never said "ducks". They've made that up.' Tracy was too young to remember much about the escape, but her mother took her to a caravan park in Devon and 'it was like being on holiday'. After forty days on the run, Zoe was recaptured and sent back to prison and Tracy went to live with a friend of a friend.

'All the gangsters and the villains looked after me,' she smiles. 'I got *great* big chocolate eggs at Easter!'

But she still didn't know about her mother's life as Britain's leading woman burglar. 'Even though I'd visited her at Holloway, I'd always thought she was at the dentist. My friends would ask, "How long has your mum gone to the dentist for, Tracy?" And I'd say, "Seven years".'

We both start laughing, but then I stop, picturing a 4-year-old child who has no idea her mother is locked up in prison.

Andy comes in with the tea and I take out a second newspaper clipping, from 1963. The headline is 'Underworld Queen says: "I abdicate"', and the photograph shows Zoe Progl elegantly dressed in black with newly bleached hair, the perimeter wall of Holloway Prison looming up beside her. She was going to look for honest work, she told the *Daily Mirror*, she'd learned her lesson and 'people who steal should be made to pay back the money'. Tracy reads the article and shakes her head, 'Bloody hell, she would have had to be paying back forever.'

I hand her a third newspaper clipping, from April 1964, entitled, 'The bride who was a gangster's moll'. This time Zoe wears a box hat with a veil; she looks beguilingly over one shoulder, clutching a bouquet of flowers and a large silver horseshoe. She has just 'secretly' married 24-year-old salesman Roy Bowman, a furtive-looking man with slicked back hair. 'He wasn't a salesman,' says Tracy, 'he'd just come out of the merchant navy. And look,' she points at the picture, 'he's wearing a false moustache and goatee because he didn't want to be recognised.'

I say this seems a bit strange when he'd agreed to be photographed for the *Daily Mirror*. Tracy laughs, then she gazes at the photo, 'Isn't mum beautiful? She was such a tiny thing, so delicate.'

According to the *Mirror*, Zoe was no longer a gangster's moll; instead, she was about to become a respectable woman and her new husband promised her children would 'have a future and complete security'.

Tracy finishes reading the clipping and makes a face. 'It was the worst time of my life,' she says, 'having him on the scene. I was safe before Roy. He was an arsehole. We were all petrified of him. He punched us. I weed myself when he came in. He broke mum's jaw and nose.' Tracy stops and shakes her head, 'Mum was such a strong woman, it was odd that she put up with him.'

Zoe eventually split up with her husband after a vicious custody battle, and when I ask what happened next, Tracy relaxes and smiles again, 'Mum went straight back to thieving!'

She did? I sit back in my chair, surprised. I've never read anything about this; I haven't found a single newspaper report on Zoe Progl after her release from Holloway and her marriage to Roy Bowman. So she refused to live the respectable life after all?

Tracy nods, 'She said crime was better than sex; it was the thrill she got. She always said she didn't regret anything.'

But, I say, at the end of her autobiography she says she's very sorry and promises to go straight.

'Mmm,' says Tracy, 'that went well then.'

After Roy Bowman left, her mother's underworld friends started coming round again. 'They were her old associates,' explains Tracy, 'and it was such a buzz, a house full of people, police crashing the door down, she loved it. Our home was a hub. Everyone met there for a roast, to talk about who had nicked what, what jobs were coming up, and all the crooks came to her flat to place orders for what they wanted beforehand.'

One day, while Tracy was sitting doing homework with a friend, three men in balaclavas ran in. 'They'd just robbed a jeweller's. They were trying to burn all the packets the jewellery came in by throwing them on the fire. But it was all normal to me, it wasn't frightening. When I went to my friend's house and had Yorkshire pudding, that was exciting to me! It was drama all the time at home, gangsters and cops, and I was part of it all.'

'Then what happened?' I ask.

Tracy sighs, as if it's inevitable, 'Mum was sent to prison again.'

'She was?' I've never read anything about this either. As far as I knew, Zoe Progl's 1960 conviction for housebreaking, and her subsequent escape and re-arrest, was the last time she was ever jailed.

'It was for fraud,' Tracy explains. 'Then when she came out, she started shoplifting again. She used to go out missing, for days on end. One time, she was caught shoplifting at Cecil Gee's, the menswear shop in Oxford Street. She'd been gone for a week when we got a call from Bromley cops. She'd pulled the sleeves off her coat, she was struggling so much when they arrested her. She went out in a coat and came back in a waistcoat!'

Tracy speaks of her mum with such fondness and a smile that fills her eyes. She's proud to be Zoe Progl's daughter and wants her to be remembered, which is why she responded to me on Twitter. But she's also worried about sounding disloyal.

'Mum lived by her own rules,' she says. 'She had a different set of morals from anyone else I knew. Nothing she did was bad or wrong, she didn't harm anyone … but for us.' Tracy looks at the vase in the corner of the room, 'Sorry, mum, but kids were pushed to one side;

it wasn't glamorous from the inside. She was good fun, but she wasn't maternal. When she was here, she was a great mum.'

Tracy is silent for a minute. 'I never cried when she died. Her funeral was in West Norwood or Croydon, I can't remember, it's all a blur. All the gangsters arrived in Rollers and people were craning their necks to see them. The Rollers stopped and all these little old shrunken men got out with fedora hats on!'

I finish my tea; it's time to go. Andy is heading off to football practice and Tracy is going for her daily swim at a local lido. I ask if she'll sign my copy of *Woman of the Underworld*, and if I can come back another day to ask more about the book.

'Was your mum really Britain's top woman burglar?' I ask, as I stand on the doorstep to say goodbye.

Tracy shrugs, 'I don't know of any others, do you?'

'No,' I say, because I've never heard of a single top woman burglar.

'You would have loved mum,' says Tracy, 'and she would have loved you.'

I smile, feeling pleased. 'Do you think so?'

'Yes. I was a bit worried about meeting you, I thought you might judge her.'

All the way home, I think about the assumptions I'd made about Zoe Progl. I'd read *Woman of the Underworld* and countless newspaper reports about her prison escape, but perhaps I'd slightly dismissed her criminal career, because if she really *was* Britain's top woman burglar, then why hadn't I heard of her? I assumed she'd given up the criminal life, as she promised to do at the end of her autobiography, but she hadn't. Her abdication wasn't true, and neither was her apology. Zoe Progl wasn't sorry, and she hadn't had any regrets; instead, she'd loved it. Crime had been better than sex.

There have been no further books about Zoe Progl; her life hasn't inspired any documentaries, dramas or films, and there has been nothing to set the record straight. I wonder if the same thing has happened with other female crooks. Have they had their stories twisted, or not had their stories told at all? And if Zoe Progl was Britain's No. 1 Woman

Burglar, then who came before and after her? Did she have any predecessors in the world of crime? What about bank robbers, or jewel thieves or smugglers, were there any women? Can I find others who pursued the criminal life, who were respected and had fun? Are there other women out there who were happy to call themselves 'Queen of the Underworld'?

When I get home, I type 'British female criminals' into a Google search and up comes a list of the 'most notorious female criminals in British history'. There are five 'serial killers', a murderer, a suspected terrorist and a pirate. I click on Wikipedia, which lists seventeen women, including several transported to Australia for theft in the eighteenth century, as well as a suffragette. A subcategory provides eighteen English female criminals, but nearly half of these were convicted of murder.

I look up *The Oxford Dictionary of National Biography*, where the category 'law and crime' has around 4,000 entries, but only 5 per cent are women, and many are victims – of murder, abduction, kidnapping, marital abuse – rather than perpetrators. But as for male criminals, they are everywhere, from Robin Hood to Dick Turpin, Jack the Ripper, Dr Crippen, the Great Train Robbers and the Krays. Male crooks have inspired fiction and biographies, feature films, dramas and documentaries. They've been taken seriously and turned into cultural icons, lionised in exhibitions, studied in academic papers, included in the national curriculum for schools. But what about their female counterparts, where are their stories?

A few weeks later, I take the train to the National Justice Museum in Nottingham, which has the largest collection of objects and archives relating to law, justice, crime and punishment in the UK. If I'm going to find some female crooks, this seems like a good place to start. I enter the museum's Crime Gallery and come face to face with the wooden dock from Bow Street Magistrates' Court, one of London's most famous courts. I step up onto the dock and take my place in the middle, holding onto the thick black railings.

Opposite is a mural of twenty people who once stood here waiting to hear their fate. I can only see three photos of women. One is a group of suffragettes; another is Katherine Gun, who exposed a US plot to spy on the UN in 2004. The third, strangely, is the singer Ms Dynamite, tried at Bow Street in 2006 for slapping a police officer.

I keep looking at the mural. Surely there are other women who could be included here? What about Zoe Progl? She appeared in the Bow Street dock in the autumn of 1960, after the Flying Squad tracked her down to a flat in London and ended her forty days on the run.

I wander around a display about the Great Train Robbers who, in 1963, stole £2.6 million from a Royal Mail train. The museum certainly has a lot of artefacts: a glass cabinet containing keys and monopoly money, a map and floor plan of the farm where the gang hid out, and a combat jacket worn by one of the robbers. I move on to another display about Cesare Lombroso, the 'father' of modern criminology, whose book *Criminal Woman, the Prostitute, and the Normal Woman*, first published in Italian in 1893, was regarded as a classic. He argued that the majority of female criminals are 'merely led into crime by someone else or by irresistible temptation'. Women were naturally conservative, he explained; we were also clumsy and lacked courage.

I walk next door to another exhibition, 'Liberated Voices: Stories of Women (In)Justice', where I read about Charlotte Bryant, hanged for poisoning her husband in the 1930s, and Beatrice Pace, acquitted of murdering her abusive husband in the 1920s. Then comes Alice Burnham, one of three 'Brides in the Bath', murdered by George Joseph Smith in 1913. And here is the actual bath she was killed in. It can't be, I think, as I walk cautiously around the Edwardian bathtub. Why would anyone put that on display?

I've been at the National Galleries of Justice for a few hours now and I've seen quite a few victims, but I still haven't found one successful female crook. I head to the courtroom, but I've missed today's performance, a re-enactment of the trial of Joan Phillips, a 'legendary Nottingham highwaywoman who passed herself off as a man'. At last! A real-life criminal woman.

I read some of the papers laid out on the tables. Joan was executed in 1685 and hanged on the gallows in Nottingham. But I later realise that the main source of her story appears to be a highly unreliable eighteenth-century book, whose author was known for making things up.

If I can't find many criminal women online or in the National Galleries of Justice, then I'll have to begin with the few women who have been remembered and start off as far back as I can go …

1

MARY FRITH JACOBEAN PICKPOCKET AND FENCE

At the upper entrance to Shoe Lane, an ancient alley in the City of London, roadworks are blocking the traffic. A lorry attempts to deliver a load of gravel and as a bus inches its way onto Charterhouse Street, drivers begin sounding their horns. I head down Shoe Lane and away from the noise, passing modern office blocks with walls of reflective glass and then the medieval church of St Andrew Holborn. The lane is wide, but no one is about, aside from a woman rattling the wheels of her suitcase along the pavement.

Back in the seventeenth century, this alley was cobbled, and lamp lit, a claustrophobic passage lined with timber-framed houses that would be burnt to cinders in the Great Fire of London. There were tenements here, as well as businesses belonging to signwriters and broadsheet designers. Street vendors gathered to sell their wares on Shoe Lane – the fishwives, orange-women and gingerbread men – while visitors flocked to the local cockpit and alehouses. Diarist Samuel Pepys, who was born nearby, described one as 'a place I am ashamed to be seen to go into'.

The area was known for thieves and 'bad women' and featured in several criminal trials. One afternoon, a gentleman strolling down Shoe Lane was thrown to the ground by a gang of pickpockets, and a few seconds later, his valuable watch was gone.

The City of London was home to around 200,000 people in the early 1600s, but there was no police force as such. Watchmen, largely untrained and ill-equipped, patrolled the dark alleys with staffs and lanterns, while parish constables arrested people after they'd already been caught. Most victims of crime had to catch the perpetrator themselves, to raise the 'hue and cry' and call for constables and passers-by to help, then take the offender to court at their own expense. If they couldn't find assistance in time, the thief simply escaped through the narrow, twisting streets.

I carry on down Shoe Lane and the alley opens up, a nearby bar advertises a five o'clock cocktail club, while a woman sits on the pavement holding a sign that says 'hungry'. The lane narrows again, and I come to a security booth and rows of City of London bollards set across the width of the street. The City has traditionally been London's financial heart, and this is a sensitive area in terms of security.

Today, Shoe Lane is home to accountancy, law and banking firms, including the European headquarters of the American giant Goldman Sachs. I look down the lane and see a man suddenly stop and take a card from his pocket, then he flicks it against a black shiny wall. Part of the wall opens, the man slips inside, then the door closes and becomes a blank wall again.

It seems like a very secretive way to go to work, and I approach the security booth to ask if the building is part of Goldman Sachs. But the guard inside doesn't answer. Instead, he looks over my shoulder as if I'm a decoy whose job it is to distract him. I point down the alley and ask again, 'Is that shiny black wall part of Goldman Sachs?' Still the security guard doesn't answer. I tell him I'm looking for where the infamous Moll Cutpurse once ran her business. Isn't it funny, I ask, that the country's most notorious criminal worked here and now it's home to investment bankers?

The security man finally relaxes. 'Nothing changes,' he laughs, 'nothing changes.'

A few moments later, I emerge onto Fleet Street, with the dome of St Paul's Cathedral in the distance. On my right is the front entrance to Goldman Sachs, an enormous columned building adorned with a gold-rimmed clock. On the other side of the road, and almost directly opposite, is Salisbury Court. So it was here, somewhere on this spot, that the most famous female criminal of the seventeenth century ran her business.

The story of Moll Cutpurse has appeared in numerous books and articles, and she is one of very few female criminals still, to some extent, known today. Yet, the reported details of her life are frequently contradictory and confusing. Her real name was Mary Frith and she was born in 1584, just north-east of Fleet Street. Her father was a respectable shoemaker, and her parents lavished their only child with tenderness and love. But Mary displayed a 'boyish, boisterous disposition' right from the start, and she couldn't endure the sedentary life expected of girls. She was a 'tomrig' – a rude, wild tomboy, who delighted only in boys' play and pastimes. While other girls were content to sit and hem a kerchief, Mary escaped to the Bear Garden in Southwark, on the south bank of the Thames, to enjoy the sport of bear baiting and other manly pursuits. 'Why crouch over the fire with a pack of gossips,' she apparently asked, 'when the highway invites you to romance?'

In the summer of 1600, at the age of 15, Mary Frith was charged with stealing 2s 11d from a man in Clerkenwell, snatching a purse from his breast pocket. She was arrested with two other women, Jane Hill and Jane Styles. Two years later, she was arrested again, this time alone, for stealing a purse. Mary was then put on a ship bound for the English colony of Virginia in North America in an attempt to reform her, but she escaped before it set sail and returned to London. Here, she joined a different sort of colony, a nation of land pirates – the cutpurses and pickpockets who haunted the city's theatres and streets. 'I could not but foresee the danger,' she recalled, 'but was loath to relinquish the profit.'

It was around this time that Mary also became an entertainer, performing inside taverns, alehouses and tobacco shops, as well as on the streets. She dressed in men's breeches and doublet, held a sword in her hands and accompanied herself on a lute. Crowds gathered to watch, while her pickpocket gang stole the onlookers' watches and gold.

Mary didn't just dress in male attire, she was said to have the manner and ways of a man. Her voice and speech were 'masculine', she loved to swear and drink ale, and claimed to be the first woman to smoke tobacco. Soon she earned the name Moll (or Mal) Cutpurse – Moll was a nickname for Mary, as well as a common term for a disreputable young woman or prostitute.

Mary's habit of wearing men's clothes was regarded by many as a sin. Preachers condemned the practice from the pulpit and quoted from the Old Testament: 'The woman shall not wear that which pertaineth unto a man, neither shall a man put on a woman's garment: for all that do so *are* abomination unto the LORD thy God.'

Dress was carefully regulated in Jacobean England; clothes indicated rank and social class. Only queens and kings, for example, could wear purple silk, gold cloth, or garments trimmed with ermine. Dress also served as a way to 'to discern betwixt sex and sex', as Philip Stubbs, a Puritan pamphleteer, explained. Women who violated the rules were 'monsters of both kinds, half women, half men'. Breeches revealed legs and a crotch, normally hidden by long skirts, and so a woman who dressed like a man was regarded as promiscuous and sexually insatiable.

A young servant in Perth was imprisoned for 'putting on men's clothes upon her', while one London woman was made to stand on the pillory after travelling round the City 'appareled in man's attire'. In 1620, two pamphlets were published to address the issue, *Hic Mulier: or The Man-Woman*, and *Haec-Vir: or The Womanish Man*. The first criticised women for becoming too masculine – in dress, mood, speech and action – while the second argued that times had changed and so had custom and fashion. If men were dressing up in ruffs and earrings, fans and feathers, then what could women do but 'gather up those garments you have proudly cast away'?

Some women donned men's clothes to follow the latest trends, while others used them in order to escape – from a violent marriage, capture or prison. On a practical level, men's clothes gave more freedom of movement; it was easier to walk, run and ride a horse in breeches than a cumbersome skirt.

Mary Frith appears to have worn men's attire both to pursue a career as an entertainer and to further her criminal activities. Soon, she attracted the attention of the nation's playwrights and in 1611, she inspired the central character in Thomas Middleton and Thomas Dekker's comedy, *The Roaring Girl*. It was performed at the Fortune Theatre, one of the largest and best-known theatres just outside the City of London. The Roaring Girl was an outlandish figure, a 'Mad Moll', a 'Mistress/Master', who frequented taverns, mocked the police and was well known in the underworld. But she also provided the moral heart of the play, saving two star-crossed lovers who'd been forbidden to marry.

Moll herself was chaste and swore more than once that she would never marry. 'A wife, you know, ought to be obedient,' she explained, 'but I fear me I am too headstrong to obey, therefore I'll ne'er go about it.'

In April 1611, Mary Frith herself took to the stage of the Fortune Theatre in an afterpiece to sing, play the flute and banter with the 2,000-strong audience. But although she wore men's clothes, Mary told the spectators that if any of them thought she was a man they could come to her lodgings where 'they should finde that she is a woman'. So scandalous was her behaviour – women would not be allowed to perform on the English stage until 1660 – that Mary was arrested and sent to Bridewell, a prison on the banks of the Fleet River.

Not long after her release, however, a showman bet £20 that she wouldn't ride from Charing Cross to Shoreditch on horseback, in breeches and doublet, boots and spurs. Mary accepted the challenge and added a trumpet and banner as well. She set out from Charing Cross on Marocco, a famous performing animal, and it was only as she reached Bishopsgate that an orange seller recognised her and set up the cry, 'Mal Cutpurse on horseback!' Instantly, she was surrounded by a noisy mob 'hooting and hollowing as if they had been mad'. 'Come down, thou shame of women!' they cried. 'Or we will pull thee down.' Mary spurred on her horse, managed to reach Shoreditch, and claimed her £20.

But she was soon back in Bridewell again. On Christmas Day 1611, Mary Frith was arrested with 'her petticoat tucked up about her in the fashion of a man' and taken to prison. A few days later, she was summoned before the Bishop of London to answer charges of public immorality by wearing 'undecent and manly apparel'. She confessed to having frequented most of the 'disorderly & licentious places in this

Cittie' and appearing at the Fortune Theatre 'in mans apparel & in her boots & with a sword by her side'. She admitted swearing and cursing, associating with ruffians and getting drunk, but she vehemently denied the charges of being a prostitute and pimp who drew 'other women to lewdnes'. Mary was 'heartely sory' for her dissolute life and earnestly promised to 'carry & behave her selfe ever from hence forwarde honestly soberly & womanly'.

Her punishment came on 9 February 1612. She was made to do penance standing in a white sheet at Paul's Cross, an open-air pulpit in the grounds of St Paul's Cathedral, during Sunday service. 'She wept bitterly and seemed very penitent,' noted one observer, 'but it is since doubted she was maudlin drunk.' Her gang, meanwhile, were busy slashing the clothes of the onlookers, stealing their goods and sending them home half-naked.

By the end of that year, Mary Frith had turned her back on the world of entertainment and in March 1614, she married Lewknor Markham in Southwark. He may have been the son of Gervase Markham, author of *The English Huswife, Containing the Inward and Outward Virtues which Ought to Be in a Complete Woman*. But it's unclear if Mary ever lived with her husband. Instead, it appears to have been a marriage of convenience for she kept her legal status as a single woman. As a feme sole, she had the right to own property, make contracts and run a business. But when she was later sued for unpaid bills, Mary claimed the status of a feme covert – a married woman. This meant she was effectively a child with no legal liability for any criminal act; a defence that would be used by female crooks right into the nineteenth century.

Within a few years of her marriage, Mary Frith established herself in a new form of crime by turning her house on Fleet Street into a warehouse for stolen goods. The house stood two doors from the Globe Tavern, a popular watering hole on the north side of Fleet Street, near the corner of Shoe Lane. It became a 'kind of Brokery', she explained, for jewels, rings and watches, all of which had been 'pinched or stolen any manner of way, at never so great distances from any person'. Highwaymen and cutpurses brought in stolen watches and jewellery to sell, while those who'd been robbed came looking for their property.

Mary compared her business to the Custom House, with its detailed record of imported goods, and boasted that she had regulated the process of crime by introducing 'rules and orders'. When a victim came for help, they were questioned about the circumstances of the theft, then Mary circulated a description of the missing item to her 'agents'. The victim was invited to call back in a day or so, to retrieve their stolen property and pay Mary a finder's fee.

The business bordered 'between illicit and convenient', she admitted, but it provided a better service for victims than the forces of law and order. If a robbery was committed in London one evening, then Mary knew all about it by early the next day – and had a full inventory of what had been taken. Among the stolen goods were gemstones, then arriving in London from all over the world, whether sapphires from India, rubies from Burma, or emeralds from Colombia.

The early seventeenth century was a time of conspicuous consumption, the city's merchants wore rich, colourful clothes adorned with diamonds, and for a thief there could be easy pickings. Most jewellery, however, was stolen through burglary or housebreaking. In 1590, a well-known gang of women – all called Elizabeth – were found guilty of stealing rings set with rubies and emeralds from houses in north London. All three were found guilty and hanged.

Mary Frith ran her Fleet Street business perfectly openly. It wasn't until 1691 that a receiver of stolen goods could be prosecuted as an accessory to theft, and only then after the thief had been convicted. She was also a useful contact for the authorities, as she knew all the thieves and cutpurses in London.

In February 1621, a gentleman called Henry Killigrew was robbed one Saturday night, and the very next day he came to Mary's house, aware that she'd helped many people who'd 'had their purses cut or goods stolen'. Henry had been propositioned by a 'nightwalker' while strolling down Blackhorse Alley, and as he was doing up his trouser buttons, he realised eight pieces of gold were missing from his pockets. The parish constable arrested the suspected thief, Margaret Dell, and took her to the Fleet Street brokery to be cross-examined. When Margaret's furious husband demanded her release, Mary explained she had a licence to examine and interrogate suspected thieves and advised him to leave before he was beaten up.

But then a farmer was robbed on Shoe Lane and when he came to Mary's house for help, he spied his own watch hanging in her window. The farmer returned with a constable, and this time Mary Frith was sent to the most feared prison in London, Newgate. She pleaded not guilty, the farmer had made a mistake, it wasn't his watch at all. When the constable attempted to produce the crucial piece of evidence, the watch had gone, stolen out of his pocket by one of Mary's thieves. The Lord Mayor was 'very much incensed at this affront', and she was warned to behave, 'which I took very good heed of, resolving to come no more into their Clutches, and to be more reserved and wary in my way and practise'. The jury were forced to acquit her, and Mary Frith went straight back to thieving. Considering she had now been operating as a criminal for some twenty years, her time in prison had been brief, for she had contacts within the judiciary and constables and prison turnkeys 'retained to my service'.

She made friends with a new sort of thieves, the Heavers, who stole shop books as they lay on a counter, and the Kings Takers, who ran by shops at dusk to 'catch up any of the Wares or Goods'. Once again, Mary mediated between thief and owner, returning the shop books, which included a record of sales, orders and receipts, to shopkeepers for a fee. She also expanded into forgery, and apparently worked as a pimp, procuring young women for men and, more unusually, male 'stallions' for middle-class wives, chosen to 'satiate their desires'.

Mary was an outlandish criminal, but she was also portrayed as a staunch Royalist who committed 'many great robberies' against the Roundheads during the Civil War. When she heard that General Fairfax, their commander-in-chief, was en route to Hounslow Heath, she rode forth to meet him and demanded he stand and deliver. When the general tried to resist, she shot him through the arm and killed two of his horses. Mary was captured and taken once more to Newgate but escaped the gallows after bribing General Fairfax with £2,000.

In the summer of 1644, Mary Frith was released from Bethlem Hospital, better known as Bedlam, although it's not known why she'd been admitted to an institution for the insane in the first place. After this, she settled down to a contemplative life, reading romances, hiring three maids and 'intending now at last to play the good House-wife'. She died a wealthy woman on 26 July 1659, aged 74, and was buried in nearby St Bridget's churchyard, with a marble stone over her grave and an epitaph composed by the great poet John Milton.

St Bridget's church is just a few minutes' walk from the site of Mary Frith's brokery. Today it's called St Bride's and its name is spelt out in gold letters above the entrance gate. I sit down on a bench in front of the church, and the noise of the city traffic softens until it sounds like distant waves. On the floor before me are tombstones, but the inscriptions are so faded I can barely read a word. A man appears, wearing a white jacket and a nametag that says 'verger', so I stop him and ask, 'Was Moll Cutpurse buried here?'

The verger looks confused. 'Who?'

'Moll Cutpurse, the most famous female criminal of the seventeenth century?'

The verger shakes his head, he hasn't heard of her.

'Her real name was Mary Frith,' I explain. 'She died in 1659, and she was buried right here at St Bride's?'

The verger shrugs, lots of people are said to have been buried here, but the Great Fire of London left the church in ruins and so did bombing raids during the Second World War. I ask if anyone has ever come here wanting to see the last resting place of Moll Cutpurse, but the verger gives a final shake of his head and disappears into the church.

Mary Frith's legend has lived on, however. Not only was she immortalised on stage in the *Roaring Girl*, but three years after her death, her autobiography was published, and it promised to tell the whole truth about her adventurous life.

I'm standing at a counter in the British Library, waiting to see the world's only surviving copy of *The Life and Death of Mrs. Mary Frith. Commonly Called Mal Cutpurse. Exactly Collected and now Published for the Delight and Recreation of all Merry disposed Persons.* I've ordered it in advance, and it turns out to be a very small book, only slightly wider than my mobile phone. It has a beautiful chestnut-coloured leather cover and I inspect the scratches on the front, impressed that this is nearly 400 years old. On the spine are the words 'Life of Mary Frith' and it seems a little odd that this is the shortened version of the full title.

I sit down at a table and open the book. The paper inside has grown beige with age and feels like cloth, while the pages are so small there is only room for a couple of sentences. It begins with an address 'To the Reader', promising a true account of the 'Oracle of Felony, whose deep diving secrets are offered to the World entire'. There has never been another woman like Moll Cutpurse, the reader is told, and the author hopes there never will. 'She was like no body … throughout the whole Course of History or Romance.' Moll Cutpurse was in a category of her own.

I flick through a short biography, until I come to Mary Frith's own diary. 'All people do justly owe to the world an account of their Lives passed,' she begins, entreating her readers to 'hear me in this my Defence and Apology'. But she quickly changes tack, and for the next 146 pages she relives her 'Pranks and Feats' with relish.

The Life and Death of Mrs. Mary Frith is a difficult document to read, and it takes me a while to follow the story. Not only is it written in script that is centuries old, but I'm not clear who is telling this tale. There are times when I think I can hear Mary Frith speaking, when she talks about her friends or beloved pet dogs, but there's also a more dominant voice, full of literary and Classical allusions.

There are also lots of stories missing from this diary that I've read elsewhere as biographical fact. It only begins at around the age of 20, so there is nothing about her childhood, and her age and date of birth appear to be wrong. Mary makes no reference to her groundbreaking performance at the Fortune Theatre in 1611, although she briefly mentions being taken to court for wearing manly apparel. She doesn't describe any attack on General Fairfax at Hounslow Heath or her admission to Bedlam. And as for her marriage to Lewknor Markham, she doesn't write about that at all.

At the end of the book, Mary Frith is on her deathbed, offering her penitence and deploring her 'former course of Life, I had so profanely and wickedly led'. She tells the reader that she has left no will – but she did leave a will, and she wrote it in her married name of Mary Markham.

I close the book and balance it in my hand again. Did Mary Frith actually write this? Did she even know how to write? The introduction says she had been taught to read 'perfectly', but that didn't necessarily mean she could write and, even if she did, would she really have written this on her deathbed? Did she, as some have suggested, dictate the autobiography to someone else? Shakespeare scholar Gustav Ungerer believes that the book was written by a team of male writers, hired by the publishers to capitalise on her fame. If that's the case, then this 'diary' can't be seen as a credible source, even though it has been repeatedly re-published and quoted from as if Mary wrote it herself.

I go up to the enquiries desk to ask for more details and wait while the woman behind the counter inspects the book. She notes that it was rebound in 1981 by the British Library, so the chestnut leather cover may not be a few hundred years old after all. The British Library catalogue names the author as Mary Frith, yet no one actually knows if she wrote it. Was she really a Royalist, or was this just because her diary was published once the monarchy was back on the throne? Did she ever ride through London on a performing horse? Did Milton write her epitaph? Was she a highway robber at all?

These questions didn't seem to bother Victorian writers, who plundered freely from Mary's 'diary'. Some two centuries after her death, Charles Whibley published *A Book of Scoundrels*, in which he included just one woman, and that was Moll Cutpurse, 'the Queen-Regent of Misrule'. Another Victorian writer, Arthur Vincent, also included Mary in his book, *Lives of Twelve Bad Women*, assuring his readers that he had drawn on 'the best available resources' and that his facts were supported by 'authentic records'. He described Moll as vulgar and brutal, a procuress whose masculine ways made her 'a pioneer'.

It is as a pioneer that Mary Frith is now being reclaimed and celebrated as a role model for girls. The Museum of London has hosted a talk for children called 'The Legend of Moll Cutpurse', while the Wallace Collection featured her in a drama and history workshop for schools. In 2014, when the Royal Shakespeare Company staged a new production of *The Roaring Girl*, actor Lisa Dillon described Moll Cutpurse as 'the original girl power, she was a dynamite cool, cool chick'. Others have reclaimed her as a queer icon, and a seventeenth-century 'gender-bending rogue'.

Images of Mary Frith can still be found in art and museum collections all over London, but as with her biography, it's difficult to pin down who is being represented and why. The National Portrait Gallery owns ten images of Moll Cutpurse, including a woodcut advertising her appearance on stage in 1611, in which she is a feminine figure with downcast eyes, theatrically dressed in male clothes, with breeches and a large hat. Reference curator Paul Cox has worked at the National Portrait Gallery for two decades, but it's only in the last few years that people have begun to ask to see the prints of Moll Cutpurse. 'The requests have increased,' he says. 'I put this down to recent academic interest in controversial women from history.'

The Museum of London holds four images of Mary Frith, including an engraved portrait made in the 1660s, in which she has the face of a slightly wizened man, dressed in a long doublet with a wide-brimmed hat on her head. 'It is a loosely Puritan look and very definitely male attire,' explains Hazel Forsyth, senior curator of medieval and early modern collections. 'Men's garb was easier to move around in and if she was thought of as a man, then that gave her opportunities and flexibility.'

Hazel first came across the portrait in the museum's print collection while putting together an exhibition on Samuel Pepys. She has since used the image during illustrated talks on seventeenth-century jewel theft, a subject she's an expert in. 'People slightly laugh when I show it,' she says. 'Generally, they have never heard of her. But her brokery was very clever.'

So what crimes did Moll actually commit? 'I think she sailed very close to the wind,' says Hazel, 'and she was clearly a pickpocket. The fact she wore men's clothing is not enough to have caused such notoriety on its own.'

But despite Mary Frith's criminal skills and her longevity in the underworld, her story has always revolved around the clothes she wore and the nature of her gender and sexuality. Was she a woman, a man, neither, or both? In the seventeenth century, she was described as a hermaphrodite in 'Manner as well as in Habit', but at her death this was 'found otherwise', suggesting her body was subjected to close examination. Victorian writers cast her in a maternal role within her gang of pickpockets and described her as the 'neatest of housewives'. But she was still a stranger to the 'soft delights of her sex', 'by accident a woman, by habit a man'.

The emphasis on Mary Frith's sexual life continues today. At London's Clink Prison Museum, she appears in a small Rogues Gallery just by the exit door, along with Colonel Blood, an 'improbable rascal', and Claude Duval, the 'Dandy Highwayman'. There is no mention of her famous Fleet Street brokerage. Instead, Mary was 'a brothel keeper, though she seems to have had no interest in sex herself'. An online war-gaming company has produced a miniature 'Moll Cutpurse – highway robber', in which she wears a large, feathered hat and breeches and holds both a gun and a sword. She's also wearing sunglasses and her shirt is half open, revealing a large naked breast. She is designed to be a 'pin-up', explain the manufacturers, and is 'not necessarily historically correct'.

The story of Mary Frith has never been historically correct. She was a performer who took part in her own myth-making; a 'Queen Regent of Misrule', who turned the social order on its head. But what do we really know about Mary Frith, and which of her portraits – if any – resemble the real person? She was clearly subversive and went places and did things women weren't supposed to do, frequenting taverns and appearing on stage. But while she may have apologised to the Bishop of London for her dissolute life and offered her penitence in her deathbed diary, she doesn't appear to have been that repentant. She was an outlaw who revelled in breaking criminal law and in breaking society's laws. But her 'masculine ways' have overshadowed any detailed analysis of her criminal career, and even today she's better known for wearing breeches than for her Fleet Street brokery.

Mary Frith seems to have worked independently as a criminal, running her own business and operating in a world largely dominated by men, whether thieves, victims or constables. But another Queen of the Underworld, who was based just half a mile north of Fleet Street, would take another approach. Unlike Mary, she worked closely with a small gang of women – and their targets were specifically men.

ANN DUCK
EIGHTEENTH-CENTURY STREET ROBBER

One snowy December evening in 1743 two young women were walking up Snow Hill, just west of the bustling Smithfield Market in the City of London, when they met a gentleman out for a stroll. 'My Dear,' said Ann Duck, 'it is a very cold Night, suppose you, this young Woman and I, were to go to a House, I know you will be so good as to give us a Dram this cold Evening.' The gentleman agreed, and off he went with Ann Duck and her companion Ann Barefoot to a pub near Chick Lane, one of the most disreputable streets in eighteenth-century London.

The landlady showed them up the stairs. A bowl of punch was called for and then another. The man began to be 'very rude' towards Ann Barefoot – ignoring her friend because he didn't like her 'tawny Complexion' – and she took affront at the gentleman's behaviour. Did he think they were 'Women of the Town'? If he did, then he was very much mistaken, for both were married and had very good husbands. They had never in their lives gone into a house with a strange man, and he should 'take it as a particular Favour'.

At this point, the landlady returned with a fresh bowl of punch, drank a glass to the man's good health and assured him that Ann Duck and Ann Barefoot were 'as modest Girls as any in London'. With the punch finished, the man began to be very merry indeed and the 'modest girls' got down to business. Ann Duck threw him on the bed and held him down with all her strength, while Ann Barefoot picked his pocket, taking his watch and 22s in silver.

Then Ann Duck gave her usual signal – a knock of the foot – and up came one of her bullies or 'husbands'. Bullies were 'lewd, blustering fellows', explained one guide to London criminals. 'Their rendezvous is among bawds and whores, they eat their bread, and fight their battles.' But while the men may have received a share of the spoils, they were hired accomplices rather than pimps.

The bully swore at the gentleman who'd been robbed by Ann Duck, and asked 'what Business he had there, in Company with his Wife', at which the victim took fright and ran down the stairs crying, 'Thieves! Murder! I am robb'd of my Watch and Money!'

Later that night, the gentleman returned with a constable and Ann Duck was carried to the local Watch House, where suspected offenders were questioned and held overnight. She was then sent to Newgate to await trial, but 'was so fortunate … to be acquitted'.

Fortune did seem to smile on Ann Duck when it came to being acquitted. But then she was a member of the Black Boy Alley Gang, one of the most fearsome groups of street criminals in the capital. Over one week in August 1744, the gang attacked and robbed dozens of men, making 'a noise like a parcel of ravening wolves'. When one gang member was captured and taken to the Watch House, the others broke in and rescued him, firing pistols at neighbours who were shouting 'Murder! Murder!' from their windows.

The press seemed intent on fuelling a moral panic about street violence, portraying the gang as insolent and barbarous, committing crimes day and night, in contempt and defiance of the law.

The Black Boy Alley Gang numbered around twenty to thirty men and boys, and their captain appeared to be 19-year-old Richard Lee, known as Country Dick, a little fellow with 'a bold and daring Spirit'. Other men included Thomas Wells, a lamplighter whom Ann Barefoot described as her husband. There were at least nine women in the gang, who were sometimes known as the Black Boy Alley Ladies, and they either led street robbery attacks or fenced the stolen goods. Many of the women were called Ann – one of the most popular female names of the time – and Ann Duck had the worst reputation of all. The young woman with a 'tawney' brown complexion would be arrested – and acquitted – nineteen times for theft, assault and highway robbery. She was one of the most notorious street robbers in London, and her base was Black Boy Alley.

I'm walking up Farringdon Street, heading north towards Farringdon Station, looking for where Black Boy Alley used to be. There were three such alleys in London in the 1740s, as well as a Black-Moor Street and Blackman Street, and this one was situated in Holborn, on the western border of the City of London. Some of the eighteenth-century street names remain today, reminders of the area's long history as a market-place, such as Cowcross Street and Cock Lane, West Poultry Avenue and White Horse Alley. But other streets, such as Chick Lane and Black Boy Alley, disappeared during Victorian redevelopment, which included the building of Farringdon Station.

I turn left into Greville Street, hear the clink of glasses from revellers outside the Sir John Oldcastle Pub, then stop at a crossing with Saffron Hill where Christmas decorations glitter over the street like falling snow. This is roughly where Chick Lane used to be, a long, narrow street running east towards the sheep pens of Smithfield Market, and one of its turnings was Black Boy Alley. Many young criminals blamed their downfall on the bad company found in Chick Lane, home to robbers, pickpockets, housebreakers, shoplifters, prostitutes and 'other masters of wickedness'.

London had been rebuilt since the Great Fire of 1666, and in the early eighteenth century the capital experienced a building boom. For those who could afford it, there were luxury shops on New Bond Street, theatres around Covent Garden, and over 500 coffee shops in the City alone. But it was still a place of dirt and pollution, where the air smelled of soot, open sewers ran through the streets, and shopkeepers lit candles at midday, such was the gloom outside.

Chick Lane was bordered by a maze of courts and interlocking alleys, its tiny houses divided into several apartments, with doors opening into neighbouring houses and side streets. One alehouse had trap doors, sliding panels and secret recesses for hiding stolen goods, as well as a tunnel to Fleet Ditch and a secret door in the garret that led to the roof of a neighbouring house. Chick Lane was home to the 'darkest and most dangerous enemies to society', according to one military officer. It was an ideal base for a republic of thieves.

I walk uphill, past a jeweller's shop promising 'best prices paid for gold and diamonds', and then turn into Hatton Garden, the traditional centre of the UK's diamond trade. Nearly every shop is advertising jewels, whether antique diamond engagement rings or 'quality watches at best prices'. In April 2015, a gang of elderly men broke into an underground safe deposit here, abseiled down a lift shaft and stole an estimated £200 million worth of jewels. It was said to be the largest burglary in English legal history and the 'OAP bank robbers' quickly became the subject of a TV documentary, a mini-series and three feature films, including *King of Thieves* with Michael Caine. But no film has yet been made about the Black Boy Alley Ladies, who ruled these streets in the eighteenth century, former servants who transformed themselves into vile and wicked street robbers.

I continue down Hatton Garden, passing a dark, open doorway with a sign for Ye Olde Mitre Pub, and step into Ely Court. The alley is cold and silent. Even though there are people on the street behind, it still feels spooky. The windows on my right are covered with rows of iron bars like a prison.

At the end of the alley is the sixteenth-century pub, tucked to one side, its wooden front like an old-fashioned sweet shop. This was the sort of watering hole that Ann Duck and her friend Ann Barefoot frequented during their evening walks, where they'd call in for a bowl of punch before getting down to business, and then split their profits with an obliging landlady.

Most eighteenth-century crime involved theft and assault, and the majority of court cases were property related. There was still no professional police force as such, although the Bow Street Runners, a small group of constables who investigated crime and arrested offenders, would be formed in 1749. According to some modern historians, women played little role in crime, except as decoys and fences, and they generally showed 'less bravado and initiative' than men. But the women of the Black Boy Alley Gang certainly showed bravado and initiative, and by the time of their robbery near Snow Hill, Ann Duck and Ann Barefoot were well known to watchmen, parish constables and court officials.

Ann Barefoot was born around 1719 in Cambridge, where her father kept an inn. She was given a good education, but after her father's death, she came to London and worked as a domestic servant. At first, she 'behaved pretty well' but then she began to walk the streets and pick up men. She was sentenced to hard labour at the Bishopsgate Workhouse, and on release became a 'noted Thief and Street-Walker', taking lodgings in Black Boy Alley. Here, she met 'a most wicked Creature' called Ann Gwyn, who had also worked as a servant before becoming 'as vile as any Prostitute of 'em all'.

The biographies of both women were provided by the Chaplain of Newgate Prison in *The Ordinary of Newgate's Accounts*, and reflected eighteenth-century theories of criminality – all 'men' were sinners and, although they might start off honest, they could be easily enticed into a life of crime through bad association.

Ann Duck appeared to be a prime example of this, and her biography was more detailed than the others. She was born in Surrey, and baptised as 'Anna' on 22 July 1717 in Cheam. She was 'the Daughter of one Duck, a Black', named John, and a white mother called Ann Brough. John worked as a servant for Edward Green of Nonsuch Park, although his position in the household isn't clear as the term 'servant' included pageboys, footmen, valets, butlers, grooms and coachmen. A few weeks after Ann's baptism, her parents married in St Clement Danes in London, a handsome church at the end of the Strand. Marriage between Black men and white women 'seems to have been common', according to historian Kathleen Chater, although there are no reliable figures because race was rarely mentioned in marriage registers.

Ann Duck grew up in Little White's Alley off Chancery Lane, and her parents had 'several' children, according to *The Ordinary of Newgate's Account*, including two sisters – Elizabeth, who died at the age of 3, and Mary. Their father taught sword fighting to gentlemen at the nearby Inns of Court, instructing trainee barristers in 'the Use of the Small Sword, of which he was a very good Master'. John wasn't the only Black Londoner to teach sword fighting. George Turner had been a fencing master at the Bear Garden in Southwark, while Julius Soubise would teach fencing and horsemanship to London's upper class.

The Duck family must have been reasonably well known around Chancery Lane. Africans had lived in Britain since Roman times, but it wasn't until the mid-eighteenth century that London began to have a substantial Black population. Black Georgians 'were numerous enough to have been a feature of city life,' writes David Olusoga, 'but still unusual enough to have remained an exotic novelty'. Population estimates in London vary wildly, from 3,000 to 20,000, and most were men, often sailors, soldiers and merchants, as well as students and diplomats.

Some Black Georgians were enslaved – at the time of Ann's birth, Britain was the dominant slave-trading power in Europe – or had escaped from slavery. However, Ann's father was a free man who may have arrived in England from the West Indies with his employer. He could have learned his sword-fighting skills at Nonsuch Park, or may have already possessed a military background. His work was freelance, and he may have just been able to support the family, but he sent his daughter to school where, according to *The Ordinary of Newgate's Accounts*, she received a 'proper Education … to fit her for Business', including reading, writing and accounts.

Ann may have attended a dame school, run by working-class women in their own homes, or been enrolled in one of around 100 charity schools in London, which provided lessons for poor children. Charity schools taught pupils to read, mainly the Bible and Book of Common Prayer, but not necessarily to write – equipping boys for a life of manual labour and girls for a future of domestic service.

Ann Duck appears to have then become a shop assistant, one of the few employment opportunities open to women, aside from laundering, street selling, or working in the clothing trade. But just like her seventeenth-century predecessor Moll Cutpurse, she was soon 'impatient of Restraint'. Not long after her father died in 1740, Ann 'launched out into such Excesses, as were beyond her Mother's Power to control; and became as expert a Mistress in all Manner of Wickedness, as Satan himself could make her'.

If her father's livelihood had been precarious, then his death would have plunged the family into poverty and Ann's options were limited. A fifth of young women in London were reportedly working as prostitutes, and she appears to have joined their ranks. Ann became a servant at a bawdy house, or brothel, then a streetwalker and pickpocket, until she 'became so bold, so resolute, and so daring, as to commit Street-Robberies even upon Men too'.

Ann Duck wasn't the only daring female criminal operating in London in the early decades of the 1700s. Moll King was a noted pickpocket and street robber, who inspired Daniel Defoe's eighteenth-century novel, *Moll Flanders*, which also drew on the life and career of Moll Cutpurse. Mary Harvey, who ran a pub near the Strand, was 'a noted virago' and prison escapee with a reputation for threatening and beating constables, while Mary Young was the renowned leader of a pickpocket gang who became known as Jenny Diver and inspired a character in John Gay's *The Beggar's Opera*. All of these women were committed lawbreakers, unafraid of arrest or imprisonment, and when it came to Ann Duck, she was more than ready to defend herself.

In January 1743, Ann made her first appearance at the Sessions House, later known as the Old Bailey. It was a 'fair and stately' building, according to one contemporary, with a courtroom on the ground floor and two large galleries for fee-paying spectators. The accused stood at 'the bar', or in 'the dock', with a mirror above their head, reflecting light from the court windows so everyone could see their facial expression and judge whether they were telling the truth.

Ann Duck was accused of highway robbery along with her companion, Ann Barefoot. They had seized hold of a man called William

Cooper in Eagle and Child Alley and stolen his moneybag containing 35s. Ann Barefoot managed to run away, but William dragged Ann Duck down the alley, where a passer-by helped take her into custody. The sequence of events is confusing, but Ann arrived at the Watch House with her arm bound up from elbow to wrist, claiming she couldn't have seized hold of anyone, 'when I am a Cripple'.

During the trial, Ann insisted she was innocent. William Cooper had come running down the alley with his shirt hanging out 'and said he was robb'd; says he to me, you are the Woman that robb'd me, for I can find no Body else. I did not touch the Man.' A witness who'd been heading to the market to buy her husband's supper testified that she'd seen William pulling Ann down the alley 'in a very indecent; Manner; his Breech were down, and his Shirt hung out'. Another witness had seen 'that old Gentleman' in the alley with two other women 'both fair', his shirt had been hanging a little indecently and the threesome were up to something 'immodest'.

Both witnesses appeared to be working hard on Ann Duck's behalf, offering evidence to corroborate her story – William Cooper was a drunken letch who'd apprehended the wrong woman and injured her arm in the process. The witnesses also identified Ann by colour. 'I took Notice of her,' said one, 'because she is a Black Woman, and so the more remarkable.' Race was rarely mentioned in Old Bailey trials, and the purpose here seemed to be to emphasise that the witnesses had identified the right woman. Black defendants received the same treatment as white defendants at the Old Bailey, and Kathleen Chater has found little evidence of prejudice in terms of press coverage. A systemic racist ideology was yet to take hold, and intermarriage had not become an obsession.

But discrimination did exist; Black people in London were prohibited from learning a trade, and one asylum for female orphans refused to accommodate 'Negro or mulatto' girls. Ann Duck alluded to racism in everyday life – the gentleman she accosted on Snow Hill had 'no liking to me, he swore he did not like my Face, being of a tawny Complexion'. She was also living at a time and in a place when African children could be bought and sold. One newspaper advertised a 9-year-old 'pretty little

Negro Boy' for sale at a tavern in Tower Street, just a mile from Ann Duck's home, while a goldsmith on Duck Lane advertised collars and 'silver padlocks for Blacks or Dogs', to provide identification in the case of escape.

It wasn't unusual to see a woman on trial at the Old Bailey – in 1744, almost half of all defendants were female – but the appearance of a Black woman was rare. Between 1674 and 1812, there were around twenty-three cases – and five of those involved Ann Duck.

The women usually faced charges involving pickpocketing, robbery and prostitution, and they spoke up confidently in their defence. In the 1770s, when Lucy Johnson was arrested for robbing a schoolmaster who lodged in Chick Lane, she argued it was a malicious prosecution. The schoolmaster hadn't found the real robber, so he was making her pay for it. She was found guilty and sentenced to death, but then reprieved.

Three years later, Esther Allingham was charged with stealing 6 guineas from John Baptista, whom she'd approached in the street. She also argued it was a case of mistaken identity, describing him as 'neither fit for God nor the devil; he is neither fit for a Black woman, nor a white woman'. The court appeared sympathetic; she was found not guilty and released.

During Ann Duck's trial in 1743, several witnesses attested to her good character, and she was acquitted. But according to a male witness, her character was 'very vile, as bad as can be', while another described her as 'a common Street-Walker', intent on 'decoying and seducing Mankind'.

Whether Ann Duck was working as a prostitute in the modern sense isn't clear. Prostitution in early eighteenth-century London 'was not about sex', writes Rictor Norton, 'it was about theft … theft rather than sex was the main object'. Prostitutes who operated from the streets regularly picked gentlemen's pockets, or assaulted and stole from potential clients, without having sex with them. The women usually worked in pairs, partly for company and protection, and partly so they could overpower and rob men. Streetwalkers were known to beat up gentlemen if they didn't agree to buy them a dram, and if they did, then they'd be taken to a local brothel or inn and robbed anyway. Women 'used their sexuality aggressively', writes Rictor Norton, but this sexuality appeared to be a role they played in order to commit crime.

The streets of London were apparently infested with predatory prostitutes, and one guide listed several types of 'Whores and Jilts'. The lowest class 'ply in the common streets, and endeavour to haul men by force to their disgustful embraces', while others 'allure a person' to petty brothels, where they ply him with alcohol 'in order to perpetrate their fraudulent designs'.

A late seventeenth-century broadsheet listed twenty-two women who worked as prostitutes in Smithfield, four of whom were described as Black or 'brown', including Sarah – 'a very Black Woman, who has several times attempted to turn honest, but her itching flesh won't let her'. *Harris's List*, however, a bestselling eighteenth-century guide to London prostitutes, included very few women of 'dark complexion'. One was from Jamaica, with 'very pleasing' features and 'considerable taste and fashion', and was popular with gentlemen actors at the Covent Garden Theatre.

Ann Duck and her friend Ann Barefoot often enjoyed evening walks together as 'women of the town', even if they weren't selling sex. On one occasion, they met a very well-dressed gentleman near Temple-Bar and told him they were cousins – which didn't appear to surprise him, despite their different complexions. The women took him to a nearby house to buy them a glass of wine and, once he'd fallen asleep, they riffled through his waistcoat and breeches, taking a watch, 6 guineas and a silver snuffbox. Then they fled to Chick Lane, where they sold the goods to a fence. Not long after, they robbed another man who belonged to one of the Inns of Court. 'What became of the Gentleman we never heard since,' explained Ann Duck, 'nor was it our Desire.'

In June 1743, Ann was again on trial at the Old Bailey, accused of highway robbery with Elizabeth Yates. The prosecutor raised the issue of prostitution, but when the victim was asked, 'Had she any Intention of Lewdness with you, do you think?' he replied, 'No, I do not think she had.' Elizabeth Yates swore that Ann had been the robber, but when she failed to appear in court, once again Ann Duck was acquitted. 'These Things gave me no great Concern,' she recalled, 'for as soon as I was discharged, I went to the old Trade again.'

A few months later, Ann Duck and Alice Norman took another man to a pub and, once inside, they 'began to pull off our masks' and 'swore "D**n our Eyes … you shall soon see what we are"'. Then they 'directly threw him by force on the Bed'. Three days later, the gentleman came back with a constable and the women were sent to Newgate. However, when he failed to appear at the trial, they were acquitted. Ann Duck and her friends clearly had contacts in the right places, who were able to threaten or bribe both victims and witnesses.

The Black Boy Alley Ladies appeared to keep a low profile after this, or at least they evaded arrest, until 17 October 1744 when Ann Duck was once again on trial for highway robbery. This time, she was charged along with four men, including Ann Barefoot's husband, Thomas Wells. They were accused of assaulting Alexander Forfar, a Headborough, or constable, and stealing a silk handkerchief, a powder horn and a pistol.

Alexander Forfar was also a thieftaker, with a reputation for corruption. Thieftakers had been around since the seventeenth century, and were hired to catch thieves, as well as negotiating the return of stolen goods for a fee. In the early 1700s, Jonathan Wild became a notorious thieftaker, opening a lost property office in Old Bailey Street and advertising his services in the press. He also led a gang of thieves, who brought in a regular supply of stolen property, and one of his warehouses may have been in Chick Lane. Jonathan Wild styled himself 'Thief Taker General of Great Britain and Ireland', and today, he's often described as a master criminal and ingenious businessman. Yet his methods were strikingly similar to those of Mary Frith, and she had devised them a century earlier.

Towards the end of 1744, the authorities began offering attractive rewards to aid in the arrest of the Black Boy Alley Gang, and many trials were initiated by thieftakers. In this case, Alexander Forfar told the court he'd been set upon by a mob in Black Boy Alley and slashed with a cutlass – 'that very woman Ann Duck in particular assaulted me and took my powder horn out of my pocket'. She had cried, 'Hamstring the Dog!' and joined in with other women when they 'fell upon him, beating and kicking him with their hands and feet'.

But the gang were not intimidated by their appearance at the Old Bailey. They goaded Alexander Forfar and subjected him to fierce cross-examination, with Ann Duck demanding to know what sort of gown she'd been wearing on the night of the alleged assault. It wasn't uncommon for Old Bailey trials to erupt into a direct confrontation between victim and defendant, with prisoners challenging the evidence and arguing with the verdicts and sentences. It was only later that defendants were encouraged to remain silent, and barristers played a more dominant role.

Despite Alexander Forfar's vivid testimony, Ann Duck and the four men were acquitted. However, the jury felt it was 'a pity such dangerous persons should slip out of the Hands of Justice', and so the male defendants were immediately charged with a separate assault on another constable and thieftaker. They were found guilty and sentenced to a year in Newgate and a 1s fine. Ann Duck, meanwhile, was then charged with another street robbery, and this one would be her last.

3

A CONSCIOUS MISTRESS OF CRIME

It's a cold afternoon in early January 2019 and I'm walking north across Hyde Park, looking for an ancient spot known as Tyburn Tree. I pass through the squat stone monument of Marble Arch, cross Bayswater Road, and reach a small traffic island on the corner of Edgware Road. The island is bare but for three spindly trees, set in squares of soil littered with discarded silver bullets of laughing gas. Then I see a circular stone disc on the ground, with words engraved round the edge: 'the site of Tyburn Tree'.

And that's it – there is no further explanation – it appears to be a memorial to a tree. But in the mid-eighteenth century, Tyburn was the main place for public hangings in London and its triangular gallows meant that several people could be executed at the same time.

I turn to face Oxford Street and the direction from which the execution procession arrived, but I can't even hear myself think as lorries constantly thunder past. I wonder what this spot would have looked like in 1744 when, on 7 November, seven people were hanged, including Ann Duck of the Black Boy Alley Gang.

Ann had been acquitted for the assault on thieftaker Alexander Forfar, but that same day she was charged with assaulting a man called George Cheshire outside a pub on Thatch'd Alley, along with Ann Barefoot. They'd draped their arms around his neck and taken fourpence from his pocket. When George resisted, the women began to beat him and when he cried out, 'Murder!' two accomplices arrived and handed Ann Duck a stick. '[She] gave me several blows upon my arms and back,' explained George, 'and particularly one upon my left eye, which swelled my eye up, and cut it pretty much.'

The women of the Black Boy Alley Gang were no longer bothering to lure men into pubs; they were becoming more violent and simply attacking them in the street. George Cheshire was so badly injured that he couldn't leave home for a week but, as usual, witnesses were reluctant to come forward, 'for fear of having damage done them'.

This time, however, Ann's luck had run out. She was found guilty of stealing the fourpence, convicted of highway robbery and sentenced to death. Alexander Forfar must have rubbed his hands in glee; he later admitted he'd received £5 9s as part of the government's reward for her conviction.

Ann was held in Newgate, along with Ann Barefoot and Ann Gwyn, who'd also received the death sentence. The three women were taken to chapel and strenuously urged to 'unlade their Consciences, confess their Guilt, and implore Forgiveness from their too much offended God'. But Ann Duck 'appear'd but little Penitent', according to Newgate's chaplain, and preferred to talk with her old companions rather than 'attend to the more serious Affair, the Welfare of her Soul'.

On the morning of 7 November, the three women were taken to the chapel for the final time, for prayers and the singing of psalms. Then they were led into the prison yard, along with four condemned men – including Richard Lee, captain of the Black Boy Alley Gang. A blacksmith removed their handcuffs and leg irons. Their hands were tied in front and a noose placed around their necks, with the free end coiled around their bodies. At 9 a.m., the prisoners were put into an open cart, sitting on top of their own coffins, with their backs to the horse. The procession then set off for Tyburn, the cart bumping over the holes and ridges of the London streets, surrounded by armed cavalry.

'Three such vile Women as Duck, Barefoot, and Gwyn, were hardly ever seen together within the Walls of Newgate,' declared the prison chaplain, 'and happy perhaps may it be to many Persons now living, that they are in Time cut off, and prevented from doing more Mischief.' It didn't matter that the assorted gentlemen had willingly agreed to buy the women drinks at notorious houses around Chick Lane and Black Boy Alley. What mattered was that the women had 'lured' them with false promises. They were not prostitutes but robbers, and this deceit made them vile and dangerous – along with their violence against men.

The journey from Newgate covered around two and a half miles, with the procession stopping at two pubs along the way, and by the time it arrived at Tyburn around midday, the crowd could number 100,000. Spectators thronged the local streets, leaned out of windows to watch, and paid to stand in carts to get a better view. Some dashed up to the condemned and offered pots of beer or fruit; others sometimes threw missiles.

When the cart carrying the women of the Black Boy Alley Gang came to a stop, the coils of rope were tied to the gallows beam. The Newgate chaplain prayed with the condemned. Ann Duck and her friends 'wept plentifully' and cried out, 'Lord have Mercy upon us! Lord Jesus receive our Spirits!' Then the horses were whipped away, pulling the prisoners off the carts and leaving them suspended.

It could be a slow and agonising death, and relatives sometimes pulled on a prisoner's legs to speed the process up, as they paddled in the air 'dancing the Tyburn jig'. The bodies of the condemned could then be suspended in a gibbet, or given to surgeons for public dissection, while some were taken to burial grounds by friends.

The Black Boy Alley Ladies were said to have 'died in Peace with all Men', but not every condemned woman went peacefully. When Hannah Dagoe, a 'strong masculine woman', was about to be hanged for burglary and theft in 1763, she managed to free her arms, seize the executioner and punch him in the chest. When he eventually got the rope around her neck, Hannah threw herself out of the cart, dying instantly.

Executions provided mass entertainment for Londoners. Hawkers sold pies and gingerbread, others sold ballads, souvenirs and freshly printed broadsides with the prisoners' 'dying speeches' and final confessions. On the day of Ann Duck's execution, *The Ordinary of Newgate's Accounts* provided a full description of her 'Behaviour, Confession, and Dying Words', available for sixpence. She acknowledged that she'd been 'in almost all the Gaols in London', and hoped that 'none will reflect on my poor Mother, for if I had taken her Advice, I had not brought myself to such an unhappy End'. She also hoped that her sister 'will take Warning by me, and take Care what Company she keeps, for ill Company has been the Ruin of me. So the Lord have Mercy on my poor Soul.'

The Ordinary of Newgate's Accounts provided a short biography and details of the robberies committed by Ann Duck, 'taken from her own Mouth'. But while her confession was recorded in her words, as with Moll Cutpurse's diary, there is nothing about her life before she reached her twenties. There is no hint of her thoughts or motivations, and the list of robberies read like sensational newspaper reports.

Where did Ann Duck live at the time of her execution? Was she still in Little Whites Alley with her mother? How did she live? Was she making money, or was it just enough to get by, to pay for a room, clothing, food and liquor? The chronology of her crimes is also confusing, and Ann's assault on the gentleman on Snow Hill may have occurred in 1742. *The Ordinary of Newgate's Accounts* included a letter, sent to her mother a few days before the execution, which was highly religious in tone. 'My dear Mother,' she wrote, 'for Christ's Sake be Comforted. Rejoyce in the Lord, for his Mercies are infinite.' Ann also wrote a letter to a cousin who had unsuccessfully petitioned the king for her pardon – her family appeared to be doing what they could to save her.

It was uncommon to see a woman on the gallows. Of the 1,232 people executed at Tyburn between 1703 and 1792, only 7 per cent were women. But press reports on the executions of the Black Boy Alley Gang were minimal, and when it came to Ann – or 'Anne' – not a single one mentioned her race. *The Stamford Mercury* announced the execution of 'Anne Duck, for a Street Robbery', while on the same page it described an attack on 'Mr Lock, a Colourman' in Whitechapel, and the capture of a French Guinea ship with '311 Negroes'. Another newspaper noted that Ann had been tried nineteen times, while the *Gentleman's Magazine* wrongly stated that she'd been executed for 'robbing Mr Forfar'. Ann's tawny complexion was of no significance to the press, despite the fact that only eight Black people were executed at Tyburn between 1684 and 1812.

But Ann Duck's story wasn't over just yet. On Christmas Eve 1744, six carts set off to Tyburn Tree, carrying sixteen men, half of whom were members of the Black Boy Alley Gang, including Ann Barefoot's husband, Thomas Wells. *The Ordinary of Newgate's Accounts* published a postscript that day, in which Ann Duck was now blamed for a far more serious crime than street robbery. According to gang member Bess Nash, who had made a confession while imprisoned in Clerkenwell, the incident had happened one evening in the winter of 1742.

She had joined Ann Duck and Bess Dawney, 'as usual upon the Scout', when they'd met a man in the Cowcross area. Bess Nash asked where he was going, to which the man replied, 'With you, my Dear.' They took him to an empty house in Turnmill Street where, after a few drinks, they fell on him. Bess Dawney set her knee against his throat, Bess Nash kneeled on his legs and picked his pocket, while Ann Duck gave him a kick on the head. 'D**n the Blood of a Bitch, he is not dead!' she cried, to which Bess Dawney answered, 'D***n him but he is, as dead as a Door Nail.' Bess Nash appeared 'not quite so bloody minded as her Sisters in Iniquity' – perhaps because this was her confession – and asked 'wherefore did you kill the Man?'

Ann Duck responded, 'D**n you, what else did you bring for, but first to rob, and then murder him.' They then went to a friend's house, called for half a pint of gin and went upstairs to 'Snack the Cole' and share out the stolen money. Finally, they went to Chick Lane to 'dispose of the murdered Carcase'.

Ann Duck was the leader of the gang in this story – both the instigator and the killer. So, perhaps her crimes had not been growing more violent, they had been murderous to begin with.

By the end of 1744, the reign of the Black Boy Alley Gang appeared to be over. The press had lost interest and moved on to other stories. There was minimal coverage of the mass hanging on Christmas Eve – the crime wave was old news. Law and order had been restored.

But Ann Duck wasn't the only family member to find herself on trial. The year after her execution, 15-year-old Mary Price, described as her sister, appeared at the Old Bailey accused of stealing a corset worth 6s. When the victim failed to appear in court, Mary was acquitted. Ann Duck had hoped that her sister would 'take Warning by me, and take Care what Company she keeps', and it seems that she hadn't.

In 1760 the *London Chronicle* reported that twenty-eight women had been sentenced to transportation to North America, including 'the noted Moll Duck, one of the Black-boy-alley gang, who has been tried many times at the Old Bailey'. Yet Ann Duck had been executed sixteen years earlier, so perhaps the paper meant the 'sister of the noted Moll Duck'? Mary Price does not appear in any further Old Bailey trials, however, unless she successfully changed her identity.

Historian Emily Brand has now discovered another family member, a brother named John Duck, who was baptised in 1719. He was a seaman who, in September 1740, set sail from the Isle of Wight onboard HMS *Wager*, heading to South America in a squadron of eight warships, during the war with Spain. HMS *Wager* ran into stormy conditions off the coast of Chile and in May 1741, the ship hit a rock while attempting to steer around Cape Horn. Some of the sailors mutinied, others made for the shore, and around 145 seamen survived, setting up camp on 'the most unprofitable spot on the globe of the earth', according to midshipman John Byron, grandfather to the poet Lord Byron.

Reports of the shipwreck and mutiny became a public sensation back in England, and in 1745 two crew members described their adventures in detail. They were part of a group of eight men, including John Duck, who had set off along the coast for Buenos Aires when they were taken prisoner by a group of 'Patagonian Indians' and carried 1,000 miles inland. They were sold as slaves but treated with 'great Humanity', and after some eight months, the men persuaded the king to allow them to travel to Buenos Aires – except for John Duck, 'whose Misfortune it was to be too near of a Complexion with those Indians (for he was a Molatto [*sic*], born in London)'.

John was 'sold by the Chief to a Master farther up in the Country', where 'he will end his Days, there being no Prospect of his ever returning to England'. What fate awaited him isn't known. Was he still treated humanely, now that he'd been separated from his comrades?

Ann Duck made no mention of a brother in her Newgate confession, and nor did the prison chaplain; the family must have assumed he'd died in the shipwreck. But in October 1744, when Ann was sentenced to death, her brother had been sold into slavery on the other side of the world.

The reign of the Black Boy Alley Gang ended in 1744, but their reputation lived on. William Hogarth included the gang in his engraving of 'Idle Tom', set in a tavern cellar, a villainous hellhole where Tom divides the spoils of a recent robbery as an accomplice throws a dead body down a trap door. The Black Boy Alley Gang was still referenced in Victorian times, when one commentator described their 'diabolical deeds' as 'a terror to the whole city'. But by the nineteenth century, the role of the women had been rewritten. Now the gang were said to 'entice the unwary by means of prostitutes', gag, rob and murder their victims, before throwing the dead bodies in a ditch. Ann Duck and her female companions had taken on a more secondary role – rather than robbing men with the occasional assistance of bullies, they had become prostitute decoys. The men were in charge and the depraved females were simply accomplices.

But, of all the members of the Black Boy Alley Gang, it is Ann Duck who is best remembered today. She is one of very few eighteenth-century mixed-race women in Britain to have left behind a significant historical record. 'Her popularity is a very recent phenomenon,' explains Rictor Norton, who first began researching her crimes nearly twenty years ago. 'It stems from the "history from below" movement. She fits the categories that are currently fashionable among historians: an outsider, a strong woman, a Black person, an anti-establishment figure, a victim of oppression.'

In 2014, students from a secondary school in south London made a four-minute documentary on Ann Duck, part of a project at the Honeywood Museum in Sutton, situated not far from Nonsuch Park where John Duck once worked. It ended with the question, 'Was Ann Duck a cold-hearted criminal who deserved to be hung or was she just a troubled girl who was misunderstood?' There was no mention of the real-life Ann Duck being mixed race, however, and the cast appeared to be all white.

A more recent portrayal of Ann Duck appeared in ITV's drama, *Harlots*, set in an eighteenth-century London brothel. The character of Violet Cross, a 'Black street girl', was 'sort of based' on Ann Duck, explained the show's co-creator, Moira Buffini. 'She's great, we love her … She's a street whore and a thief.' Violet is a glamorous figure, striding along in a gold dress and bright red cloak, snatching a man's purse as she brushes past him. The theft is skilful but bears little resemblance to the methods used by the real Ann Duck.

'She was an intelligent, calculating and assertive woman,' says Montaz Marché, a PhD researcher at the University of Birmingham. 'Ann Duck had a firm knowledge of self and also how to manipulate others. She is a rare example of a Black woman who had control over her own narrative.' While her criminal career may have begun as a consequence of circumstances, her confession suggests it 'became a sport, a thrill, a hunt and very much a way of life'.

Ann also played an active role in constructing her own legacy:

She decided what crimes we know about, how we know about them and how we know about her. Her last words could almost be interpreted as a boast, a final 'two fingers' to the judicial system of which she had escaped so many times before. Ann Duck was a conscious mistress of crime.

Ann Duck's career was far shorter than that of her predecessor, Mary Frith. She didn't die a wealthy woman, and no portraits of her exist in national art collections. No book has yet been written about her life, although she will feature in an upcoming children's book on Black British history, and actor Cush Jumbo is developing a musical through National Theatre Studios about an eighteenth-century, all-female criminal gang, inspired by Ann Duck.

While Mary Frith was portrayed as masculine and chaste, the Black Boy Alley Ladies were the other side of the coin – sexual figures who lured men to their downfall. But by the beginning of the nineteenth century, female criminals were about to become notorious for a very different sort of crime, and one that was regarded as specifically suited to the 'weaker sex'.

4

LADIES GO A-THIEVING

In the summer of 1814, an 'extraordinary instance of female depravity' was reported in the north-west of England, with the arrest of the 'most daring gang of female depredators ever recorded in the annuals of the Police!' A group of women, led by 54-year-old Phoebe Price, had travelled some 40 miles from Manchester to Liverpool, where they'd embarked on a two-week crime spree.

Like the Black Boy Alley Ladies, the women worked in small, all-female gangs, but they didn't need to lure gentlemen or use physical force: their targets were haberdashers and linen drapers. 'Their practice was to frequent the shops of tradesmen,' explained the press, 'and while one was engaged in looking at different things, or purchasing some trivial articles, the other watched her opportunity to purloin whatever was within reach.' The women committed over a dozen thefts in Liverpool, hiding stolen goods under their cloaks and petticoats, and within two weeks they'd made £4 profit each, roughly half the annual wage of a housemaid.

Phoebe Price and her companions fled back to Manchester, where they led an 'idle life' until the money was gone, before returning to Liverpool for another four days of shoplifting. Next, they headed to Chester for the July Fair of 1814, where they stole lace, shawls, silk handkerchiefs and yards of cotton. There was little difficulty in robbing Chester's shops, explained 21-year-old Sarah Rockley, as 'the tradesmen were not sufficiently sharp to strangers'.

Shoplifting was hardly a new activity and it can be traced back to at least the sixteenth century, when groups of men called 'lifters' would 'lyft' cloths and fabric from city merchants. Mary Frith described befriending Kings Takers, who ran by shops at dusk to 'catch up any of the Wares or Goods', and towards the end of the seventeenth century there were a number of shoplifting cases at the Old Bailey.

Two women were said to possess 'profound experience in the mysteries of Shoplifting', and soon the crime become so common that, according to the press, 'a Tradesman scarce dares trust his Wares to Customers view'.

In 1699, in response to pressure from traders, the Shoplifting Act was introduced, part of the 'Bloody Code', which radically increased the number of crimes punishable by death. Those convicted of stealing goods worth 5 shillings or more – and who took the items 'privately', without being observed – could now be transported or hanged. Shoplifting would remain a capital offence for 120 years, although juries could value stolen goods under 5 shillings, so the accused faced a lesser penalty.

Despite the death sentence, shoplifting increased in the eighteenth century and was often viewed as a form of organised crime. Only a minority were professionals, however. It was 'overwhelmingly an amateur, occasional crime', writes historian Shelley Tickell, 'and one primarily driven by need'. Female offenders tended to steal to support their family or wider community, and sometimes stole goods to order. In northern England, around 60 per cent of shoplifting took place at linen drapers', mercer or woollen drapers' shops. Cotton was particularly in demand – it was more fashionable and practical than woollen clothing – while silk handkerchiefs and stockings were easy to conceal. The stolen goods were then sold to fences, hawkers, street sellers and pawnshops, for around a half to two-thirds of their value.

Phoebe Price hailed from Denbighshire, in North Wales, and she appeared to run a family firm of criminals, including two sisters and three daughters. She was portrayed as a cunning professional, who had already been imprisoned several times for shoplifting, including the theft of seven cotton handkerchiefs and a shoulder of mutton. During her imprisonment in Chester Castle while awaiting trial in 1814, she managed to hide money in the feet of her stockings, and several pawn-brokers' duplicates – suggesting she'd sold stolen goods – were found 'carefully hidden in the grey *ringlets* of her hair!'

Sarah Rockley, her co-accused, was from Newcastle-under-Lyme. She'd been brought up by her grandmother, a charwoman, and then put into service at 14. She too had a criminal record, having first been imprisoned for stealing a flannel waistcoat.

Phoebe and Sarah were described as former cotton batters – factory workers from the cotton mills of Manchester where, by the mid-nineteenth century, half of the workforce were female. Mill work was preferable in many ways to domestic service, with fixed hours and better pay, but shifts lasted up to thirteen hours, women were often paid a third less than men, and conditions could be dirty and dangerous. At some point, Phoebe and Sarah decided to stop making cotton – instead, they would steal it.

In August 1814, the 'daring gang of female depredators' were arrested for stealing several items from two shops in Stockport, near Manchester, including 37yds of printed calico. Shoplifting convictions often relied on one gang member giving evidence against the others, and when the case came to trial, Susanna Price testified against her mother. Her words were not reported by the press, but they must have been damning, for Phoebe Price and Sarah Rockley were sentenced to death.

Several other people received the death penalty that day – men convicted of house breaking, robbery, burglary and highway robbery – but the judge singled out Phoebe and Sarah, who were 'inured to crime and plunder' and had 'carried on your depravity for a very long period … excepting at those periods when you were shut up & in prisons, your career remained unchecked'. However, the two women were saved from the gallows and reprieved, and in July 1815 they were among 101 convicts onboard the *Mary Anne*, heading to the British penal colony of

New South Wales. Instead of execution, Phoebe and Sarah were to be transported for twenty-one years, to a country from which few convicts ever returned.

Some transportees refused to go. In 1789, a woman who received the death sentence for robbery said she'd rather 'die by the laws of my country' than be sent to Australia. Campaigner Elizabeth Fry described desperate scenes of 'brutal, debasing riot' as female prisoners were taken from Newgate to the convict ship.

The *Mary Anne* arrived in New South Wales after a six-month voyage, and Phoebe and Sarah were assigned to the Female Factory in Parramatta. The factory had been established a dozen years earlier to house women who'd not yet been employed, and to punish those who broke the rules. Two rooms above a jail were turned into a wool and linen factory, where 150 women worked and slept with their seventy children on the floor.

Unlike convicts in England, however, those in New South Wales could hold property, and they could earn wages through other employment. In 1820, Phoebe Price and Sarah Rockley were given a Ticket of Leave, which allowed them to move freely around the colony, but not to leave it. Two years later, it appears that Phoebe was pardoned, and in her early sixties she married a fellow convict, William Holden, who'd been transported for possessing forged bank notes. The former Welsh shoplifter who'd once hidden pawnbroker receipts in the grey ringlets of her hair, had narrowly escaped the death penalty and now she had to make a life for herself in Australia.

Some serial shoplifters managed to evade both the death sentence and transportation. Ann Gregg, one of Cumberland's most determined felons, was jailed in at least ten prisons, escaped four times, and used over a dozen aliases. She was also the mother of thirteen children, four of whom were born inside jail. Like the Manchester-based cotton batters, Ann Gregg came from a background of poverty, and she was also described as having 'a swarthy dark' complexion. A few years before her birth, two of her relatives had been transported as members of the notorious 'Gang of Faws', who were sometimes described as Gypsies. 'Ann was part of a Travelling family and they were persecuted,' explains David Cooper Holmes, her five times great-grandson. 'If anything went missing, or a crime occurred, they were the first to be accused.' The family were potters and hawkers who followed the trades and traditions of Romany people and Irish Travellers, and their forebears had been subjected to centuries of victimisation and oppression.

Gypsies had arrived on the Scottish borders at the beginning of the sixteenth century, originating from northern India but frequently described as Egyptians. They were treated as illegal aliens, and described by one pamphleteer as 'wretched, wily, wandering vagabonds ... all thieves and whores'. Men and women could be hanged just for being a Gypsy, while those arrested under vagabond laws could be branded with a 'V' on the breast. In the early nineteenth century, Gypsies continued to be portrayed by the press as liars, cheats and thieves, and 'vagrant Egyptians' could be arrested on sight.

Ann Gregg was first convicted at the age of 21 and sentenced to death for stealing several handkerchiefs from a shop in Wigton. She was reprieved, but by 1785 she'd been involved in so many shopliftings and thefts that the press complained a full report would 'fill half a newspaper'. She was certainly smart and determined. In January 1794, she was sentenced to seven years' transportation and taken 300 miles down to London. But Ann managed to avoid being put on the boat and returned home, where she continued her criminal career well into her 80s. 'She was painted as a rogue and thief from birth,' says David Cooper Holmes, 'but generations of racism and poverty made her this way. She had strength, tenacity and ingenuity.'

As far as the justice system was concerned, women like Ann Gregg and Phoebe Price were hardened career criminals. When they stole cotton and lace, handkerchiefs and ribbons, they were whipped, sentenced to hard labour, transportation and death. But they weren't the only female shoplifters operating in the early nineteenth century, and it was one thing to arrest a cotton mill worker, quite another to accuse a lady.

One Friday afternoon in 1827, Miss Elizabeth Walls, a beautiful and elegantly dressed young woman, entered a grocer shop in Marylebone, west London. She explained her aunt would join her in a few minutes to buy some tea, so the grocer offered her a seat. After a while, Elizabeth announced she was going to be measured for a pair of shoes and would return very soon. But as she was leaving the shop, the grocer noticed that 3 ounces of tea were missing and followed her out. He watched as Miss Elizabeth Walls went in and out of several more shops in this upmarket district of London, then he confronted her and she was searched. 'The unfortunate young lady seemed to possess the mania for shoplifting in the highest degree,' explained the press and 'a kind of large pocket at the back of her silk cloak' was filled with fowl, a piece of pickled pork, a book, a pair of gloves and several pairs of stockings. Elizabeth faced six charges of shoplifting and 'seemed to feel most acutely her disgraceful situation'. The only defence she could offer was that 'she knew not what she was doing at the time'.

By the early 1800s, shopping had become a leisure pursuit for those with money. London's population was nearing 1 million and the city's shops, bazaars and emporiums were a visitor attraction. Industrialisation and improved transport had led to a wider range of goods, and the West End was known for its fashionable milliners, tailors, linen drapers and goldsmiths. 'Shopping is the amusement of spending money at shops,' explained *Punch*, 'it is to a lady what sporting is to a gentleman.'

There was little security in place, although some shops fitted bells to doors, installed glass spy-panels, placed mirrors behind counters, and used code words to alert staff to suspected thieves. But on the whole, shop assistants had to watch customers as best they could, and if they suspected a wealthy client of stealing, then it put them in a very difficult position indeed. Respectable-looking women like Elizabeth Walls 'threw tradesmen off their guard', noted one magistrate. They were assumed to be above suspicion – even though they'd adapted their clothing for the purpose of shoplifting. Wealthy women also received preferential treatment – following her arrest, Elizabeth was permitted to sit in a private office, 'instead of being locked up' until the prison van arrived. What happened next is unclear, for she disappeared from newspaper reports.

The following year, when another elegant London lady was accused of stealing a gold brooch from a jeweller's in Pall Mall, the press described her clothing in some detail. She was dressed for her court appearance in a blue silk gown, a fur stole and a velvet bonnet ornamented with artificial flowers. The lady's name, however, was reported only as 'Julia M'. She had 'once moved in a sphere of great respectability' and revealing her full name might 'wound the feelings of several respectable individuals'. Again, there don't appear to be reports on any subsequent conviction, so perhaps Julia M's social status helped in an acquittal. A lady couldn't possibly be a thief; it had all been a dreadful mistake.

Shoplifting was a degrading charge, so it was natural that a respectable woman would want to avoid it, and soon there would be a medical defence – kleptomania. '*Klopemania*', the 'thieving madness', had been identified in 1816 by Swiss doctor, Andre Matthey. It was defined as the inability to resist stealing – an emotional impulse that was not motivated by the desire for money. Kleptomaniacs had an uncontrollable urge to steal; they were suffering from shoplifting fever. They didn't need the stockings or the brooch and, unlike Phoebe Price or Ann Gregg, they didn't intend to profit by selling them on. By the end of the century, kleptomania was recognised as a mental illness which could be used as a defence in court, but this applied only to women – and as long as they were well connected.

Shoplifting was beginning to be viewed as a peculiarly female activity. According to the experts, and particularly Victorian psychiatrists, its roots could be found in biology. Pregnant women had a 'violent impulse' to steal, as did those who had recently given birth, and those going through the menopause. Kleptomania was caused by hysteria, and that was caused by a disease of the uterus.

Shoplifting was also presented as a strangely sexual activity. Women had an 'erotic passion for fabrics', explained one psychiatrist, and silk was particularly arousing. Female shoplifters were linked with prostitutes – both were immoral and operated in public places. A late eighteenth-century print by John Collet, *Shop-Lifter Detected*, depicted a well-dressed young woman grasped from behind by a male shop assistant, while another male assistant kneels to one side, in the process of pulling a length of lace from beneath her dress. The woman has her hands firmly held between her legs, and her expression is hard to read: is it coquettish, pleading or humiliated?

Today, kleptomania is recognised as a rare and serious mental health disorder, and its causes are sometimes attributed to changes in the brain, such as low levels of serotonin. But in Victorian England, it came down to women's natural lack of self-control and suppressed sexual desires. Women had an 'organic inability to resist stealing', explained criminologist Cesare Lombroso, and shoplifting 'quickly becomes a habit'. But if shoplifting was dictated by biology, then why were most women able to resist it? The sexual nature of shoplifting continued to be claimed well into the twentieth century. Sigmund Freud declared that 'all women … are clothes fetishists', while others attributed kleptomania to 'ungratified sexual instinct'.

But none of this explained why men were shoplifters, or the fact that men were just as likely to appear at the Old Bailey accused of shoplifting as women. In 1814, the year that Phoebe Price was sentenced to death, nearly half of those on trial for shoplifting were men.

Respectably dressed male shoplifters usually operated alone, stealing bundles of neckties or parcels of gloves and hiding them under their coats. They rarely played the part of the genuine shopper, talking to staff and asking for help; instead they stole from open shop windows, broke in at night, or created a diversion while an accomplice ran in and grabbed the goods.

But it was the lady thieves who were apparently becoming endemic, and some doctors laid the blame on consumerism. Women were tempted by 'streets of gorgeous shops', explained psychiatrist John Charles Bucknill; they were almost persecuted 'to buy, buy, buy …'

Middle-class women were overstimulated by what was on offer; they became victims of their own desire and their natural vanity turned them into thieves. One woman, who stole seventy-two silk laces, as well as a bracelet and necklace from the Soho Bazaar, could 'not tell what had induced her to disgrace herself in such a manner, except that she must have been mad at the time'.

In 1845, Miss Elizabeth Osborn, a baronet's daughter, was arrested for stealing potted meat from a shop in Brompton. She told the magistrate, 'I am Sir John Osborn's daughter … of course you will allow me to go home.' The magistrate was put in a distinctly uncomfortable position. 'It is painful – most painful,' he apologised, 'but I must do my duty', and he sent Elizabeth to prison to await trial. On her second appearance however, she arrived with her father in a carriage at the court's private entrance. They were immediately shown into the magistrate's room, and instead of standing in the dock, she was provided with a chair. After that, Elizabeth Osborn disappears from newspaper reports.

The press continued to cover 'curious and extraordinary cases' of shoplifting, such as the trial of 50-year-old Mary Ramsbotham, the 'wife of a physician', who was caught slipping four handkerchiefs into her pocket at a draper's shop on Baker Street. The shopkeeper, John Moule, was accused of laying a trap and tempting Mrs Ramsbotham to purchase goods when she already had enough. Mary was experiencing a 'constitutional change', according to her defence, she had been 'much excited and confused' and a doctor testified that imprisonment would 'induce mental aberration'. The jury could not agree on a verdict, and so she was acquitted.

For many shopkeepers, prosecuting lady thieves just wasn't worth it. They could be vilified in court, lose a fortune in bringing a prosecution, and then be shunned by wealthy customers for treating a lady like a common thief. In 1860, an Association for the Prosecution of Shoplifters was formed in London. Shop proprietors paid an annual subscription and the association prosecuted on their behalf. Nearly forty cases went to trial in the first year, and only two ended in an acquittal.

The street ballad, 'Ladies Don't Go Thieving' summed up the differences when it came to prosecuting different classes of women:

If a woman very poor,
Who never had a veil, sirs
Only stole a skein of thread,
They'd send her off to jail, sirs …

A woman who was a lady, on the other hand, was simply given a licence to go on thieving. She was searched in a private room, remained anonymous in court, pleaded mental or physical ill health, and persuaded juries of her innocence. Ladies stole because they couldn't help themselves, they were 'mad', but poorer women stole because they were criminals – and they needed to be stamped out. Shopkeepers, police and magistrates seemed to have no difficulty in distinguishing between the two groups of women.

But what if a lady thief was only pretending to be a lady?

5

EMILY LAWRENCE
VICTORIAN JEWEL THIEF

I'm walking across a small park in the middle of Hanover Square, past construction workers eating their lunch and two boys on a bench smoking a joint. In the mid-nineteenth century, this Mayfair square was a fashionable address, home to aristocrats and learned societies, with concert rooms and a gentlemen's club. The area doesn't look quite as grand now. Instead, it's partly a building site for Crossrail, a new railway line.

I'm heading for No. 5 Hanover Square, a gleaming modern building just outside the park that's currently occupied by property investors and asset managers. I peer through the glass door. A sign says to ring the bell, but when I do, the man watching me from behind a glass desk doesn't move. When I push on the golden door handles, he still doesn't move and nor does the door. Perhaps I look like an undesirable.

One January afternoon in 1860, Emily Lawrence and her gentleman friend James Pearce pulled up to this spot in a horse-drawn carriage. Emily was expensively dressed in a velvet cloak and bonnet, with a dark-coloured veil covering much of her face. The couple entered the showrooms belonging to Mr Emanuel, jeweller and silversmith to the queen. It was four o'clock and just getting dusk. The gaslights had not yet been lit and they were the last customers of the day.

James and Emily asked to see some lockets and the shop assistant, one of twelve who worked on the premises, showed them a great many. But the items were not expensive enough, the couple wanted to see more, and soon there was a great deal of jewellery on the counter, including a diamond locket in a blue velvet case.

The assistant noticed Emily Lawrence moving along the counter, putting down her muff and examining jewellery cases. 'Oh,' she said, 'these are empty.' She moved further along and put down her muff again. After half an hour of deliberation, James and Emily ordered two diamond and turquoise lockets with earrings to match, which they would return to collect later. James opened an account and gave his address as Portland Place, and the shop assistant noticed that 'his hand trembled very much' as he wrote it down. But James explained he'd been at the opera the night before and was still in shock after a diamond had been 'stolen out of my pin'.

After the couple left, the jewellery boxes were closed, taken down to the strong room and the key locked in an iron chest. It was only the following morning that staff realised a diamond locket was missing, valued at £2,000, equivalent to around a quarter of a million today.

This wasn't the first time that 21-year-old Emily Lawrence had robbed a jeweller's. A couple of months earlier, she'd visited Messrs Hunt and Roskell on New Bond Street, an eminent silversmith's which held the royal warrant of the queen.

New Bond Street is just a few minutes' walk from Hanover Square, and as I head down St George Street it's like entering a film set for an eighteenth-century aristocratic drama. The Georgian façades are new, their windows surrounded with fresh cream paint. I go up to a grand, white building, but its occupants are so discreet that the house has no number or name, just a gold-coloured intercom. Further on is a sign, 'Images are being monitored for the purposes of Crime Detection'.

I pass Sotheby's, the auction house renowned for dealing in fine art and jewellery, and then arrive at the most expensive retail street in Europe.

New Bond Street has been a wealthy shopping area since the eighteenth century, and by Victorian times it was a parade ground for fashionable women. Its fine and elegant shops, with dazzling window displays, advertised their wares to the nobility and gentry, from hunting outfits and shooting suits to silk umbrellas and kid gloves from Paris in all the latest colours. Her majesty's tradespeople were numerous on New Bond Street, including silk mercers, tailors, upholsters, perfumers, and Mr Grove, purveyor of fish.

Today, the street has a festive air. Flags flutter in the breeze, advertising Chanel and Dior, Givenchy and Louis Vuitton. The pavements are as clean as if they've just been sandblasted and the only noise is the gentle purr of black cabs going by. I walk along, past window displays of Rolex watches and gold necklaces. Security guards stand behind every glass door, immaculately dressed in black suits, their hands folded in front of them.

I'm trying to find No. 156 New Bond Street, but the numbering is confusing and I'm about to push at the door to Hermès when a security guard pulls it open. I get a glimpse of a young man lounging on a leather sofa, while a woman tries on a pair of pink high-heeled shoes. The guard tells me this is No. 155 New Bond Street, and directs me next door to Miu Miu, where another security guard lets me in. Two women approach from behind a desk and I feel like an imposter – I haven't come to buy anything. They tell me this is No. 150 and send me back off down the street to Chanel, where an assistant explains their shop is definitely No. 158. I thank him, and he calls me 'Madam'.

Next door at Dior, a French assistant explains they are Nos 160–62, and I'm so frustrated now that I'm sweating. I've never been into so many luxury shops in my life. The assistant asks what I'm looking for and I explain there was a famous robbery here in the nineteenth century, when this was the site of the jewellers, Hunt and Roskell. He shakes his head, he hasn't heard of them. A group of young women come in behind me and I'm conscious of my cheap trainers and old grey jumper. I have no jewellery, no designer handbag, nothing to indicate disposable wealth. The staff on New Bond Street have all been polite, but I wonder how they've classified me. Do I look like someone who might pay fifteen grand for a Hermes bracelet or £1,100 for a Chanel straw hat? How easy is it to spot which shoppers really have money to spend?

One November evening in 1859, Emily Lawrence arrived at Messrs Hunt and Roskell, accompanied by an unnamed male companion. They asked to look at a selection of jewellery, including several diamond and emerald bracelets, and then they left. A day or so later, the staff realised four bracelets valued at £600 were missing, one of which had a large emerald surrounded by diamonds. The police were informed, but nothing more was heard until the following January when a man came into the shop and offered an emerald for sale. The employees recognised the stone: it had come from one of the stolen bracelets.

James Pearce, who accompanied Emily Lawrence on her Hanover Square theft, had sold the emerald to a lapidary, a specialist in cutting and polishing gemstones. He had handed it to a commission agent to sell, unaware that it belonged to the New Bond Street jewellers.

Before long, the police were on the trail of the daring jewel thieves, led by Inspector Jonathan 'Jack' Whicher. He was one of the first in a new breed of police officers, a detective at Scotland Yard, the headquarters of the Metropolitan Police. Policing in London had changed significantly since the days of the Black Boy Alley Gang, and the capital was now the biggest city in the world.

The Metropolitan Police were newly trained professionals, who had first stepped onto the London streets to begin their beat patrols in 1829. They dressed in blue trousers and a blue single-breasted coat and were armed with a wooden truncheon and a rattle. They looked like respectable tradesmen, according to the press, and they strolled at a slow pace along Holborn and the Strand, with none of that 'offensive inquisitiveness and unnecessary meddling' which had characterised the old watchmen. Their job was crime prevention; they could stop and question anyone acting suspiciously and arrest those 'about to commit a felony'. But it wasn't that long before constables were mocked in the music hall as corrupt cowards who stole gentlemen's watches and associated with prostitutes.

In 1842, the Metropolitan Police established a Detective Department, consisting of eight men. They had 'no specific beat or round', explained one Victorian dictionary, but were 'concerned with the investigation of specific cases, or the watching of particular individuals or classes of offenders'. Initially, these plain-clothes officers were regarded as spies intruding into citizens' private lives, but with the rising popularity of detective fiction, their image became far more favourable. Unlike the brutish constables, detectives were intelligent men, with sharp minds and a vigilant eye.

When Inspector Jonathan Whicher set out to catch Emily Lawrence, he had already headed a number of high-profile investigations, including the theft of a Leonardo de Vinci painting and two murder inquiries. He was 'quiet, shrewd and practical', according to one colleague, and would soon become famous for solving the Road Hill Murder in Wiltshire.

Inspector Whicher had also been responsible for the arrest of Louisa Moutot, a 'travelling companion to aristocratic families' who, the year before, had stolen a diamond bracelet from the very same New Bond Street shop as Emily Lawrence. When Louisa was searched, police found a man's wig, a pair of false whiskers and moustaches and a man's travelling cap, while her dress was 'fitted with the pockets usually worn by shoplifters'.

Inspector Whicher tracked the Mayfair jewel thieves to a house in Stoke Newington, east London, where he found Emily Lawrence and James Pearce at home. He politely asked them to 'go a little way with me for some people to see you', at which Emily announced she had to go upstairs to get a pair of boots. The inspector accompanied her, but she couldn't find the boots, so they went back downstairs and he told her to put on her things.

'I noticed something strange in her movements,' he recalled. 'She kept her back turned towards me, which made me suspect she had got something in her hands which she wished to conceal.' When Inspector

Whicher took hold of her hands, Emily 'struggled to disengage herself and screamed', while James Pearce seized a poker and cried, 'God blind me, if he touches my wife, I will smash his b***** brains out!'

Emily threw up her hands and declared, 'There now, you see, I have got nothing.' But when the inspector looked down, he spied a diamond ring lying by her feet, and another two close by. The police also found a 'large number' of diamonds and other precious stones in the house, along with gold watches and chains, and forty silk dresses in Emily's bedroom. Just who was this lady, and where had she got such an impressive collection of clothing and jewels?

Biographical facts on Emily Lawrence are hard to come by. She was 5ft 4in with brown hair and hazel eyes, and she appears to have been born in 1839 in Clerkenwell – or possibly Southampton. Her date of birth often changed in official records, as did the spelling of her name: sometimes she was Laurence or Lawrance. Her mother was said to be Amelia Brewer, who resided at a coffee house on London's City Road, while her brother James lived at another coffee house in Hoxton, described as a haunt of prostitutes and 'suspected persons'. According to some reports, Emily had one child, but no details were provided, not even the child's sex or age.

James Pearce was a few years older than Emily. He was born in Manchester, had trained as a lapidary and already had a criminal record. In 1855, he'd been sentenced to three months as a rogue and a vagabond, after trying to steal a diamond ring from a London shop. He'd been charged along with a young woman, but the court found she'd taken no part and she was acquitted. Two years later, James was jailed in Manchester for stealing six gold chains from a jeweller's with his common-law wife.

He appears to have met Emily Lawrence in Southampton where, according to the police, she lived under the name Eliza Durant. In February 1859, an Eliza Durant took her employer, Peter Rainier Esq., a Royal Navy lieutenant, to court and attempted to sue him for one month's wages. She had left service without giving notice on account of her master 'constantly abusing her from morning to night'. But the lieutenant argued that Eliza had arrived in 'a state of rags and great poverty'. He'd kindly lent her money and now she owed him. Her hopes of retrieving her wages failed, and she lost the case. If this *was* Emily Lawrence, then she was certainly skilled at transforming herself. At the end of 1858, she was in 'a state of rags and great poverty' – a few months later, she was heading to Paris.

On 30 March 1859, Emily Lawrence and James Pearce visited a shop belonging to Mr Joseph Fontana, a jeweller in the Palais Royal, a shopping arcade for luxury goods. Press reports varied as to what happened next. Some said James and Emily arrived with another woman and man and asked to look at some opera glasses. James eventually bought one and, while the assistant was busy, Emily emptied a case of loose diamonds worth a staggering £12,000. Other reports said there were four women involved, one of whom, a French woman, was arrested.

James and Emily immediately returned to England. But their male companion, Eugene Edmunds, an American who'd previously been jailed at Chester for 'robberies committed in bed-rooms of gentlemen', was caught and sentenced to six years.

Emily and James settled back in Southampton as Mr and Mrs Durant. Perhaps they'd spent their share of the £12,000, or perhaps Emily just couldn't resist a further theft for, in June 1859, she was convicted of stealing a silk mantle from a shop in the high street, under the name Eliza Durant. She was sentenced to four months' imprisonment and not long after her release, the couple set off to London to steal more jewels.

When Emily Lawrence and James Pearce stood trial for the two Mayfair robberies in May 1860, the Old Bailey was dense with spectators, including many jewellers and West End tradesmen. The couple were part of 'a little society', explained the press, intent on plundering jewellers' shops in England and Paris and 'most of the actual robberies appear to have been committed by the women'. The thieves were 'of very low origin', but Emily Lawrence was 'rather good looking' and able to dress and 'come the lady' in a manner that prevented all suspicion.

The French jeweller, Joseph Fontana, identified both James and Emily, but, the press explained, 'the Paris case, of course, could not be gone into in this country'. Emily repeatedly asserted that her 'husband' was innocent and she alone had committed the Mayfair robberies. The press agreed, 'It is very probable that, so far the fact of the property being taken by her hand, the statement is correct.'

But what was the nature of the relationship between James and Emily? He was a lapidary and had already been caught stealing jewels with two other women, so had he persuaded her into a life of crime and taught her how to 'come the lady'? But if James was the instigator, why had his hand trembled during the theft at Hanover Square? And what happened to all the jewels stolen from the Mayfair shops? Only one 'small' emerald had been recovered, according to the press, so presumably the gemstones found at the house in Stoke Newington were from another robbery.

On 11 June 1860, James Pearce was sentenced to ten years in prison, and Emily to four. When the sentence was pronounced, she screamed out, 'I am guilty; he is innocent. Oh! My dear James!' and was removed, 'shrieking', from the court.

Prison had now become the main form of punishment in Victorian Britain. Transportation had largely come to an end and offenders could be sentenced to penal servitude – a fixed length of imprisonment with hard labour. Female inmates made up around 20 per cent of the country's total prison population, often sentenced for drunkenness or lodging in the open, with the vast majority receiving short sentences of under a month. Emily Lawrence was unusual, as most defendants at the Old Bailey in 1860 were men, and women were more likely to be charged with passing counterfeit coins, stealing from a master or concealing a birth.

The aim of Victorian prisons was to correct women's impulsive nature and replace a life of vice with a 'truer life' of respectable pursuits. Female inmates were subjected to constant surveillance and, as Professor Lucia Zedner explains, every aspect of their appearance, manner and conduct was required to conform to Victorian ideals of femininity. But Emily Lawrence refused to conform, and while her character at

Newgate was 'good', on her transfer to Millbank, she became increasingly troublesome.

Millbank was the largest prison in Britain, built on 16 acres of damp, marshy soil, and with the highest rate of disease of any London jail. Its prisoners, both men and women, were supposed to be isolated at all times, under a system of separation and silence, and required to work twelve hours a day. Female prisoners picked oakum for the first few months, stripping old ropes into fibres, and were banned from receiving visits and writing or receiving letters.

Emily's first appearance in the prison's misconduct book was for laughing and talking during divine service in the chapel. Then she was caught writing to a male prisoner, and five loose diamonds were found 'secreted' in her corset. She must have hidden them well as she'd already been a prisoner for around six months, at two different prisons. Emily apparently hid more stolen jewels behind a brick in her cell wall, a story that was given credence by a later Millbank governor, Major Arthur Griffiths, in his novel *A Prison Princess*: 'You've 'eard tell of Emily Laurence?' asks Sappy Sal, an elderly prisoner. 'She was a famous one, a real, tiptop, high-flying dona; she was in all the big things a-goin.'

Emily had lived like a swell with horses, carriages and a big house in the West End, and once in Millbank she'd hidden stolen gems under the floor of the punishment cell. In a later non-fiction book, *Mysteries of Police and Crime*, Major Griffiths described Emily as 'a dashing adventuress and adroit, daring thief'. He also admitted the story of the hidden jewels was probably 'a fable'.

Emily Lawrence didn't settle down at Millbank, perhaps it was the frustration of trying to contact James Pearce. She was an 'affable, lady-like, fascinating woman', according to Major Griffiths, but her conduct inside was 'atrocious'. She was repeatedly put on a diet of bread and water and locked in the punishment or 'dark cells'.

The cells were used for 'refractory prisoners whom nothing else will subdue', explained one journalist, and once inside, 'the sensation was that of living tomb'. The cells were so dark that even with a lit candle it was impossible to see the walls, while overhead came the sound of the weaver's looms, 'like the quivering of a legion of water wheels'.

Emily's crimes included idleness, wearing her muslin cap contrary to prison rules, talking during exercise, impudence, laughing loudly outside chapel and attempting to strike an officer.

She was soon transferred to Brixton, a women's prison, where her behaviour became increasingly desperate. She made a 'feigned attempt' to strangle herself, followed by a 'feigned' attempt to hang herself. Suicide was a crime in the 1860s, and those who tried to 'commit' it in jail were dismissed as 'attention seekers' and further punished. But Emily's refusal to obey the rules continued. She lit the gas in her cell 'for the purpose of cooking' and hid stolen goods including scented soap, hair oil, tea, sugar, sweets, a bottle of spirits, a song book and a bottle of ink. In 1862, Emily made sixteen appearances in the prison's misconduct book. The Brixton authorities had had enough, and she was sent back to Millbank where her behaviour remained disorderly.

In 1864, Emily and James were both released, and they headed straight to Brighton, where they robbed a silversmiths in Ship Street. The shop manager spotted them and took chase, apprehending the couple in the street. Emily 'asked me to let her alone', explained the manager, 'saying that was not the way to treat a lady'.

In court, the couple took on a new identity, giving their names as Charles and Catherine Percival. Their lawyer argued that, as they were married, 'Catherine' may have been acting under the influence and control of her husband and if that were the case, a jury would have to acquit her. But London police identified 'Charles Percival' as none other than James Pearce, and although Emily produced a marriage certificate, this was rejected, and she was sentenced to another seven years in prison.

This time, she was locked up in Lewes Gaol, and she didn't intend to stay there for long. One Saturday afternoon she had a visit from her 'brother', which took place in the company of a warder called Mary Ann Jenner. That evening, Emily Lawrence went missing. The alarm was raised, and the prison searched, and while she mysteriously reappeared in her cell, the authorities discovered two carpetbags outside the prison, one with clothing and the other with cord and ropes, ready to be thrown over the wall. The warder was accused of assisting an attempted escape but was discharged because of lack of evidence. Perhaps Mary Ann Jenner had been tempted by the offer of an illicit diamond.

Once again, Emily's behaviour meant she was moved from one jail to another. At the end of 1865 and now in Brixton, she was caught dropping a letter out of her cell window, intended for a matron. The letter was addressed to 'my dear friend C' and promised there were 'bright days coming yet for us'. Emily thanked the matron for having 'always done the uttermost of your power', wished she could 'run and steal a kiss', and was very 'glad you take no notice of me no matter where I am'. Unsurprisingly, the prison authorities underlined a number of passages in the confiscated letters. The matron appeared to have carried out several favours for Emily Lawrence, who was very grateful for 'those little things you gave me last'.

Emily was transferred to Millbank where, once again, she was in trouble for hiding things in her cell, writing secret letters, quarrelling and fighting. As a result, she was put in a straitjacket for twenty-four hours and restrained in 'hobbles', or handcuffs for the legs.

In 1869, Emily Lawrence was released from prison, but I can't find what happened to her after this. She was apparently spotted by a Millbank warder six years later, in a carriage passing along Park Lane. She was also suspected of being involved in the Great Post Office Robbery of 1881, when thieves stole registered letters containing £40,000 worth of diamonds. According to some reports, she fenced the jewels in Amsterdam and Antwerp and retired on the proceeds.

Emily Lawrence had been a Queen of the Underworld for at least ten years, committing several high-profile thefts and netting thousands of pounds' worth of diamonds from jewellery shops in London, the south coast and Paris. She was a skilled performer, able to 'come the lady' and convince shopkeepers she had money to spend. Despite being imprisoned for lengthy periods, locked in punishment cells, hobbled by the ankles and tied up in a straitjacket, she'd remained defiant. She also took full responsibility for her crimes, declaring her partner James innocent. Yet although she left behind a detailed record of her thefts and time in prison, Emily Lawrence has been forgotten as a jewel thief, and rarely appears in any compendiums of crime. Many leading female crooks followed in her footsteps, however, reinventing themselves as wealthy ladies in order to steal from Mayfair's luxury establishments.

In the late 1880s Sophie Lyons, the American Queen of Crime, arrived in London with a British swindler known as Lady Temple. Sophie was in her early 40s and a leading player in the American criminal world, as a thief, pickpocket, bank robber, prison escapee, shoplifter and conwoman.

The two women took a suite at Claridge's, hired a carriage and a coachman in livery and drove to nearby Bond Street where they stopped outside 'a famous jewellery store'. Lady Temple selected several diamond necklaces, explained that her husband had an account, and instructed the jewellery to be sent to Claridge's. After two weeks touring London's finest shops and dressmakers, Sophie Lyons and her companion returned to the Continent.

Another American thief targeted Christie's auction house, just half a mile from New Bond Street, which prided itself on being 'safe as the Bank of England'. In the summer of 1905, it offered a valuable collection of jewels for sale, and one afternoon a stylishly dressed lady asked to inspect a pearl necklace, valued at £2,000. But a few moments later, an attendant noticed her walk away, and realised the necklace had been replaced with 'imitation pearls of rather bad quality'.

The lady refused to be questioned. Instead, she expressed great indignation and 'took to her heels', dashing out of the saleroom and into King Street, throwing the necklace away just before she was caught

Her identity appeared to be a mystery, and the press speculated that she was Belgian, French or German. She gave her name as Annie Grant, an actress from Chicago, but when the case came to court, the police revealed her name was Gleeson, and her husband was a bank thief. Annie was a professional shoplifter, who had recently fled America while on bail in New York, and she was also a notorious 'penny weighter'.

The judge was confused. 'A what?' he asked. The police explained that a penny weighter went into jewellers' shops, inspected jewellery and then, with 'some sticky substance on the fingers', palmed an article and hid it under the counter for a confederate to pick up. 'Well,' said the judge, 'we are always learning something', which was met with laughter in the court.

Annie's defence attempted to argue that it had been a case of 'sudden temptation', but the theft had taken a significant amount of planning. First, she'd visited Christie's to inspect the goods for auction, then she'd bought an imitation pearl necklace from a shop in the Burlington Arcade for £5. She'd returned to Christie's to inspect the genuine necklace again and asked the arcade to alter the clasp before making the switch. But Annie had failed to notice that the genuine article had a yellow tab attached to it, while the fake had a white one.

Some press reports were admiring, saying the audacity of the act 'puts it on a pedestal among such crimes', and it had shown surprising ingenuity and skill. Annie was sentenced to three years' penal servitude. She was later arrested for shoplifting under the name Mary Ferguson, along with a Russian 'prince'. 'The woman is a devil,' he told the police. 'She is a thief and made me a thief. It is very hard on me.' The prince, however, already had convictions in London, Paris and Brussels. Annie later became involved in a far more violent crime, and was sentenced to ten years after a brutal attack on an elderly diamond merchant, who was beaten, bound and gagged.

Scotland Yard, meanwhile, might have caught the Mayfair diamond thief Emily Lawrence, but soon they were facing an entire gang of British female crooks – and these ones were as lawless and immoral as the Black Boy Alley Ladies.

6

MARY CARR QUEEN OF THE FORTY THIEVES

Near the banks of the River Thames, in the picturesque parish of Stone in Kent, there once stood a House of Mercy for fallen women. St Mary the Virgin Female Penitentiary was a Church of England establishment, offering a sheltering home for sixty girls and young women on a 6-acre site of beauty and quiet. Here, it was hoped, sinners would become penitents. Their souls would be saved, and they would leave as honest, respectable women.

Female penitentiaries had started in London in the early 1800s, not as prisons or places of punishment, but religious charities for those who had 'lost their innocence' – prostitutes, mistresses, unmarried mothers, thieves, vagrants, alcoholics and those who had been sexually abused. For some, Houses of Mercy were a refuge, providing shelter, food and clothing, and while inmates were expected to stay for around two years, they were free to leave if they chose.

Most of those at St Mary's came from a background of domestic service. Some were as young as 12, and they were reformed through hard work – trained in needlework, washing and scrubbing – as well as religious reflection.

The early years at the Kent House of Mercy proved successful, but then several girls were dismissed for robbing the female staff and superintendent Harriet Nokes grew concerned. Inmates were being drawn from 'a lower class of society' than before. Some were 'girls wishing to hide from the police … or they want a little rest and a wash-up of themselves and of their garments, and know where to get it!'

The 'low-class' inmates were more difficult to manage. In one instance, a group became openly disrespectful and were 'deprived of a portion of their tea'. As a result, nine girls refused to attend prayers or come in from the garden. The superintendent called on the aid of a local policeman and when four of the ringleaders were threatened with expulsion, the others exclaimed, 'Please, sir, we're all as bad as one another, and if four are to go, we will all nine go.'

The inmates of the House of Mercy showed solidarity, and they knew they were bad. One girl had been 'led astray' by an army captain and then 'went from bad to worse'. Another had tried to poison herself after witnessing her friend's suicide in the River Thames. Some were restless and disliked 'settled occupation and restraint'. 'I never did knock under to nobody,' explained one girl, 'and I aint a-going to.'

In around 1881, a young woman named Mary Carr arrived at the House of Mercy in Kent. It's not known why, how or exactly when she came, but she was around 18 years old and had previously been in trouble with the police.

Mary was born in Holborn in 1862 and her mother had died when she was 10. Four years later, Mary was cautioned for stealing from shops, and she also spent time in the City Road Workhouse, along with her elder brother, John, and sisters, Ellen and Annie.

Workhouses were intended to provide work and shelter for people in poverty, but conditions soon resembled those of prison. Inmates slept on wooden platforms or hammocks, wore coarse uniforms and received a bath once a week. They were governed by strict rules and frequent punishment, while couples were separated, and children over the age of 7 removed from their parents. Mary Carr's father is believed to have been John Carr, an international thief and forger who, in 1882, was found in possession of £1,000 worth of bonds, stolen from a ship en route from Rotterdam to Essex, and jailed for five years. Yet confusingly, official records show her father John, a tailor, died inside the City Road Workhouse in 1876.

At some point, Mary Carr left Kent and returned to London, where she worked as a flower seller on the Strand. Victorian flower girls were often romanticised as rosy lasses offering bunches of primroses to passers-by, but they were more likely to be middle-aged women, dressed in ragged clothes, with two or three hungry children by their side.

In the warmer months, around 1,200 flower girls worked on the streets of London and many were said to sell flowers as a 'covering for immorality', particularly alcohol and prostitution. On the Strand, some were known for pursuing gentlemen for 100 or 200yds, offering bouquets and 'mixing up a leer with their whine for custom or charity'.

Mary Carr bought her flowers from Covent Garden Market before daybreak, then arranged them into 'button-holes' and bouquets to sell. She earned a few shillings a day, perhaps 10 if she was lucky. But she became 'noted for her good looks and engaging manners', according to *Lloyd's Weekly*, and she also 'managed to get round her a gang of young women who gave her complete obedience as their leader'. The House of Mercy had not reclaimed her from the path of vice. Instead Mary Carr was about to become the first Queen of the Forty Thieves.

The Forty Thieves – or simply the Forties – were famed for luring and assaulting men, much as Ann Duck had done in the 1740s. But while Ann's bullies had burst into pubs and accused gentlemen of indecency with their 'wife', Mary Carr's gang operated on the street, and threatened to call the police.

Younger girls were sent to approach well-to-do gentlemen and ask for directions, and when the man set off to show the way, two or three other gang members appeared and accused him of assault. The victim usually handed over his valuables, rather than be publicly involved in 'such a disgraceful affair'.

It was a difficult charge to prove. In 1860 there were nearly 700 cases of 'larceny from the person by prostitutes', and just thirty-nine convictions. On the rare occasion that a man suggested calling the police himself, the Forty Thieves simply stole his watch and ran.

Mary Carr was said to be particularly skilful. Smartly dressed, with an 'innocent pleading smile', she targeted elderly gentlemen who were 'proceeding home in a genial frame of mind after a particularly good dinner'. She explained her purse had been stolen while she was leaving the theatre and asked for the bus fare home. Then she led the elderly gentleman into a quiet street and accused him of assault. 'As a black-mailer,' explained one American journalist, 'she was merciless.'

It's not clear why the gang were known as the Forty Thieves. The title may have come from the folktale, *Ali Baba and the Forty Thieves*, which was a popular Victorian pantomime featuring a robbers' cave with a secret store of gold. There were various criminal gangs called the Forty Thieves in the early nineteenth century, and according to historian Brian McDonald, Mary Carr's were one of several 'sub divisions' of the Elephant and Castle Gang.

The Elephant and Castle Gang had begun in the 1780s as a band of highway robbers and grown into a violent network of gangsters, thieves and receivers based south of the River Thames. Their leader was Alf Gorman, described as 'a good-looking, smartly-dressed man', who'd first come to police attention as an 11-year-old pickpocket. Alf had then joined a garrotting gang, one of the most feared types of street robbers, with victims seized from behind and choked while their pockets were picked.

The female Forty Thieves appear to have started out as part of the Elephant and Castle Gang, initially operating as pickpockets, and then establishing themselves as an independent group under the leadership of Mary Carr. They retained close links with the Elephant and Castle Gang, however, many of whom were their fathers, boyfriends, husbands and accomplices.

In 1888, Mary married a man named Thomas Crane and the couple lived in Buckingham Street, off the Strand. She took on a new career as a model to 'various artists of repute', using the name Annie Leslie or Jenny Lesley. She had 'an exceptionally fine figure', reported *Lloyd's Weekly*, and carried her head in such a stately manner that she was nicknamed 'Swan Neck'. Mary sat for Dorothy Tennant, whose paintings had been exhibited at the Royal Academy and whose book, *London*

Street Arabs, published in 1890, included a portrait of a young flower seller who may have been Mary Carr.

Mary was also painted by Lord Frederic Leighton, President of the Royal Academy of Arts, and some believe she is the subject of 'The Maid With the Yellow Hair', in which a young woman in a high-necked white dress sits reading a book, her auburn hair cascading down her shoulders. Mary Carr had 'a luxurious crop of auburn hair', recalled Detective Tom Divall, and she was exceedingly handsome with 'rather small features'. If she had stuck to being an artist's model, 'she might have done well and lived in luxury', but instead she enticed men 'into filthy and foul places' and became involved in 'everything too horrible to mention'.

In September 1890, Mary Carr was convicted of stealing a gold watch and chain from an elderly gentleman in Soho. The police found her hiding under the counter of a greengrocer's shop and she was sentenced to four months with hard labour.

On her release, Mary refined her skills as a blackmailer. A 'clever mimic and actress', she would 'get herself up like a very young girl', explained the press, and lure gentlemen to a house in Pimlico kept by an 'aunt'. The gentleman would be shown into the parlour, then Mary would 'shriek' and her aunt would burst in, much like one of Ann Duck's bullies. When the man was accused of assault, he'd pay up, to the extent that Mary Carr was reportedly making around £40 a day – a fortune compared to life as a flower girl or artist's model. The 'sufferers' included several Members of Parliament and one 'well-known legislator', who paid £400 'in order to preserve his previously spotless reputation'. Such stories were certainly titillating, but the press provided few details, and the identities of Mary's male clients were not revealed.

Crime had become a hugely popular topic in Victorian England, and broadsides that covered murder cases could sell millions of copies. In

1888, journalists created the terrifying figure of 'Jack the Ripper', after five women were murdered around Whitechapel. The case 'caused the greatest sensation throughout the civilised world', according to Detective Tom Divall, and the victims were 'of the most filthy and depraved class'. But as historian Hallie Rubenhold has shown, there is no real evidence that three of the women were prostitutes at all – the police simply assumed that they were. Journalists based their reports on rumour and speculation, fabricating quotes and twisting statements in order to reinforce Victorian moral codes of right and wrong.

There was a rising obsession with prostitution in Victorian Britain. In 1857, one house in every sixty in London was a brothel, according to *The Lancet*, and one woman in sixteen worked as a prostitute. Journalist John Binny described a 'low class of women who prowl about the streets at midnight', using methods that were 'obscene and shameless'. But, as with the Black Boy Alley Ladies, it was hard to tell the women's true motives. John Binny found it 'impossible to draw an exact distinction between prostitution and the prostitute thieves'.

Prostitution was not illegal, but women could be arrested for soliciting, obstructing a public thoroughfare, causing a public nuisance, or disorderly conduct. Any woman apprehended for being drunk or out alone after dark was labelled a prostitute, too. Solicitation laws were used to control 'unruly' women, and suspected prostitutes could be convicted and jailed on the evidence of a single police officer.

As well as blackmail, Mary Carr became involved in fencing stolen goods, a branch of crime in which women predominated. There were around 3,000 houses of 'bad character' in London, where stolen property was received, including public houses, beer shops, coffee shops, lodging houses, brothels and Dolly shops, run like unlicensed pawnshops. Stolen jewellery was generally taken to pieces, the name of the owner erased, and then it was often sold abroad.

In 1893, Mary Carr reportedly travelled to Antwerp to dispose of a diamond necklace, after a male companion was convicted of stealing jewellery from a hotel bedroom in Charing Cross. By now, she had left her husband and was living at 118 Stamford Street in Lambeth, south London, with Alf Gorman, the leader of the male Elephant and Castle Gang.

Lambeth was the home of the criminal underclass, according to detectives, and the local hotels were 'little else than brothels'. Mary's house was already a well-known address. Dr Thomas Neill Cream, the Lambeth Poisoner who was executed in 1892, had met two of the women he later murdered at 118 Stamford Street.

In the spring of 1896, Mary Carr appeared at Southwark Police Court, dressed in a rich velvet cloak trimmed with fur and a broad Rembrandt hat adorned with five ostrich feathers. As the leader of the Forty Thieves, Mary had an image to live up to. But this time she had not been arrested for blackmailing men or fencing stolen jewels; instead she was accused of kidnapping a 6-year-old boy.

When the case came to trial at the Old Bailey, Mary was defended by the aptly named Mr Lawless. According to the prosecution, a young boy called Michael Magee had been stolen from his mother, Bridget, the previous April during the City and Suburban Race at Epsom. The case was widely reported in the press, but the coverage was deeply confusing, as was the trial itself. Witness statements were contradictory in terms of who had been involved, when the events had happened, and who had informed the police.

Phil Jacobs, who had a history of convictions for theft, said he'd met Mary Carr at the Epsom Races and she'd asked him to take a young boy to Stamford Street. But his testimony made for bizarre reading – 'I am a general dealer; I buy things, children included – I do not mean that.' The court was told that the 'Gypsy boy' had been found in a 'shocking state' and was 'suffering from a terrible disease'. The disease was left unstated, but a doctor attested that the boy had not got it from 'riding a bicycle'.

Mary Carr agreed she'd been at Epsom, where Phil Jacobs had asked her to look after his 'son'. The child was covered with vermin and all his clothes were 'lousy', but she agreed to keep him for a week or two, as she was used to looking after children. The jury didn't believe her and Mary Carr was found guilty. When the judge sentenced her to three years in prison, she simply smiled and said, 'Thank you.'

As for poor Michael Magee, he was put into the care of the Society for the Suppression of Vice, with his mother's consent.

So, had Mary cared for him, or was she responsible for his terrible unnamed disease? A later report by Scotland Yard described the boy as having been well looked after at Stamford Street. It seems the police had simply welcomed the opportunity to finally bring down Mary Carr.

Detectives informed the court that she was the queen of 'a gang of young females who infested the Strand'. She lived in a 'disorderly house' in Stamford Street with 'notorious characters' and had previously been in prison.

Mary Carr fitted the profile of the 'born criminal', as identified by criminologist Cesare Lombroso, whose book *The Female Offender* had been published in English the year before. He argued that while women were law abiding by nature, there was a small sub-species, the 'female born criminal'. She was more masculine than normal women, and at the same time she was also a prostitute, and this 'exaggerated eroticism' formed the starting point for a life of vice and crime. The 'female born criminal' was preoccupied with the satisfaction of her own desires – she was a 'lustful' savage, whose ultimate goal was self-satisfaction.

Cesare Lombroso's ideas weren't new. He drew on the biblical idea of the sinful woman leading men astray. But he presented his theories as scientific truth, and he also provided a way to identify born criminals by their physical characteristics. After Mary Carr was convicted for the Epsom kidnapping, her 'paramour', Alf Gorman, was charged with robbery, along with several other men. The press noted that one had 'the broad head and low set, large ears described by Professor Lombroso'.

Alf Gorman was sentenced to five years and the 'great Stamford Street criminal gang is practically broken up', declared *Lloyd's Weekly*. Confusingly, it described the men as members of the Forty Thieves, under the leadership of Mary Carr. Now the Queen was in prison, however, a new woman would have to take on the crown.

One evening in 1899, 22-year-old Minnie Duggan was enjoying a drink with a female friend in a public house in St Pancras, north London. As the women left, a man realised that his umbrella, worth 10*s*, was missing and Minnie was arrested. She adamantly denied taking it, until a constable found the umbrella hanging from a loop at the back of her dress. 'Oh!' she exclaimed, 'I have made a mistake: I thought it was mine.'

According to the police, Minnie Duggan was the new Queen of the Forty Thieves – a fearsome band of women who 'molested and assaulted all the respectable people they come across'. Minnie already had a string of convictions under several aliases. In 1895 she'd attacked two sisters on Tottenham Court Road, pulling a baby out of one of their arms and 'throwing' it on the ground, then stabbing the other in the head with a tin opener, 'causing the blood to flow freely'. Minnie also stabbed one of her friends in the process, 'apparently by mistake'. It was a dispute over a man, according to the press, and she was sentenced to twenty-one days' hard labour.

While Minnie was in prison, another gang member, Annie Horrigan, sold off all her goods – including a feather bed and couch – and the moment Minnie was released, she took her old friend to court. 'You are one of the "forties" and the biggest thief of the lot,' protested Annie. 'None of us are any good, we are all thieves.' This led to laughter in the court, and the case was dropped. Like the girls of St Mary's House of Mercy in Kent, the Forties knew they were bad – and they had no interest at all in being reformed.

Mary Carr, meanwhile, had now become so notorious that, like Moll Cutpurse before her, she inspired a play, *The Worst Woman in London*, written by Walter Melville. It opened in 1899 at the Standard Theatre in Shoreditch, and from the moment the curtain rose, the audience were captivated by the central character of Frances Vere – beautiful, unscrupulous, irresistible and scheming. It was a sensational tale featuring crime and sexual intrigue, as well as ornate scenery, circus acrobats and firefighters. Frances attempted to rob her wealthy employer, bewitched him into marriage, shot him dead in his sleep, helped to set fire to a house, then escaped via an overhead telephone wire. She was a most fascinating creature, reviewers agreed, 'She has great worldly desires, but little of the wealth necessary for their satisfaction, and so she exercises her power of fascination to gratify her love of luxury.'

The plot bore little resemblance to Mary Carr's life, aside from her 'fascination' over men and a desire for wealth. Instead, *The Worst Woman in London* reflected deep-seated fears about the changing role of women in late-Victorian England. A married woman could now own her own property and money, and she could legally separate from her husband if he was violent. Women were earning university degrees, becoming dentists and doctors, and in 1897 the National Union of Women's Suffrage Societies was formed to lobby for the right to vote.

It was the dawn of the 'New Woman' – independent and educated, with control over her own life. Yet, at the same time, audiences couldn't get enough of debauched female characters, and when *The Worst Woman in London* opened in the West End in 1903, it was the 'greatest success of the season'. Publicity was extensive, with brightly coloured posters, programmes and handbills portraying Frances Vere as both a 'lady' in her rich clothes, and a dangerous, threatening presence. Walter Melville had hit on a winning formula and more plays on a similar theme followed, *The Female Swindler*, *A Disgrace to Her Sex* and *The Girl who Lost her Character*.

As for Mary Carr, she'd been released from prison in 1898 and it wasn't long before she was involved in a series of thefts from West End hotel rooms. Her companion in crime, Charles Harvey, a frock-coated, smart-looking man in a silk hat, had been seen knocking on bedroom doors at a hotel in Piccadilly, while Mary sold the stolen goods to a pawnbroker. The spree lasted for around eight months and the couple targeted nearly every hotel in the West End. In August 1900, she was sentenced to twenty months and condemned as 'one of the most dangerous women in the metropolis'.

London certainly seemed to have its fair share of dangerous women. A year earlier, the self-styled Queen of Crooks, Chicago May, arrived in the capital, and she had many similarities with Mary Carr.

She was born Mary Anne Duignan in County Longford, Ireland, and had run away to America at 19, where she made a living as a 'badger'.

Badgers operated much like the Black Boy Alley Ladies and the Forty Thieves, enticing men into hotel bedrooms where an accomplice burst in, pretending to be a landlord, irate husband or police officer. In the ensuing panic, the badger robbed the man and ran. Chicago May was also a blackmailer and, like Mary Carr, she too had a 'wealth of auburn hair … artistically arranged about her baby face'.

The American Queen of Crooks continued her activities in London, based at hotels such as the Langham and the Russell, and she regarded the city as one of her 'chief headquarters', along with Rio de Janeiro. If a man attempted to take advantage and 'tried to buy my body', she explained, then 'it was up to me to pretend to go along, but to do my best to thwart him and to *make him pay dearly*'. She also joined a gang who were 'working the pennyweight', which included stealing jewels and substituting them with fakes – as Annie Grant would later do at Christie's – earning the nickname 'Diamond May'.

Then, together with Eddie Guerin, an international criminal, she robbed the American Express office in Paris and was jailed for five years. In 1907, there were 'wild scenes in court' when Chicago May was convicted of attempted murder, after Eddie was shot on a London street. The press revelled in her reputation for enticing men into compromising situations – 'several' had killed themselves, including 'a rising young barrister'.

Mary Carr, meanwhile, had now turned to shoplifting. In 1905, she was arrested in Bournemouth, along with 19-year-old Louisa Long, for stealing lace collars. The two women vehemently denied the charges. 'I don't want any lace,' declared Louisa, 'I have plenty. I can have diamond rings or anything I want.' Mary asked to see the proprietor alone in private, where she offered to pay, 'Do for God's sake take the £2 10*s* or whatever it is, and let us go.'

Both women were playing the role of the lady, deeply affronted at the charge of shoplifting. They didn't need lace when they had diamonds – perhaps they were suffering from kleptomania. During the trial, Louisa explained she'd been sent to Bournemouth for her health, but if this was a defence it failed. She also accused Mary Carr of threatening her in the police cell and telling her to stay quiet. The two women were jailed for four months with hard labour.

This appears to have been Mary Carr's last prison sentence and she reportedly died in 1924, after a career that had lasted at least thirty years. She'd been a flower seller and an artist's model, a pickpocket and blackmailer, but most importantly she'd formed the Forty Thieves, and their criminal activities would continue well into the twentieth century.

After Mary Carr's arrest in Bournemouth in 1905, and the imprisonment of Minnie Duggan the same year, once again a new queen was needed, and she too was fatally alluring to men. One evening in 1906, Charles Steng, a spice merchant, met a beautiful young woman on the streets of Lambeth and was so 'fascinated with her society' that he invited her home and introduced her to his sister. They enjoyed 'refreshment and conversation' for several hours until the merchant fell asleep, the keys to his bedroom safely tucked away in his pocket. He woke with a terrible headache, the fascinating lady had left, the keys to the safe were lying on the dressing table and £215 worth of cheques, cash and jewellery were missing. The merchant was certain he'd been a victim of 'hocussing', a crime often associated with women, when robbery victims were drugged with laudanum added to gin.

Detectives arrested Helen Sheen, or 'Fair Helen', as the press dubbed her, during a funeral at Kensal Green Cemetery. She was regarded as a 'very dangerous character', who frequented high-class hotels and dressed very fashionably and associated with thieves. 'The money is spent,' she told detectives, 'but you might get the jewellery back', and she alluded to others being involved.

When it came to sentencing, however, Helen changed her mind. The judge urged her to make 'a clean breast of it' and provide information on the robbery. But Helen replied, 'I have got none.' The judge didn't believe her and sentenced her to eighteen months of hard labour. But if he thought this would silence her, he was wrong. 'That won't break my heart, old tallow face,' said Helen. 'Good bye, dear!' Her taunting response was widely reported in the press. Like Ann Duck and the Black Boy Alley Ladies, she was bold, brazen and not afraid to stand up for herself in court.

The Forty Thieves had now established themselves as a force to be reckoned with and, while Helen's role as leader was short-lived, the next queens of the Forties would turn a gang of pickpockets, blackmailers and robbers into a highly successful, professional operation.

ALICE DIAMOND AND MAGGIE HUGHES THE FORTY ELEPHANTS

I'm sitting at a table in the National Archives in Kew, staring at a page of mugshots from 1921. They form part of a supplement to the *Police Gazette*, a thick heavy book, bound in red leather and stamped with gold capital letters: CONFIDENTIAL. A notice on the first page repeats the warning, 'CONFIDENTIAL. For Police Only.'

The *Police Gazette* was a daily publication circulated to all police forces in Great Britain, while the supplement was issued fortnightly and provided a description of 'Expert and Travelling Criminals', their names, aliases, methods and 'Personal Weaknesses, Peculiarities, etc.' The first page of mugshots shows six men, and so does the next. They look surprised or resigned, menacing or afraid. They wear working-men's flat caps, some have boaters, trilbies or bowler hats – one even wears a top hat.

I turn another page and there, among the men, is the person I'm looking for – Maggie Hughes. She is in her early twenties, a fresh-faced young woman, far fresher looking than the men. She wears a luxurious fur coat, its collar turned up to her ears, and her expression is utterly unfazed. She looks like a gangster.

I peer more closely at the photo, distracted by the rustle of someone walking past my table and the man opposite chewing on his fingernails.

What is Maggie Hughes wearing on her head? It looks like a velvet Tam O'Shanter, a cross between a turban and a beret, made famous by American film star, Clara Bow. Maggie is staring right at the police photographer, as she must have been told to do, her gaze a little hypnotic. She is described as an expert shoplifter, who is 'suspected of being concerned with a gang of shop breakers using motor cars and vans'. Her peculiarities include 'sometimes dyes her hair a light colour; addicted to drink; of a violent disposition and loose morals'.

I flip through more mugshots of men until I come to the second woman I'm looking for – Alice Diamond. She's also enveloped in a fur coat, and she wears a stylish cloche hat embroidered with flowers, a wisp of hair escaping from under the rim. Alice's previous crimes include stealing fur coats worth £100 and applying for a job at a wartime munitions factory using another girl's Labour Bureau card. Her eyes are slightly droopy; she does not look bothered at all. And no wonder, for Alice Diamond was the new Queen of the Forty Thieves and 'Baby-faced Thief' Maggie Hughes was her fearsome lieutenant.

They made a striking pair. Alice was an Amazon and 'the tallest woman criminal in London', while green-eyed Maggie was petite, demure, always tastefully dressed and one of the most beautiful crooks in the capital.

In February 1920, the two women had stood trial for shoplifting from four West End establishments. They'd only been left alone for a few minutes while an assistant was called and managed to steal a fur stole, a large skunk fur coat, two fur wraps, a mole jacket and five silver fox skins, all from one shop. None of the property was recovered and 'so clever are their methods', explained Detective Inspector George Cornish, 'they have never been seen to steal anything'.

Six years after their mugshots appeared in the *Police Gazette*, Alice Diamond and Maggie Hughes had earned such a string of convictions that, according to the *Illustrated Police News*, 'their past records, too long to quote here, make one gasp for breath'. Together, they masterminded military-style raids on department stores, from London's West End to Newcastle, from the city centre of Manchester to the shopping districts of Derby and Bristol. The Forty Thieves had started out as Victorian street pickpockets under the leadership of flower seller Mary

Carr; now the women travelled in chauffeur-driven cars, dressed to the nines in furs and silk, and were celebrated for their 'good looks, fine stature, and smart clothing'.

Alice Diamond and Maggie Hughes both came from humble beginnings and grew up in families who were used to evading the law. Alice was born in Lambeth on 20 June 1896, one of eight children. Her mother, Mary Ann Alice Blake, was a jam packer, a seasonal and badly paid factory job, while her father, Thomas Diamond, was a porter at Borough Market. He'd served five months in prison for stealing lead and zinc and was described as part of a gang of south London 'savages' after attempting to rescue another market porter from the police.

Alice's parents married in April 1896, but around a week before her birth, her mother was admitted to St George's Workhouse on Mint Street, a place previously condemned by *The Lancet* for the 'grossest possible carelessness and neglect'. The workhouse authorities wrote a note next to Mary Ann's name, 'in Labor – Deserted?' Perhaps she told them the father of her child had disappeared and she needed free medical help while giving birth. But on 17 June she left the workhouse, and her daughter was born three days later.

Alice's parents appeared reluctant to provide accurate details. Her mother was registered under the surname Black and the family frequently moved lodgings, at one point living in a road which ran off Stamford Street, the former residence of Mary Carr and her paramour Alf Gorman.

By the age of 14, Alice Diamond was a domestic servant, as were a third of working women in Britain. New sectors of employment had opened up towards the end of the nineteenth century, including nursing, shop work and clerical jobs, but for most working-class girls, opportunities had barely changed. The annual wage of a London maid could be as low as £7, and girls like Alice Diamond had to wear the uniform of servitude, the apron and cap that signified their status in life. She would later give her occupation as tailoress, and many members of the Forty

Thieves similarly worked in the clothing trade, as dressmakers, milliners and needlewomen. It was unreliable work and poorly paid, but it meant the Forties knew how clothes were patterned, cut, fitted and finished, and they recognised valuable cloth when they saw it.

Alice Diamond's criminal career appears to have started in 1912, when she was cautioned along with a friend for stealing chocolate from a shop counter in the Strand. That same year, when the suffragettes launched a window-smashing campaign as part of an increasingly militant fight for the vote, Alice Diamond's mother and aunt took advantage of the disturbance to help themselves to gowns and coats in a West End store. In 1913, Alice was sentenced to six weeks for stealing blouses, and then cautioned again on a similar charge. Two years later, she was convicted of stealing a watch and sentenced to one year of hard labour at Holloway Prison.

Holloway was the largest prison for women in Britain, an imposing castle-like building on a 10-acre site in north London. It had first opened in 1852 as a prison for men and women, and its foundation stone was inscribed with the words, 'May God preserve the City of London and make this place a terror to evil-doers.' By the time Alice Diamond arrived, it had become a female-only jail and was known far and wide for its brutal treatment of the suffragettes and its regime of force-feeding.

Alice Diamond was only 19 years old, but according to Scotland Yard, she was the new Queen of the Forty Thieves. Like Mary Carr, she'd become a leader at a very young age. She was also fearless and strong – during one arrest it took three policemen 'to hold her down in the station' – and she was well connected to the criminal underworld through family, friends and tenement neighbours.

Alice used a number of aliases, alternating between Blake and Black, changing her first name to Dolly, Diana or Maud, and often altering her date of birth. Official descriptions of her physical appearance also varied: sometimes she had a dimpled chin and a scar on her forehead, in others a scar under her left eye, or no scars at all. But in the popular imagination, it was her height that became the defining factor. The tallest she grew, according to prison records, was 5ft 10½in, a significant height when the average woman was around 5ft 2in. But as her fame increased, so did her size, and soon the press insisted she was over 6ft tall. Alice Diamond was portrayed as exceptional, her physical difference from 'normal' women was repeatedly emphasised and, by implication, her moral difference as well. She was a terrifying modern example of the 'female born criminal'.

Maggie Hughes' background was similar, although she came from north of the River Thames and her family were said to be 'one of the toughest in London'. She was born Margaret Lilian Hill on 29 July 1898 in Westminster. Her father James was a bricklayer and housepainter from Chichester, and her mother Amelia was from Dublin or Limerick. At the age of 5, Maggie was admitted to the St Pancras Workhouse, along with three siblings, but not her parents. People often arrived at the workhouse in a 'dying condition', and while conditions had improved since the mid-nineteenth century, when the fetid air was 'enough to knock you down', government inspectors had recently found inmates locked up in padded rooms for weeks on end.

The Hill children were removed after a few weeks, and Maggie and a sister were later sent to a school in Hertfordshire to be trained for domestic service. By 1911, the family was back together, sharing two rooms off Tottenham Court Road. Maggie's younger brother, Billy, who would eventually adopt the title 'Boss of Britain's Underworld', described their childhood home as 'one of the favourite visiting places for all tealeaves and crooked people'. Their father received numerous convictions for 'belting cozzers', while their mother 'was a buyer of bent gear'. Billy boasted that the Hill children were 'the best fed and best dressed in the district', and when they were bullied by local children, their mother advised them to 'get the bleeding chopper and go out and murder them'. If they didn't, then 'we'd get another belting from our mother'.

At 14, Maggie ran away from home and, three years later, she married thief and gangster Alfred Hughes. He was nine years her senior and said to be one of the best 'screwsmen' – burglar or safebreaker – in England. Six months after the marriage, Maggie received her first prison sentence – one month for 'damage'. Then, in 1919 she was arrested in Bristol after a constable saw her acting suspiciously in the street. Maggie was in the process of receiving a parcel from another member of the Forty

Thieves, containing thirteen new silk blouses. 'We got them from a shop,' Maggie told the police breezily, 'and we came to Bristol from London for the purpose.'

It was around this time that Billy Hill visited his elder sister in Holloway, neatly dressed in a sailor suit and carrying a potted plant, unaware that small containers of snuff were hidden inside the soil. Once Maggie retrieved the snuff, she was able to exchange it for other goods and 'it made her top girl in the nick ... she got whatever she wanted'. Prison did little to deter the Forty Thieves, the women had friends inside and support from the outside, and as one member explained, 'You'd be surprised what a few nicker spread in the right direction will do to make life easy in the nick.'

The Forty Thieves were involved in various crimes in the early decades of the 1900s, stealing from hotels, warehouses and jewellery shops. But their favourite occupation was large-scale shoplifting, and by the 1920s they had turned it into an art. The women were professional hoisters – or 'oysters' – a term that had been used to describe shoplifters, who went 'on the hoist', since the late eighteenth century. Only now their targets weren't individual drapers' shops but enormous department stores with an assortment of luxury items under one roof.

The first department stores had appeared at the end of the eighteenth century, when some drapery shops began dividing their premises into separate departments. By 1870 Debenham & Freebody in London had twenty-seven departments, including silks, furs, shawls, gloves, parasols and ribbons. Seven years later, Bon Marché opened a shop in south-west London, said to be England's first purpose-built department store, and situated just a few miles from Alice Diamond's family home.

The more opulent stores were destinations in themselves and shopping became entertainment, as enticing as going to the theatre. There was a new emphasis on marketing, with window displays and seasonal sales, and customers could browse the items on sale, rather than ask an assistant to bring them.

Selfridges, on Oxford Street, resembled a palace or museum and by the 1920s it had 100 separate departments, as well as restaurants and a roof garden, a post office and theatre booking office, and 12,000 employees. Behind the scenes, meanwhile, were the working-class women like the Forty Thieves who made the luxury clothing, while some apprentices were paid no wages at all.

Shoplifting was a problem right from the start, and shortly after Selfridges opened one magistrate accused the store of setting out goods 'in such a manner as to be a temptation to theft'. It was no wonder that Selfridges became a playground for the Forty Thieves, as did Liberty, Whiteley's, Harrods and Bourne & Hollingsworth. The women timed their visits to coincide with busy periods such as lunchtime and teatime, or the opening day of a sale. 'Dressed to kill, those girls would descend on a West End store like a swarm of locusts,' recalled Detective John Capstick. 'They would roll up in taxis and chauffeur driven limousines and practically clean the place out inside an hour.'

Like the lady thieves of Victorian times, the Forties adapted their clothing, using specially designed skirts with deep pockets, as well as 'grafter's bloomers'. 'If you knew your graft,' explained one member, 'you could stick a grand piano up 'em.' They fixed webbing under their coats, inserted hooks to petticoats and corsets, tied belts around the waist from which to suspend parcels, and made slits in stockings to conceal smaller goods.

The Forties weren't the only female thieves using ingenious new methods. Some shoplifters filled hollow boot heels with beeswax to hide stolen rings, while others concealed clippers in parasol handles to cut the strings of bags and purses. By the late 1920s, there were said to be at least 10,000 regular professional women shoplifters in London.

The Forties often operated in teams of three, with their driver parked by the store's side door. The hoister walked up to a rack of dresses, slowly examined each one and then slid the ones she'd chosen to the end of the rail. A second member of the team, the 'smother', approached the rack and waited for a signal that the coast was clear. Then she reached across the hoister, took a dress from the rack and turned around as if looking for an assistant. The hoister, now screened from view, took the clothes and stuffed them into her bloomers. All three then strolled to the door and once the hoister had gone and the goods were in the car, they progressed to another department.

Like Victorian jewel thief Emily Lawrence, there was a strong performance element to their raids, and they were experts in disguise. As working-class women, they operated in establishments designed for privileged shoppers, and they had to blend in perfectly. In the arena of Harrods or Selfridges, the Forty Thieves changed status. They were no longer former workhouse girls and domestic servants but finely dressed ladies wearing the latest styles, bought with the proceeds of shoplifting.

Once their day's work was done, the women sold the goods through a network of receivers all over London. 'They do well out of their activities,' remarked Detective Lilian Wyles, 'live under the most comfortable circumstances, rub shoulders with the wealthy in the best hotels and restaurants, and have a thoroughly good time while it lasts.'

Unlike Victorian lady thieves, however, the Forties were not portrayed as being sexually aroused by fur or silk, and while they used similar methods to Phoebe Price's shoplifting gang, their raids were responding to the demands of fashion. The Forties wanted stylish clothing for themselves, and their criminal activities made top-end designs available to other working-class women.

The gang was so successful that they also created jobs for other women, for what better way to catch a lady hoister than to employ a lady detective? A male detective could not 'frequent parts of a store given over to the fair sex', explained journalist Sidney Felstead, so 'women have to be employed to keep watch on them'. Policewomen had only just begun to work on the London streets and still had limited powers, but larger department stores hired plain-clothes female detectives as part of their 'special inquiry staff'. Like their criminal adversaries, they too had to learn to play a role. Lady detectives took on various guises, pretending to be a customer or the head of department supervising assistants. Discretion was key and shops were reluctant to publicise the fact they employed detectives. When a London magistrate advised stores to display notices of shoplifting convictions as a warning, it was feared this would scare away honest but nervous women. Advertisements recruiting female assistants for detective work therefore stressed the need for 'SECRECY and TACT'.

As with Victorian shopkeepers, the twentieth-century female detective had to tread carefully. If 'some foolish woman of weak moral balance' was tempted by the pretty things all around her, explained the *Dundee Courier*, it was 'not desirable to create a scene' and prosecution was to be avoided 'if possible'. Female detectives also had to be prepared to 'meet plenty of thrills'. 'Struggles' often took place between shoplifter and detective, and offenders were known to threaten to 'bash your face in'.

Annie Betts, one of London's most prominent store detectives, was often seen hurrying after a suspected shoplifter as fast as she could go. Annie had begun her career working for a retired police inspector who ran a detective agency, taking part in undercover investigations into fraudulent fortune tellers. She then moved into department stores and when she caught two women stealing silk from a store in Kensington, one alleged that she'd been handled so roughly her arms were 'black and blue … it was like a navvy pulling me about instead of a woman'. Annie Betts, it seems, was as fearsome as a man.

One day, she bumped into Alice Diamond, who was awaiting trial. 'You haven't been to see us lately,' she remarked. 'No,' retorted Alice, 'but I will.' An hour later, Annie Betts was on her way back to work when she saw Alice Diamond in a teashop surrounded by her confederates. The Forties had made a lightning raid on the detective's Oxford Street store and were arrested with a large number of rolls of silk.

Larger department stores began to experiment with new security techniques, such as the 'coloured light code' introduced in the late 1920s. A row of coloured electric light bulbs were installed on a wall, each colour signifying a different part of the store. The moment a shop detective recognised a shoplifter, or an assistant began to feel suspicious, they rang the shop's private phone exchange. The coloured light, which showed the location of the thief, was switched on, and detectives and shop assistants throughout the store were put on alert. If a professional hoister felt she was being watched, however, she'd often drop a stolen article into an innocent person's pocket or handbag.

But aside from lady detectives and the coloured light code, security at department stores was still minimal. Alice Diamond and Maggie Hughes were arrested numerous times, with hundreds of pounds' worth of 'stuff' about their persons but, according to the *Sunday People*, they had 'never been actually seen to steal as much as a farthing's worth'.

One day, they arrived by taxi at a firm of court furriers in Hanover Square, where Emily Lawrence had stolen a diamond locket in 1860. Alice asked for an estimate to have her fur coat relined and the assistant went off to get a quote. When he came back, the women had gone, along with a fur coat worth nearly £500.

As the Forties became well known to London police, they began to venture further out of the capital. One former member, who recalled stealing a £2,000 mink coat in Manchester, described their methods. The women hired a driver to pick them up at 6.30 a.m., usually a man in his late forties 'who'd done quite a lot of bird and so knew all the answers'. He was paid a weekly wage, plus expenses and a bonus, and drove the women using a forged licence. Just before they reached their destination, the driver stopped so the Forties could put on their grafting bloomers. They spent the day shoplifting, before moving on to the next town, and then returned to London.

When one of their younger drivers proposed marriage to three different gang members, and one was arrested trying to hoist a wedding dress with a 20ft train, the women took revenge. On the way back from Birmingham, they asked the driver to stop in a quiet wood where they stripped off all his clothing. They threw him a pair of grafting bloomers to 'cover up his bits and pieces', jumped back in the car and drove off.

The Forties averaged £30 each a week on these shopping trips, after expenses had been paid. It was well-paid work when a dressmaker could expect just 30s a week, and 'you see places you'd never visit if you were living an ordinary life,' explained one member. In London there were plenty of ways to spend their hoisting money, particularly in the West End. The Forties danced the tango and the Charleston at Murray's in Beak Street, drank cocktails and listened to jazz. They were regulars at venues run by 'queen of the nightclubs' Kate Meyrick, such as the famous 43 Club on Gerrard Street. Its clients were described as 'officers of distinguished regiments, members of the peerage, experienced Men about Town or rich young City magnates'.

Alice Diamond and Maggie Hughes were as exquisitely dressed as film stars, with bobbed hair and kohl-rimmed eyes, fox stoles round their shoulders and sapphire rings on their fingers. The rings served another purpose as well. Alice was a 'formidable brawler', according to Brian McDonald, and aside from showing off her wealth and good taste, the rings made a fearful knuckleduster.

It was around this time that the women acquired a new name – the Forty Elephants. The title was attributed to Albert McDonald, with whom Alice had a brief relationship, and stemmed partly from the fact that most of the women came from the Elephant and Castle area. It was also because the gang had the habit of emerging from department stores several sizes larger than when they'd arrived. 'They went into a draper's like sylphs,' explained one constable, 'and came out like heavyweights.'

The 'Forty Elephants' suggested power and strength, but the title was also used to mock the gang of women, who were becoming increasingly professional. The Forties were operating in cells and abiding by the Hoister's Code, a set of rules as noted down by Dan Johnston, an associate of the Elephant and Castle Gang: members were to be punctual; there was to be no drinking before a raid; and any sign of 'treachery' meant a woman would be expelled. The Forties were not to steal from each other, either money or boyfriends, and they were not supposed to wear any of the stolen clothing. The proceeds of crime were shared equally among the cell, and if a member was arrested then others provided alibis. As the queen, Alice Diamond was 'not to be held responsible' if things went wrong, it was simply part of the 'misfortunes of war'.

The Forties paid subscriptions, with the money used to hire defence lawyers and look after a woman's family if she was imprisoned. On their release, there was a reception committee waiting at the prison gate, followed by an all-night party and 'a week down at Brighton to get the taste of porridge out of your system'.

Dan Johnston clearly admired the Forty Elephants and their use of 'battlefield tactics'. He noted the similarity between professional criminals and legitimate business people and explained the women 'look at it as going out to work', planning their raids 'with the exactitude of a board meeting'. Crime gave the Forties independence. They earned their own money and spent it as they chose, so there was no need to rely financially on a man.

But while the gang were disciplined and organised, they could also be vicious, and particularly baby-faced Maggie Hughes. Maggie had always had a reputation for violence, as did her brother, Billy. He described himself as one of the 'best chiv merchants in the business', known for slashing men's faces with a razor, leaving his trademark long, thin, red line.

In September 1922, Maggie had received a twelve-month sentence for wounding a woman called Ethel Martin. The argument appeared to centre on Ethel's ex-husband. Maggie confronted her at a tram stop, produced a razor from under her fur coat and slashed Ethel in the face.

The following year, when Maggie was arrested for stealing a tray of thirty-four gold rings from a jeweller on Shaftesbury Avenue, police found a 'large pocketknife, with the blade open' in her handbag. Her case was 'absolutely hopeless', declared the judge, she was a 'dangerous person', who had been in and out of prison for years. 'From your appearance you look like a baby,' he said, 'but you are a bad thief', and he sentenced her to three years. 'It cannot make me any better,' shouted Maggie, 'it will make me a villain!' Then she 'burst forth into a torrent of abuse' and was forcibly removed from the dock. Another newspaper reported her words more threateningly. 'It won't cure me,' she shouted, 'Wait til I come out. I'll be a regular villain.' Maggie Hughes was growing increasingly volatile, and it appeared to only be a matter of time before Scotland Yard closed in on the Forty Elephants.

It's a crisp lunchtime in April 2019 and I'm walking down Lower Marsh, one of London's oldest market streets, near the back of Waterloo Station. This was the commercial heart of Lambeth in the days of the Forty Elephants, and Lower Marsh Market was a lively place, with stallholders selling old clothes and cast-off bedding, as well as dates, peanuts and cough drops made on-site. It was less sinister than the nearby New Cut, where ramshackle stalls sold stale pieces of soap and the occasional dog-fish, and where local houses were blackened with grime. Today, Lambeth is described by estate agents as a cosmopolitan, culture-packed borough for young professionals, with wine bars, theatres and galleries, and Lower Marsh is full of office workers and students, queuing beneath green and orange awnings for curries, wraps and dim sum.

I stop at a pub called Vaulty Towers, on the corner of Johanna Street, with brightly coloured painted walls and a sign that promises 'fun, food & drink'. I hear the pub door open, and a woman comes out to place a placard on the pavement.

'Are you coming in?' she asks.

'Sorry?'

'To the life drawing classes,' she points to the placard. 'Life Drawing. Drop-in. Here and now.'

'No,' I say, apologetically, 'I'm looking for No. 35 Johanna Street.' I glance down the street. It's so short that there is only one house, a slim building of red and brown brick, right next to the pub. 'There was a riot down there,' I tell the woman from the pub. 'It involved the Forty Elephants.'

'Who?' she laughs.

'The Forty Elephants, they were a female crime syndicate. Their leaders were Alice Diamond and Maggie Hughes, they ran a massive shoplifting gang that worked all over England.'

'Wow!' says the woman from the pub, 'I've never heard of them. But we're No. 34.'

I take a few steps down Johanna Street and stop in front of the house, its bottom windows covered in bars. I look up at the second floor, imagine a mob of fifty people in this street today – there wouldn't be room to turn round, let alone escape.

In December 1925, a dispute between two of the Forty Elephants, Marie Britten and Bertha Tappenden, led to a pub fight in which Bertha was slashed in the face with a glass. The trigger was unclear, but according to police, Marie had recently married an outsider and decided to go straight.

On 19 December the women fought again, this time at a nearby social club on New Cut, and others joined in, including Marie's father, William Britten. The following night a crowd set off, led by Alice Diamond, Maggie Hughes and Gertrude Scully, a long-time member of the Forty Thieves. The three women, armed, angry and drunk, marched to the Britten house at No. 35 Johanna Street, throwing stones and bottles at the windows and smashing down the front door. Then the men went after William Britten and his son, slashing them with razors, in what became known as the 'Battle of Johanna Street'.

Three months later, Alice Diamond, Maggie Hughes and seven others stood trial at the Old Bailey, now a lavish new building with oak-panelled courtrooms and marble floors. The atmosphere was 'electric with half-hinted revelations of London's underworld', and the women were blamed as 'the fomenters of the disturbance'.

Alice was sentenced to eighteen months of hard labour, and Maggie and Gertrude to twenty-one months. The *Sunday People* printed mugshots of Alice and Maggie looking suitably menacing, while a Parisian paper explained that London had been 'terrorised by Women Apaches', a gang of 'enormous women', who carried razors in their blouses and were led by 'Queen Diamond', nearly 6ft tall and 'of an extraordinary corpulence'. An American report was more reassuring, 'The Forty Elephants have at last been trapped, London at last breathes more easily.'

But while the 'Women Apaches' had been jailed for now, the 1930s were on their way and so too was a new fear. 'Women as criminals invading the special domain of men offenders', declared one newspaper, which warned of 'alarming visions of a new criminal type springing from the ultramodern young women of to-day'.

Now female crooks wouldn't just play the part of the fashionable lady in order to steal from inside department stores, they would smash their way in from the outside, just like a man.

8

LADY JACK
SHOP BREAKER

At 7.30 a.m. one Sunday morning, Police Constable Reynolds was keeping observation on Messrs Marks & Spencer in Upton Park, east London. The nationwide retailer had just launched a major expansion and its new 'super stores' boasted everything from pure silk stockings to felt hats, gramophone records and china tea sets. Constable Reynolds and his colleague were keeping a close eye on the store because four local shops had had their locks sawn through in the past two months.

All of a sudden, he saw a young woman come to the middle door, shade her eyes with her hand and look through the glass into Messrs Marks & Spencer. Then she took an instrument from a parcel under her arm and began to saw at the lock. Each time someone passed by the woman walked away – but then she returned and continued to work at the lock. Eventually, after she'd been disturbed five times, she gave up and walked off.

The police passed a description to detectives and, a few hours later, the woman was arrested while waiting at a bus stop in Plaistow. Inside her attaché case was an array of housebreaking implements – a jemmy (crowbar), a saw and seven hacksaws. The police identified her as Elsie Florence Carey, a 'cunning and dangerous thief' and the head of a sinister gang of shop breakers.

If it seemed reckless to attempt a break-in in broad daylight, Elsie had good reason. Those found in possession of housebreaking implements by night were charged with burglary, whereas those who operated during the day were treated more leniently. When the police went to Elsie's home in Canning Town, they saw her stepmother, Georgina Carey, and two men, 'sorting and inspecting articles of women's underwear', stolen earlier from a draper's in Forest Gate. All four were charged with stealing and receiving £50 worth of clothing, and Elsie was also charged with attempted breaking and entering.

When the case came to trial in September 1934, the courtroom was filled with detectives from all over London, including Detective Superintendent Frederick Bennett, one of the 'Big Five' of Scotland Yard and head of the Metropolitan Police Flying Squad. The Flying Squad had been formed in 1919 as an elite group of detectives whose mission was the destruction of criminal gangs. Initially, they had travelled in two horse-drawn wagons, but by the 1930s the Flying Squad were known for their fast cars and ability to get round London at high speed. They were generally portrayed as tough and tenacious men, relying on a network of paid informers and mixing closely with criminals, much as thieftakers had done in the past. The Flying Squad was a 'corps of ace detectives', boasted Chief Inspector Frederick 'Nutty' Sharpe, who watched 'the haunts and the movements of people who may tomorrow commit a big crime'.

When Elsie Carey appeared in court, she faced further charges, including breaking and entering British Home Stores in Ilford. Her stepmother, Georgina, insisted she hadn't been involved at all. Elsie had come running into the front room with a suitcase, thrown it down and run out. Georgina had simply been putting the goods back into the case when the police appeared. Elsie was sentenced to a year of hard labour at Holloway, while her stepmother received three months, and the men one month each.

Elsie Carey was 'a menace to the community', and she was apparently known for 'hating men and ruling crooks'. So, was this the new face of the female criminal that the press had warned about, invading the special domain of male offenders?

Elsie was operating in the 'male' world of shop breaking, and she also sported an 'Eton crop', a short, bobbed hairstyle worn by glamorous performers such as Josephine Baker. It was the ideal style to fit under a cloche hat, but it was also regarded as daring, bold and decidedly 'mannish'. The Eton crop was 'a flag of revolt', according to one American newspaper, while a British vicar warned his parishioners 'never marry a girl with bobbed hair, the glory of woman is in her hair, and the devil likes her to get it cut off'.

Female criminals were said to be on the rise in the 1920s and 1930s. 'Like the suffragettes of old, the modern woman crook is out for "equality",' announced the *Lincolnshire Echo*. Women had 'new freedoms and new lives', explained *Pathe News*, including the right to vote on the same terms as men.

There was also renewed interest in the nature of the female offender, and in 1928 Harry Ashton-Wolfe wrote a lengthy feature for the *Illustrated London News*. Harry was assistant investigator at the Marseilles Scientific Police Laboratories (now the French Forensic Police Office) and had extensive experience of criminal trials in Europe and America. He was also the author of true crime adventures such as *The Thrill of Evil* and *The Cask of Death*, and his criminology theories turned out to be as fanciful as his books.

As a rule, he explained, women were 'mere confederates' in crime. They only took part under the orders of a violent gang, or because they were blindly following the instructions of the men they loved. Their primary role – as long as they were pretty – was to distract a watchman so he became oblivious to the grind of drills, the hiss of a blowpipe or the snapping of locks carried out by male crooks in another part of the building. Women were also useful as spies. They could obtain valuable information about the habits of employees, make rough sketches of a building's layout, including burglar alarms, electric wires and switches, and take impressions of locks.

But Harry Ashton-Wolfe struggled to resolve the contradictions inherent in his theories of female crooks. On the one hand, women were incapable of initiating crime, yet their criminal schemes were now so varied and dangerous that the police had created 'special departments' to deal with them. Female criminals used subtler methods than men and were adept in cunning, but oddly this also made them easier to catch. Women lacked 'the power to visualise the result of their crimes from the investigator's point of view', and their vanity meant they left obvious and distinctive traces. They refused to wear rough men's boots and left the marks of narrow feet and small heels. Their long nails produced 'characteristic scratches', while their use of perfumes and powder made them easy to track. In addition, women's fingerprints were 'quite different' from a man's, a theory that is still being tested and investigated today.

According to Harry Ashton-Wolfe, female criminals were inept, vain and stupid. But what about Alice Diamond, Maggie Hughes and the rest of the Forty Elephants? They were well known by 1928, and they were not decoys or spies for men. The women were rarely caught in the act, frequently evaded arrest, and most of the stolen goods were never found. But shoplifting was a feminine activity and could just be dismissed, no matter how professional or well organised, so Harry Ashton-Wolfe simply ignored the Forty Elephants altogether.

Netley Lucas, another self-appointed expert, also wrote extensively on the character of the female criminal, and his book *Crook Janes* offered an international gallery of beautiful rogues who were 'not so much immoral as unmoral; women to whom the ordinary laws and convention of society mean nothing'. Only 10 per cent of crooks in London were women, Netley explained, but many more hovered on the borderline between vice and virtue. And while the woman criminal might have beautiful clothes and a life of pleasure, she would never enjoy children, an affectionate husband, a home of her own and 'everything which makes life worthwhile for a woman'. Netley Lucas, meanwhile, had his own shady past – he was a liar and confidence trickster who would soon be in prison himself.

The two criminal theorists shared many views, except when it came to women burglars. Netley estimated that there were around 100 operating in London, particularly in the East End. The most renowned was 'Fluff', the Queen of the Burglars, followed by 'Molly of Poplar', a fair-haired, blue-eyed, comely screwsman in the 'Sleever Gang', and 'what she does not know about burglary and housebreaking is not worth knowing'. But Harry Ashton-Wolfe dismissed the idea of women burglars because, when it came to female criminals, anything 'requiring skilled labour, is beyond her'.

It certainly wasn't beyond Elsie Florence Carey, as she repeatedly proved both in London and on the south coast. She was a 5ft 6in, 7-stone 'Eton cropped bandit', according to the press, who 'queened it over her gang of thieves'. She became almost a mythological figure, like Moll Cutpurse, the Jacobean outlaw; Mary Carr, the blackmailing Queen of the Forty Thieves; and Alice Diamond, the Amazonian shoplifter. Elsie Carey 'ruled men twice her age and hypnotised them with her daring'.

Elsie Florence Carey was born in Canning Town on 26 February 1910. She grew up not far from the Royal Victoria Dock, and her father James was a cooper, making barrels for boats. Canning Town was one of the most populated boroughs in England, home to nearly 300,000 people and officially a 'distressed' area of London, with slum housing, high poverty and regular outbreaks of disease. One commentator described 'the long grey streets, with anxious eyed women standing at the doors, children eating scraps of dry bread and an atmosphere of gloom and despair'.

When Elsie was 10, her mother, Elsie Ellen, died, leaving four young children. Two years later, her father married Georgina Benbow.

Elsie's first conviction came at the age of 19, for stealing a quilt from outside a shop. In 1931, she was sent to a hostel for six months for stealing cash from ticket boxes on tramcars, and the following year she was jailed for three months for stealing jerseys and handbags.

After serving her time for the attempted break-in at Marks & Spencer's in Upton Park, she worked as a shop assistant. But then, in 1936, she was charged under the name Elsie Jacqueline Marsden for breaking and entering a lock-up shop on Stratford's High Street, and taking off with sixty-seven men's shirts, twenty-one woollen pullovers and fifty-five gents' ties. At the police station, Elsie asked to go to the lavatory, where she attempted to dispose of a key, 'which could be used to open shop window fastenings'.

She was also convicted of stealing gold jewellery from her land-lady and sentenced to two counts of six months of hard labour. Elsie seemed unperturbed by her conviction. 'You wait,' she said to Detective Sergeant Muir. 'We will get you.'

After her release from Holloway, Elsie settled nearby in Tufnell Park, where she shared accommodation on Carleton Road with Phillip Ames, a 24-year-old butcher who'd been previously convicted for living off immoral earnings. In the autumn of 1937, they took a trip to Oxford, with a 21-year-old driver named Leonard Arthur Swan, timing their arrival with early closing day. Elsie climbed through the window of a gown shop in George Street and opened the main doors, then she gath-ered up some dresses, snatched £4 from the till, and the gang sped off.

But the owner of a nearby snack bar had seen two people loiter-ing, and he passed the car number to the police. At 5 p.m. that day, Constable Hobbs spotted the vehicle and took chase, jumping on the running board and forcing the driver to stop. Inside, he was surprised to see Elsie Florence Carey sitting on the back seat, wearing a dark blue trilby hat, a dark blue overcoat with square shoulders, a light fawn sports jacket, flannel trousers, and blue and white shoes. Now she would be known not just for her array of shop-breaking implements, but for 'masquerading' in men's clothes.

Word must have spread, for when Elsie appeared in court several journalists were there to describe her apparel: a squarely cut blue reefer coat of the type normally worn by sailors, and a white silk men's muf-fler or scarf. The *Daily Herald* was particularly vicious with its coverage: 'poker faced' Elsie Florence Carey was a 'hard-bitten West End woman gangster' and the leader of a bandit gang, whose 'mannish tightfitting tailored costume' made her look 'so like a man that even the clerk of assize momentarily mistook her for one'. The press dubbed her 'Lady Jack', supposedly the name by which her associates knew her.

The 'Lady Jack' figure of popular culture was a 'mannish' lesbian, often upper class, who wore tailor-made men's clothes, cut her hair short and smoked cigarettes. Women who wore trousers were no longer committing a crime as such and, unlike Moll Cutpurse, they could not be forced to do public penance. But they could be charged under vagrancy laws or arrested for indecent or disorderly behaviour.

Several cases of women 'masquerading in male attire' appeared in the press in the 1920s and 1930s. A Glasgow woman who put on her husband's clothes 'for fun', drank a couple of glasses of port and went to visit her neighbour, who was 'easily frightened', was fined 10s. Others were deliberately rebellious. When 22-year-old Londoner Margaret Kenyon threw a pair of roller skates through a café window after she'd been barred, the constable said he didn't know why she wore men's trousers. 'Well, I do,' replied Margaret. 'We can please ourselves in this country.'

Trousers and short hair were in vogue for women, just as they had been in Moll Cutpurse's day, and there were heated exchanges in the press. Women had worked in munitions factories during the First World War, and on farms and in the docks, wearing military uniforms and driving ambulances. Now they were meant to revert back to the domestic sphere, and that included wearing dresses and skirts. One letter writer described trouser-wearing women as disgusting, ugly and degenerate, and cited the same biblical passage that had been used to condemn Moll Cutpurse, 'The woman shall not wear that which pertaineth unto a man.' Some commentators were appalled at the 'epidemic' of women 'parading' in trousers – soon they would be 'the superior sex, and the dominant partners in human relationships'. But another letter writer, who signed herself 'Normal Modern Woman', said she found trousers extremely comfortable and hygienic and would continue to wear them.

There was a defiance about adopting men's clothes, and it was a brave stance to take when homophobia was on the rise. Sexual relations between women had never been criminalised in the UK, although the Criminal Law Amendment Act of 1921 had attempted to make 'acts of gross indecency' between women illegal. The bill was rejected by the House of Lords because, explained Lord Desart, it was better not to 'tell the whole world that there is such an offence' and thereby encourage other women to follow suit.

In 1928, Radclyffe Hall's novel *The Well of Loneliness*, the story of upper-class Stephen Gordon's affair with a young ambulance driver, was deemed an 'obscene libel'. 'A large amount of curiosity has been excited among women,' noted the Director of Public Prosecutions, 'and I am afraid in many cases curiosity may lead to imagination and indulgence in practices.' The British authorities were deeply afraid of the 'spread of lesbianism', and when Elsie Carey appeared in court with her Eton crop and flannel trousers, she embodied social anxieties about both gender roles and sexuality.

The police described her as clever, determined, cunning and dangerous, as well as an inveterate liar and an associate of prostitutes. At the time of her arrest, she'd been living on the proceeds of crime for two years and had recently spent £177 on 'the purchase of cars'. Elsie and her co-accused, Phillip Ames, asked for two further cases of shoplifting to be taken into consideration, at Bognor Regis and Worthing. Her lawyer pleaded for leniency – Elsie had fallen in with a gang 'who threatened her with violence if she did not stay with them'. But this sounds unlikely, considering Elsie had taken a leading role in her gang's crimes.

Phillip Ames was sentenced to twenty-one months, the driver was acquitted as an 'innocent dupe' and Elsie received four years. The judge was certain that if only she would make the effort, her time in Holloway Prison would help her to 'break free – I hope for ever – from a past that has been stained by so much that is shameful'. It's not clear what element of her life the judge found most shameful, Elsie's criminal career or her clothing. She received her punishment in silence. 'Only the muscles of her jaws twitched,' reported the press, 'then she half bowed to the judge, turned sharply and was led below.'

Elsie Carey was barely back in her prison cell before she was returned to court to face another charge. A few weeks before the Oxford theft, she'd committed a 'daylight robbery dressed as a man' in Slough. She'd broken the lock on a costumier's shop on the High Street and stolen £100 worth of dresses and furs. Again she was charged along with two men, Albert Ames and a driver, Alfred Dover. Her driver pleaded ignorance, insisting he'd been hired to teach Elsie to drive her brand new red Standard saloon, and on the way back from Slough she told him she'd broken into a shop. When he 'kicked a bit and said I had always gone straight', she responded, 'Ah, well, you are in it now.'

Elsie dismissed the new allegations. She'd simply been visiting Slough to look for a caravan for her holidays. Both men had 'used her car on occasions without her consent', and she'd fired Alfred for that very reason. When a witness described seeing two men, one of whom was 'effeminate' and wore a three-quarter-length overcoat, Elsie walked across the courtroom, picked up the overcoat produced by the police and pointed out 'this coat is a full length coat'. She was sentenced to a further three years, Albert Ames received another twelve months of hard labour, while their driver was found not guilty and discharged.

Initially, the sentences were to run consecutively, which meant Elsie faced seven years in prison, a significant stretch when the vast majority of Holloway's prisoners were serving under a month. In January 1938, she took her case to the Court of Appeal, still 'dressed like a man', and insisted they should run concurrently. The thefts from Oxford and Slough were the same type of offence, she argued, and if she'd been charged with both at the same time then her sentence would have been far less than seven years. The judges agreed, Elsie won the appeal, and she shook Albert Ames by the hand as she was led from the dock.

The case was reported as far away as Australia where, according to one paper, Elsie grasped her 'boyfriend's' hand and whispered, 'Good luck, Bert!', to which the tall, good-looking young man gave a cheerful, 'Cheerio, dear'. The paper also reported that while Elsie wore a man's overcoat and a white silk muffler, she'd replaced her usual trousers with a skirt. The Australian press appeared to be trying to feminise Lady Jack – her male associate had suddenly become her lover.

But the British press had an alternative story to tell, and particularly the *Daily Herald*. When Elsie arrived at Holloway Prison after her conviction for the Oxford theft, she'd had a stroke of luck. The window of her cell overlooked her flat in Carleton Road, where she'd been living with a Miss Queenie Day. The two women spent happy hours shouting across the 200 yards that separated the flat from the prison, and had 'such noisy talks that the neighbours couldn't hear the wireless'.

Elsie was moved to another part of the jail, where her window looked out onto a blank wall. 'It was the toughest break they could give her,' Queenie Day told the *Daily Herald*. 'I had hoped to be able to entertain Elsie every day with music from my radiogram, but our plans have all been defeated. Poor Elsie, I would not have had it happen for the world.' Then she gestured at the prison, 'Poor kid. That's one place I'll never go back to.'

Was Queenie Day aware that she was talking to a journalist? Had he made her an offer she couldn't refuse? The *Daily Herald* was a hugely successful paper, originally founded in 1911; it had recently relaunched with a new emphasis on human-interest stories, along with more photographs, features and advertising. Its daily dose of scandal, as well as free gifts and competitions, meant that in 1933 it became the first daily newspaper to sell 2 million copies.

Like other popular papers, the *Daily Herald* was keen for first-person revelations of a life in crime, and its editors could afford to offer attractive sums of money to sources. They knew a sensational story when they saw one. Lady Jack, the shop breaker who dressed like a man, appeared to have a very close relationship with Miss Queenie Day. And while she had vowed never to go back to Holloway, a few months later, Queenie too was inside, condemned as the 'worst woman in England'.

9

QUEENIE DAY
THE TERROR OF SOHO

Queenie Day was a 'coffee coloured beauty', with high cheekbones and a 'svelte figure', who, like many queens of the underworld, was wickedly fascinating to men. She was also, according to Scotland Yard, 'a violent criminal with no respect for the laws of this country or for those whose job it is to enforce them'.

In January 1938, Queenie joined her friend Elsie Carey in Holloway after attacking a white woman in Soho. 'You don't like us nigger girls, do you?' Queenie had reportedly asked, before cutting the woman's face twice with a penknife. Queenie Day would have been only too familiar with the N-word. It was used on the radio, and in music halls, in literature and song, as well as in fashion and advertising to describe the colour of frocks, hats and shoes. And then, of course, it was well established as a vicious, inflammatory racist insult, having been used as a term of hatred in the United States since the seventeenth century.

Queenie Day had grown up in a very different Britain from Ann Duck of the Black Boy Alley Ladies. Racist theories, developed to justify the slave trade in the 1800s and then used to serve the purpose of Empire, were far more entrenched. When Queenie was 11 years old, there were sustained outbreaks of racist violence in nine British cities, including Glasgow, Cardiff and Liverpool. Black seamen were attacked on Cable Street in London's docklands and mobs targeted Black families' homes, as well as white women who lived with Black men. One seaman, William Samuel, reported a police sergeant threatening 'we want you niggers out of our country, this is a white man's country and not yours'. The violence was partly sparked by a perceived competition for work, as well as fears about 'inter-racial' relationships, with alarming headlines warning of the perils of 'racial mixing'.

When Ann Duck was put on trial in the 1740s, the marriage between her white mother and Black father had not seemed remarkable. Now 'mixed colour marriages' were scandalous, a 'thing of horror', according to a former colonial administrator, and their children were cast as delinquents.

When Ann Duck was described in court as 'a Black woman', it was only for the purposes of identification, and there had been no reference to race in any newspaper report. But Queenie's colour frequently defined her, along with the suggestion she was an outsider, a foreigner with 'no respect for the laws of this country'. She was sentenced to ten months' imprisonment for the attack on the white woman and condemned as 'the terror of Soho'.

Queenie Day was two years older than Elsie Carey, born on 22 January 1908 at Queen Charlotte Hospital on the Marylebone Road. Her father, Edward, was a waterside labourer, born in Lambeth, and her mother, Edith Mary Watts, was from Pimlico. Queenie was the youngest of seven children, and grew up in Shepherd's Bush, west London.

Her first arrest came in October 1918, when she was convicted under the name Dorothy Farley, after breaking into a home in Ealing and stealing £50 worth of silver and plated goods. The press reported she was 14, but according to her birth certificate, Queenie Day was just 10 years old – and already using an alias. She was removed from her family and taken across the country to Ipswich Reformatory, where she would spend the next three years.

Nearly half of the female cases at juvenile courts involved girls under the age of 14. One 12-year-old was sent to an industrial school in Oxfordshire after stealing clothes from the workhouse, another was convicted for stealing 2lb of grapes from a shop on the Isle of Wight.

Most juvenile court cases resulted in a fine, dismissal or probation, and the rest were sent to Home Office certified schools, either industrial schools for children in need of 'rescue' and offenders under the age of 14, or reformatories for adolescent criminals up to the age of 16. Girls who appeared in juvenile courts were 'wayward', explains historian Pamela Cox, and often accused of offences against decency, including using language that was 'unbecoming' and 'offensive to chastity or delicacy'.

Inmates at certified schools wore uniforms and their hair was cropped, they could write one letter every fortnight and receive a visitor once a month. If they broke the rules they were caned, and put in the punishment room. Queenie Day appears to have been an inmate at St Matthew's in Ipswich, founded in Victorian times, where girls received classroom lessons and training for domestic service. Wayward girls needed to be domesticated, just as in the nineteenth century, and some certified schools were established in former homes for fallen women. At St Matthew's, the girls were urged to aspire to 'the qualities of womanhood' and to be gentle, kind, pure and good, holy and obedient.

When Queenie Day returned to London, she worked at the new Lyons factory in the western suburb of Greenford, alongside hundreds of other 'trousered workgirls' in a tea warehouse and cocoa factory. Lyons boasted the latest technology in factory automation, and its staff were provided with a dining room, rest and recreation rooms, a doctor's and dental surgery, and a room for manicures. But Queenie didn't stay long in the job.

In 1922 she was again convicted of housebreaking. This time, a Miss Penn came back to her Ealing home just after noon to find Queenie Day in her dining room, when she had 'no right whatever to be there'. Miss Penn demanded to know what was going on, to which Queenie replied, 'A boy brought me here ... Now he has bolted I don't see why I should have all the blame.'

There was a 'struggle' in the hall and Queenie rushed out, but Miss Penn followed and called for help. The gas meter had been damaged by a pair of garden shears, and a cupboard had been 'burst open', but the only stolen goods were a handful of apples and oranges.

According to police, Queenie then gave 'information which … led to the apprehension of three other young prisoners, with whom, no doubt, she had been associated and carried out thefts'.

Her parents were respectable people, explained Detective Sergeant Cracknell, and 'they had tried to keep her from these companions, but without success'. There had been no mention of her parents when Queenie was tried as a 10-year-old, but records suggest they were respectable, baptising all seven children and dutifully filling out census returns. Their oldest son, William, fought in the Rifle Brigade of the Yorks & Lancs Regiment during the war, and then became an artificial flower maker at the British Legion Poppy Factory.

Queenie was found guilty of housebreaking and sentenced to another three years, this time at Aylesbury Borstal in Buckinghamshire. Borstal detention had been introduced in 1908, as a way to separate offenders aged 16 to 21 from older convicts. The regime was supposed to be educational rather than punitive, with school lessons, physical exercise and training for work, but conditions were often brutal. Billy Hill, brother to 'baby faced' shoplifter Maggie Hughes, was sent to borstal as a 16-year-old in the 1920s and described it as 'the finest finishing school for criminals any underworld could hope for'. Inmates were pushed around like animals, and handcuffed and whipped when they misbehaved. 'Do you think I was in love with society,' asked Billy, 'when I came out?'

Aylesbury Borstal was housed in a wing of the women's prison, which was known for its inhumane regime. Chicago May, the American Queen of Crooks, described fellow inmates attempting to hang themselves with ropes used for making mailbags, setting fire to cells and being restrained in straitjackets. The governor was frequently so drunk he could barely walk, while prisoners survived on bread and cold tea.

Some women were 'driven insane' by their treatment and sent to Broadmoor asylum, while others were removed there as punishment 'for telling the truth'. But 'the acme of cruelty', according to Chicago May, was 'the eye which never slept'. Every cell at Aylesbury had a human eye carved and painted onto the inside of the door, 'complete in every detail, pupil, iris, eyelashes, eyebrow, etc. … to add to the realism of the thing'. From the outside, a wardress could 'slide a disk and substitute her own eye for the artificial one', while the rest of the time, 'no matter how you would place yourself in your cell ... that cursed eye seemed to follow you'. When Chicago May was released in 1917, after surviving ten years inside, her one desire was to be 'revenged on society'.

By the early 1920s, there were increasing concerns about the use of solitary confinement and handcuffs at Aylesbury. A number of girls had been 'leading wild and dissolute lives', according to prison commissioners, and their treatment presented 'extraordinary difficulties'. In 1920, the 'body belt with swivel handcuffs' was used thirty-three times, including on girls who were 'mentally deficient'. But conditions radically improved with the appointment in 1923 of a new governor, Lilian Barker, whose focus was education and guidance rather than punishment. 'Let us realise that the problem of these Borstal girls is our fault,' she declared, 'because we are not caring, and have not cared sufficiently about them.'

After Queenie Day's release from Aylesbury, she began working in the entertainment industry in Soho, as a chorus girl, dance partner and dance hostess. This was 'the very crust of London's Underworld', explained journalist Sydney Horler, and the mean shabby streets, darkened alleys, cheap lodging houses and gambling dens were dangerous places for the unwary.

Soho was also known as the resort of the 'low-class' prostitute, many of whom were ex-borstal girls like Queenie Day. Their numbers had increased during the Great Depression of the 1930s, but their economic motivations were largely ignored. Instead, women were pathologised as immoral, driven by a desire for excitement and a dislike of honest work. American sociologist William I. Thomas explained that delinquent girls 'used their sexuality' in a 'socially unacceptable way to get what they want from life'.

But working as a Soho prostitute was a dangerous job. 'It would be difficult to find a street prostitute in the West End without bruises even around the neck,' commented one chief constable. 'They daily come up against vicious men.' They were also subject to police harassment, especially women who were considered 'foreign', like Queenie Day, and who already had a criminal record. A woman could be labelled a 'common prostitute' after a single conviction for soliciting, and the stigma followed her through any future court appearance. A common prostitute could be arrested while simply walking down the street, or if she was seen being accosted by a man.

In 1928, Queenie Day was sentenced to three months of hard labour for being 'a suspected person who loitered with intent to commit a felony' on Charing Cross Road. A detective told the court she already had nine convictions for street walking, prostitution and assaulting police. In response, Queenie flung her handbag across the court and it struck a police inspector. She was immediately charged with assault and removed, 'screaming and struggling'. Her outburst earned her a further two months of hard labour.

She may then have worked with Billy Hill, who describes 'a girl named Coloured Queenie', who was 'playing in a leading West End musical', and whose job it was to knock on doors to see if anyone was at home before Billy burgled their house. She worked with his gang for several months and 'no one in the world would have suspected an olive-complexioned coloured girl, a smashing looker she was too, of drumming for a burglar's gang.'

By 1936, Queenie was living in a Bloomsbury boarding house with a young waitress called Alice Welch, and now she was organising house-breaking raids herself. In the spring of that year, the two women were arrested, along with another young waitress called Kitty Benjamin, and charged with breaking into the Edgware home of Patrick Aherne, a former leading man of the silent screen, and stealing property worth £174. When the police went to Queenie's flat, they found her in bed with Alice Welch. On being cautioned, she jumped out and brandished an automatic pistol. A police officer seized the weapon, to which Queenie declared, 'You can't blame me. It was given to me last night. I suppose this means a "packet".' Queenie was sentenced to a year in prison with hard labour, and Alice to six months.

But Queenie had barely come out of Holloway when she was in trouble again, this time during a hot summer's night at Dreamland

Amusement Park in Margate. Queenie and Mrs Jean Hales, a 'coloured woman', who was 'said to be' her sister, had come to the seaside for the day, along with Joan's husband. The press pointed out that Mr Hales was white. The press rarely – if ever – identified anyone as white, but then Mr Hales was married to a coloured woman.

According to Queenie, the trouble started when she was greeted with racist taunts and someone pushed her. George Slater, an attendant on the rocket plane, one of the 'amusement devices' in the 20-acre site, testified that the women were drunk and aggressive. When a man tried to 'restrain' Queenie, she grabbed his tie and nearly choked him. She then struck a young woman hard in the chest, at which another man in the crowd lost his temper and cried, 'You must not hit white women like that!' and pushed Queenie over. In a fury, she assaulted seven or eight people, with one witness crying out, 'She has got a knife and is going to stab someone!'

During the trial, the park inspector displayed a cut stretching from his elbow to wrist. Queenie Day had been 'mad drunk' and her language 'the filthiest I have ever heard, and I have had some experience'. Queenie explained that she 'could not stand them calling me a nigger and pulling me about'. But the court wasn't interested in this. What mattered was the filthy language used by two 'coloured' women, which was so terrible that a police constable could not even repeat it out loud but had to write it down on a piece of paper. Queenie and Joan were sentenced to twenty-eight days in jail.

So, when Queenie Day was arrested the following year for assaulting the white woman in Soho, had she again been provoked and subjected to racist abuse?

Yet, in January 1940, she was back in court again, this time for maliciously wounding a 'coloured' doorman at the 'Stepin Fetchet' Club. She was tried alongside two men for wrecking a table, five chairs, four ashtrays, two sauce bottles and a quantity of crockery. 'I was there,' she admitted. 'I didn't do anything; I only looked on … I'm the unlucky one; I suppose you pick on me because I was the only woman who was with the 16 men.' Her words sounded very similar to the day she was caught in Miss Penn's Enfield home at the age of 14 and didn't see why she should have all the blame then. This time, however, she was found not guilty and acquitted.

A couple of months later, Queenie was arrested for housebreaking in Hampstead, along with her old friend Kitty Benjamin. She told detectives, 'I don't know nothing about the breaking and entering. What are you trying to do? Pull something I haven't done.' But on the day of sentencing, Queenie and Kitty wrote letters to the judge, asking for leniency. Kitty's letter was apologetic, 'I will be very grateful if you could possibly give me probation. If you could, I know I won't get into trouble again.'

Queenie's letter was slightly more combative, 'I have been in trouble before, I have never had a chance in life.' She'd been offered a good situation in war work and, having 'never had work offered to me before', she'd thought it over and wanted to go straight. Then she added, 'The police won't leave me alone … I can't stand being hunted from pillar to post any longer.' There is a sense of desperation behind Queenie's words, she was in her early thirties now and had been in and out of reformatory, borstal and prison since the age of 10. But Divisional Detective Inspector Oxland described her as 'one of the worst women I have ever met', violent and vicious, with nineteen previous convictions. She was sentenced to two years in jail. 'Not so bad,' said Queenie, as she left the dock.

I can't find what happened to Queenie Day after this. Did she take up war work? Did she go straight? Did the police finally leave her alone? As for her former flat mate, Elsie Carey, she settled down to life in Holloway Prison to serve her sentence for shop breaking.

The prison regime had improved since the 1920s. Holloway's inmates no longer wore clothing marked with the traditional arrow or slept on wooden planks. The grim castle had been redecorated, and there was physical exercise, concerts, educational classes and lectures. In April 1939, the *Sunday Pictorial* ran a feature by Mrs Alice Coningsby, who'd been sentenced to three months for having 'foolishly borrowed money from a church friend'. Alice described playing the piano for a singsong among prisoners, and then she coached the Easter choir in the prison chapel. One of her choristers was Elsie Florence Carey. She had a fascinating personality, and Alice could 'well understand how she brought so many men – and women – under her control'. One friend 'broke windows every now and again', in order to get into Holloway and spend a few days near 'Lady Jack'.

Elsie was taking her sentence 'most philosophically', still wearing her hair in a severe Eton crop, 'twisting' her prison clothes 'to make them as masculine as possible' and smoking a pipe in her cell. Elsie didn't serve all of her sentence at Holloway. She was moved to Aylesbury, where she gave her occupation as 'motor driver – cars & lorries'. Most of her fellow inmates were domestic servants, jailed for petty crimes, but one prisoner was just as famous as Lady Jack, for 'baby-faced' Maggie Hughes of the Forty Elephants was in Aylesbury at the same time.

Elsie Carey was released in 1941 and, like Queenie Day, she too disappeared from the pages of the press. All I can find is a death certificate. Elsie Florence Carey died on 19 February 1999 in Rainham, Essex. Her occupation was 'assistant Warden retired'.

So, had she continued a life of crime but evaded capture? Or had she gone straight? And how had a former Eton-cropped gang girl become an assistant warden?

Despite her frequent appearances in tabloid crime reports, and the avid interest from both the *Daily Herald* and the *Mirror*, I can find no photos of Elsie Carey. I have no idea what Lady Jack or Queenie Day looked like – no face to put to the name – and no idea what happened when the two women eventually came out of prison in the middle of the Second World War.

10

RESCUED FROM THE FOOTNOTES

I'm sitting in a coffee shop in east London, my notebook on the table, about to have a conversation with Elsie Carey's niece. A few months ago, I wrote to Elsie's nephew, Alfred Webb, whose name and address appear on her death certificate. I wasn't sure how to word the letter. Did he know about his aunt's criminal career as the Eton-cropped gang girl? And if not, then what would he say when I told him?

When I didn't hear back from Alfred I was about to give up, until I realised he had a half-sister and found someone matching her name listed as a member of a Waltham Forest charity. A few days later, I was speaking to Linda Sansum on the phone and now we're in an East End coffee shop.

Linda has no problem talking about her infamous aunt, and she's brought along two mementos to show me. She carefully lifts a small, black jewellery box out of her bag and sets it on the table. I lean over as she opens it up.

Inside is a thick, gold signet ring embossed with E.C. – Elsie's Carey's initials. 'This is what we got when she died,' says Linda. We both stare at it for a moment, then she allows me to try it on. It's surprisingly heavy and feels tight on my finger. I hold out my hand and admire the ring. I can't believe this was once worn by Lady Jack, the daring shop breaker of the 1930s.

'Auntie Elsie never told me a single thing about her criminal life,' says Linda, 'not a thing.' I put the ring back in the jewellery box, and Linda bends down to take another object out of her bag: a photo frame. At last, I'm going to see an image of the Eton-cropped gang leader. I wait as Linda props the photo on the table, then she turns it towards me and here she is, Elsie Florence Carey. She looks like a handsome young chauffeur in a white shirt buttoned up to the neck, a slim black tie and black jacket. Her hair is lightly waved and slicked back from her forehead, her mouth is slightly open with the beginning of a smile. Elsie's large round eyes seem to look right through me. Her expression is youthful, hopeful and cheeky.

'What do you think of her?' asks Linda. 'Was she what you were expecting?'

'No,' I say, 'I wasn't expecting this at all.' She's much softer than I'd imagined. She looks nothing like the poker-faced hardbitten West End gangster described by the press. I pick the photograph up. Elsie appears to be in her twenties, but there's no date on the back so it's hard to know her age. I ask if I can take a photo of Linda with the picture of her aunt, and as I do I realise there's a resemblance – they both have such large, expressive eyes.

Linda's mother, Irene, was Elsie's younger sister. She was just 6 years old when their mother died in 1920, and the sisters remained close throughout their lives. 'They had an awful childhood,' says Linda. 'They were so young when their mother died and their father quickly remarried, to Georgina. She was horrible, that's what Elsie and my mum used to say.' Linda laughs, 'She was a nasty piece of work.'

'I thought she might be,' I say, showing Linda a news report on Elsie's arrest in 1934, when her stepmother insisted that she had nothing to do with any theft.

Linda puts on her glasses to read the article, then she sighs. 'They were tough women, Elsie and my mother. They didn't do hugging or kissing. My aunt wasn't an easy woman; you wouldn't want to mess with her. She would say what she thought. She was a bit of a rough diamond and she wasn't scared of people. But she would do *anything* for you. Elsie would always give you money, but not necessarily affection. But then she was only 10 years old when her own mother died.'

I ask when Linda first found out that her aunt had a criminal past, and she puts down her coffee and sits back in her chair. 'My mother never said a thing about her sister. Mum was a working-class woman, she was respectable, and she worked at Selfridges. She had aspirations. She corrected the way I spoke and told me not to talk cockney. She wouldn't have wanted to talk about her sister being a crook. But I was always nosey, I picked up snippets. As an inquisitive teenager I started thinking about class. No one talked about it, but I wondered how my Aunt Elsie had met someone as posh as her partner, Anne. I asked my brother, and that's when I found out that Elsie had been in prison. I thought she'd been a bank robber.'

'Who was Anne?' I ask.

'Anne Barker,' says Linda. 'She was her partner. Elsie met her in Holloway Prison.'

'She did?'

'Yes, Anne was very posh.'

'Do you know what she was inside for?' I ask.

Linda laughs, 'Oh she wasn't a prisoner. Anne Barker was a prison welfare officer.'

'What?'

Linda nods. 'She had originally trained as a nurse, and she went on to become assistant director of social services in Kensington and Chelsea.'

'She did?' I laugh at the unexpectedness of this, that the Eton-cropped gang girl fell in love with a prison welfare officer, who went on to become a head of social services. 'They actually met *inside* Holloway?'

'Yes,' says Linda. 'Anne's father was a prison officer, too, although we don't think he was at Holloway.'

'Wow,' I say. 'She must have been risking her job. And the relationship continued after Elsie was released?'

'They were *always* together,' says Linda. 'They were my godmothers and they looked after me. I stayed with them when my mother was in hospital. When I had pneumonia as a 6-year-old, it was Elsie who took me to Jersey to recuperate. Elsie was butch and wore suits, while Anne was femme – those were the roles then. But she was never particularly "masculine". She may have dressed in men's clothes in her criminal days, but I certainly never saw her in men's clothes. The word "lesbian" was never mentioned, but Elsie was into the London gay scene in the sixties. She knew Quentin Crisp, and the Beatles' manager Brian Epstein. When I was 16, she got me tickets to see the Beatles!'

Linda smiles at the memory, but then she looks serious. 'When Anne died in 1985, Elsie was devastated. They absolutely loved each other. She had a locket made, it had a picture of Anne inside and she always wore it.'

What was Elsie like, I ask, what sort of things did she enjoy?

'Well,' Linda picks up her coffee, 'she enjoyed going to boxing matches and she was a bit of a gambler. She liked to gamble on the horses. Once she won £1,000 – that was in the 1940s, it was a lot of money.'

Linda believes Elsie gave up her criminal career on her release from Holloway, but the Carey family 'didn't go without during the war', as her aunt acquired goods on the black market.

'Did Elsie love to drive?' I ask.

'No,' says Linda. 'She never drove.'

'What, never?' I'm surprised. 'But when she was in prison in Aylesbury, she put her occupation as motor driver.'

'No,' Linda shakes her head. 'Elsie never drove a car. Anne was always the driver.'

Although the family didn't speak about Elsie Carey's criminal past, when Linda trained as a probation officer in 1970, her mother was worried. 'You had to write down your mother's maiden name when you applied for a job,' she explains, 'and Mum said, "Don't fill it out", because of Elsie. She felt the Carey name was a bit notorious in the East End. She told me not to tell anyone about Elsie whenever I applied for jobs.'

In the end, Linda didn't become a probation officer; instead, she qualified as a social worker, her choice of career inspired by Anne Barker. Since then, Linda has had plenty of experience of courts, as a children's guardian, an advocate for children's rights during cases involving social services.

I ask about Queenie Day, who appears to have been Elsie's lover in the 1930s. Did the two women stay in touch? Does she know what happened to Queenie? But Linda has never heard of her. I show her a newspaper clipping from 1938 that describes Queenie as a 'coffee coloured beauty'.

'That's interesting,' says Linda. 'My husband is a Black South African and when we got married my parents didn't like it at all. But Aunt Elsie used to invite us round for meals.' Linda's husband, Lingam Moodley, also has experience of prison. He was remanded in jail for six months as an anti-apartheid activist in the 1970s, and when the charges were dropped he came to the UK as a refugee. His brother, Strini Moodley, was a co-founder of the Black Consciousness Movement and was sentenced to five years in prison, part of which he spent in the same Robben Island cellblock as Nelson Mandela.

Linda still knows very little about her aunt's criminal career, although she once came across a reference in James Morton's book, *East End Gangland*. Then, a few years ago, she went to an event run by the TV programme *Who Do You Think You Are?* 'I gave Elsie's name and date of birth to one of the researchers. He looked her up and said, "This is the best story of the day!" That was when I read that she'd been a menace to society. I don't know exactly what she did, but I'm not ashamed. Why would I be?'

Linda's daughter Leilah joins us in the coffee shop. She's fascinated by the story of her great aunt, who died when she was 14, and she keeps her portrait on her bedroom wall. I ask what memories she has of Elsie and she laughs. 'I just remember her chain smoking, and her thick, gold-topped cane! She was immaculately dressed in a suit, and she was a bit scary and fierce. She always told me money didn't buy happiness.' Leilah laughs and mimes passing me something under the table, 'Then she'd slip pound notes into my hands and whisper in my ear ... "You know, money won't make you happy", in a growling voice.'

I show Leilah a clipping from the *Sunday Pictorial* of 1936, in which an ex-Holloway prisoner describes Elsie's habit of smoking a pipe in her cell. 'She's a rebel really, isn't she?' asks Leilah, admiringly. 'She was against the system. She obviously didn't care what people thought of her, and she didn't sound repentant.'

Linda and her daughter both agree that the idea of Elsie hating men is ridiculous. She had several close male friends and was extremely devoted to her brother Jack, who was a merchant seaman on a New Zealand ship that was torpedoed during the Second World War. Elsie later bought a house a fifteen-minute walk away from her brother in Hornchurch, in order to be near him.

When Elsie died in 1999, she left two-thirds of her estate to Jack and one-third to her sister, Irene. 'We were clearing out the house after she died,' explains Linda, 'and my mother said, "We're sure to find a lot of money".'

'And did you?' I ask.

'No! What we found was wardrobes full of nylons and unwrapped bed sheets, while one room was full of unopened presents.'

If Linda could ask her aunt a question today, what would it be?

Linda thinks for a while, then she picks up the framed photo and stares at her aunt. 'I would ask, what started you off? Was it poverty? I would say, tell me all about it.' Linda puts the photo down and sighs, 'You have to see it in the context of their environment and their times; you feel more sympathy if you see it in that context. Canning Town was very poor. All the children in their family were literate, but when her brother James got a scholarship to a school he couldn't go because they had no money.'

What would Elsie have thought of my book, I ask? Would she have wanted to be called a Queen of the Underworld?

Linda considers this for quite a while. Eventually she smiles, 'My mother wouldn't have liked it. But Elsie would, she was notorious.'

The next day, Linda emails me a photograph of Anne Barker, the former prison welfare officer. She looks like my primary school headmistress from the 1960s – very smart, with rimmed glasses and freshly applied lipstick. Linda also sends me a picture of Elsie and Anne outside the Hotel de la Plage in Jersey in the 1950s – their favourite holiday destination. Anne is wearing a polka-dot dress and beaming, one hand resting on Elsie's shoulder, while Elsie looks tanned and relaxed, a slight swagger in the way she stands beneath the hotel sign. They make a happy couple, the ex-criminal and the head of social services. Elsie was lucky, she stayed out of prison and she found love.

Linda sends me an attachment – a notice that Elsie put in the local paper in memory of Anne:

> Like falling leaves, the years go by. But memories of you will never die. No longer in my life to share. Yet in my heart you are always there. I cannot bring back the good days, when we were together, but memories keep you very close and they will last forever.
> All my love dear Anne.
> Elsie.

A couple of days later, Linda's daughter Leilah sends me a text. She's spoken to her Uncle Alfie, and he's agreed to speak to me as well. He didn't receive the letter I sent months ago because the address I used was several years out of date.

'What I know about Elsie is second hand from other people in the family,' Alfie tells me on the phone, 'and what I gleaned from conversations that I shouldn't have been listening to.' His father, Alfred Webb, was Irene's first husband who died in the war, while Linda is the daughter of Irene's second husband, Albert Sansum.

In the summer of 1939, when Alfie was around 6 years old, he visited his Aunt Elsie in prison, 'though I didn't know it was a prison. I thought it was a railway station because she was behind glass, like a ticket office. It was grim, but I was just a kid, I just followed my mum and dad in there. I worked out later that it was Holloway Prison.'

Elsie was released early because she volunteered to do war work, and then she became manager of a fruit store in Kilburn. After the war, she ran a stall selling newspapers and taking bets on the side.

Alfie also remembers visiting his aunt when he was around 15. 'She had a cellar where she kept food and she said, "Come and have a look at this." It was a Webley pistol! I said, "Great, can I have it?" She said, "No you can't", and she gave me a pair of binoculars that she'd got from somewhere.'

Where had she got the gun from?

'She'd had it a long time,' says Alfie. 'It was probably a bit of protection during the war. Aunt Elsie was a great character, I can tell you that.'

Elsie and Anne moved around quite a bit, living in Sheerness and then Earls Court, where their next-door neighbour was the actress, Hattie Jacques. Eventually, the couple settled in Hornchurch, where Elsie worked at a day centre for the elderly, which explains why her death certificate describes her as a retired warden.

'Elsie was very gregarious and comical,' says Alfie. 'She had a great sense of humour; she was a piss taker, in the nicest possible way. She was just my aunt really. I didn't know anything about her sexual persuasion. I loved her; she was a lovely lady.' As for Anne Barker, she was 'very beautiful and gentle; she was a bit of class. Mum said she had thirteen letters after her name, she was very well educated.' But her relationship with Elsie 'didn't go down too well with the Barker family,' Alfie chuckles. 'She was from Lytham St Annes in Lancashire, and Elsie was from Canning Town!'

Unlike Linda, he has heard of Queenie Day. He says her father was Black, and worked as a seaman at the London Docks. 'There was a consortium, you could call it, of Elsie, her second youngest brother, Fred, and Queenie. In one case, Fred was their driver. He was just 16 and he was sent to borstal in Surrey.' But while Elsie and Queenie were close, their relationship soon soured. 'She turned king's evidence,' says Alfie, 'and got a lesser sentence.'

I'm shocked to hear this. Why would Queenie have turned on her lover? And which case was this? I haven't come across any crime reports where Queenie and Elsie were charged together. But then I think of her housebreaking arrest in 1922, when Queenie apparently provided the police with information that led to the arrest of three young associates.

Alfie says he read about it in a newspaper article when he was around 10. 'Auntie Elsie was going to get her for that when she got out – there were quite a few people looking for Queenie Day. Yes, they were good friends, until she turned king's evidence.' He thinks Queenie might then have been put under police protection because 'she totally disappeared'.

Alfie has fond memories of Elsie's stepmother, Georgina. 'She was a big woman, 20 stone. I loved her, she was a lovely lady. She always gave me bars of chocolate, so I would say that. She told me that when the police came to bang on the door at their home in Canning Town, she opened a window and poured a chamber pot of urine over them,' Alfie chuckles. 'Then they broke in and arrested them.' Elsie's father James, however, 'wasn't involved in any skullduggery', and he died in 1944 after falling off a bus on Christmas Day.

Alfie also believes Elsie gave up crime after her last sentence in Holloway, 'or at least she wasn't caught'. But the Carey name remained well known. 'Her brother, Jim, was courting a girl in Canning Town. She told me that she'd been courting him for two years before she found out his name. Carey was such a stigma.' Alfie remembers lining up at the docks to get work one morning, 'My Uncle Fred told me to stand on the stones, the cobbles outside the dock gates, it was like *On the Waterfront* with Marlon Brando. All of a sudden, the key foreman calls, "Webb!" The others were thinking, "Who the fucking hell's that?" Because I've gone out in front of them. And someone told them, "Don't say anything, it's one of the Careys".'

A few days after speaking with Alfie, I come across a copy of James Morton's *East End Gangland* in a charity shop. This is the book in which Linda first read about her aunt, but when I look in the index there is no reference to Elsie Florence Carey or Lady Jack. I flip through the 415 pages, and it's only right at the end that James Morton decides to add 'some mention of a few of the matriarchs and other women who have helped to fashion East End crime'.

This edition of *East End Gangland* was published as recently as 2006, but the description of female criminality sounds straight out of the 1920s. Women generally restrict their activities to shoplifting, or push-ing stolen cheques and credit cards, and 'few can actually be said to have been major players in their own right'. A woman's role was 'breeder, girlfriend, bail arranger, surety and minder of the ill-gotten gains in the enforced absence of the master. Few have achieved fame on their own account.' I stand in the charity shop and read the chapter twice – there is still no mention of Elsie Carey. But then I see a footnote on page 408 and a reference to her trial of 1937. She was apparently known as 'Queen Jack', and she dressed as a man. That's it – a footnote? The Eton-cropped gang girl whose shop-breaking trial in 1934 drew detectives from all over London, including the head of the Flying Squad, is reduced to a footnote? The woman who wore what she wanted and loved who she wanted, who single-handedly broke into major department stores in London, Oxford, Slough, Bognor and Worthing has been dismissed.

This is how women criminals get lost. At the time of their crimes they're portrayed as the embodiment of all that is wrong with society, but then society changes, their stories aren't passed down, their significance shrinks, and they start to disappear. The Carey name still carried stigma in London's East End in the 1970s, yet today it's as if Elsie Carey never existed. But she was an important figure, making a place for herself in the 'male' world of crime, carrying a jemmy and seven hacksaws in her attaché bag, hiring men as her drivers and sitting in the back of her red sedan in flannel trousers and a trilby hat.

East End Gangland does mention another underworld queen, however, and her story is told in more detail. She, too, was a bandit with an Eton crop, but rather than a hardbitten East End gangster, she was a glamorous 'driver and nurse' for a celebrated male jewel thief. Her career started in the mid-1920s, and despite the best efforts of Scotland Yard and the corps of ace detectives at the Flying Squad, it would be fifteen years before she was finally caught and put on trial.

11

LILIAN GOLDSTEIN
SMASH-AND-GRAB RAIDER

One June evening in 1940, a 37-year-old woman called Lilian Goldstein left her Wembley home and set off on a clandestine journey through the streets of north London. She had been at a restaurant on Wembley Park Drive, popped into her flat on the same street, and then at 8.20 p.m. she headed to the local train station with a friend. It was at this point, recalled Detective Inspector Edward Greeno, that 'the fun started'.

The Flying Squad had already placed a twenty-four-hour watch on Lilian Goldstein, a 'most alert woman', who used various 'devious routes and cunning actions' in an attempt to throw off the police. She stopped 10yds from the train station, looked around, retraced her steps and then returned. She loitered inside the station, suddenly came out and jumped on a bus, alighted near Neasden Lane and finally ended up at the Ritz cinema.

It was here that she'd arranged a rendezvous with Britain's Public Enemy No. 1, Charles 'Ruby' Spark. He was a smash-and-grab raider, known by the police and press as 'Ruby Sparks' or 'Sparkes', and six months earlier he'd escaped from Dartmoor Prison. He had apparently earned his nickname after giving away a haul of rubies believing they were fakes, although it may have been because he had a florid face.

As Lilian walked past Ruby, the police noticed that she 'spoke out of the side of her mouth like a convict at exercise'. When he ran off, the Flying Squad pounced, arresting him outside the Spotted Dog Public House, and his 170 days on the run were over.

At 5 a.m. the next morning, the police called on Lilian Goldstein and arrested her for harbouring an escaped convict. 'What!' she protested. 'I have not seen the man.' She explained she was now living with 'a good man, Jim Duggan, and I don't want to see the other man'. But the police found various items linking her to Ruby Spark, as well as several suits of clothes which were 'not all of the same trouser length'.

According to Detective Sergeant Robert Higgins of the Flying Squad, the police left the bedroom while Lilian got dressed, and at 7 a.m. she was taken to the police station. She was held in solitary confinement for thirty hours before being charged, and her repeated requests to see her solicitor were denied. 'It was necessary that no one apart from ourselves should know that she was in custody,' explained Detective Inspector Edward Greeno. The Flying Squad had finally caught the 'Bobbed Haired Bandit' and they were not about to let her go.

The police had been on her trail ever since the mid-1920s, when a mysterious woman was spotted behind the wheel during a series of smash-and-grab raids and country house robberies. An unidentified woman also helped Ruby Spark escape from Strangeways Prison in Manchester in 1927, and she'd been his getaway driver when he'd attempted to break out of Wandsworth Prison, three years later.

Lilian and Ruby were the 'British Bonnie and Clyde' and the King and Queen of the Smash and Grab. But her only conviction had been a minor sentence for shoplifting in 1933. Now she would be charged with a more serious offence – harbouring an escaped convict.

Lilian's defence was a familiar one when it came to female criminals. She'd been forced against her will, and all because of the man she loved. She had asked Ruby to stay away after he'd escaped from Dartmoor – she was afraid of him and he'd threatened to kill her twice. Then, Lilian Goldstein broke down in the Old Bailey dock and sobbed.

Witnesses, however, painted a different picture. Her landlady described Ruby Spark as a regular visitor to the flat on Wembley Park

Drive, 'I have seen him there having his food and doing the garden.' But Ruby told the court he had threatened Lilian and broken into her home, and agreed he was a very dangerous man.

The couple were defended by Geoffrey Lancelot Hardy, a well-known barrister who was deeply unpopular with the police and who'd been representing members of the Forty Elephants for years. Geoffrey criticised several aspects of the prosecution's case. In their eagerness to catch the Bobbed Haired Bandit, the police had failed to obtain a search warrant; three male officers had remained in Lilian's bedroom while she dressed; and she'd been denied legal representation for thirty hours.

But Detective Inspector Edward Greeno was furious with Lilian's performance in court and didn't believe a word she said. Prosecution witnesses had been 'got at', and it was nonsense that she'd been involved against her will. Her 'husband' James Duggan, meanwhile, was known to work for gangster Billy Hill. As far as the police were concerned, Lilian Goldstein was no innocent bystander; she was the famous Bobbed Haired Bandit.

Yet confusingly, the *Sunday Pictorial* had already revealed the identity of the Bobbed Haired Bandit, and she was a woman called Joyce Alexandra Powys-Wilson. They'd published her story shortly after Ruby's escape from Dartmoor, under the headline: 'I confess: I Was the Bobbed Bandit!' It was spread over three pages, coming second only to the question of whether Britain should declare war on Russia.

The 'signed confession' continued for several weeks, accompanied by a large photograph of Joyce Powys-Wilson, gazing wistfully into the distance like a debutante. 'I am not going to pretend there is anything romantic in this story,' she began, 'for girls who think they can lead such a life as mine and get away with it are fools.'

Joyce was the cousin of a baron and her name appeared in *Debrett's Peerage & Baronetage*. Her mother was related to Lord Lilford, a cousin was a bishop, and 'lots' of her relatives had married into titled families. But she'd thrown away the chance of marrying a wealthy young peer for the excitement and thrills of fighting the law, as Ruby Spark's getaway driver.

But who was Joyce Powys-Wilson? And why was she pretending to be someone she wasn't? She appeared to give accurate information about her background, although she didn't mention her divorce in 1925, when Peter Greenblatt, a London tailor, had taken her to court on the grounds of adultery. The judge had been sympathetic to Peter's plight – his wife had spent the night away from home and 'seemed perfectly worthless'. He assessed the damages at a farthing and granted the divorce – Joyce Powys-Wilson was officially worth a quarter of a penny.

However, she seemed to have bounced back from this humiliation, and in 1940 she turned up at the offices of the *Sunday Pictorial* to confess she was the Bobbed Haired Bandit. According to gangster 'Mad' Frank Fraser, Lilian Goldstein had arranged the confession herself while Ruby was on the run. She 'set up a really good smokescreen, getting a woman to write to the papers saying how she'd abandoned Ruby and begging him to give himself up – and all the while he was staying at her place in north London!'

Joyce's confession failed to create a smokescreen, though, and on 18 July 1940 Ruby and Lilian were convicted at the Old Bailey. He received a further twelve months, and she was sentenced to six months. A week later, however, Lilian was brought back to court, her prison sentence was 'cancelled' and she was placed on probation for three years instead. 'No doubt you found it difficult to act otherwise in assisting this old lover of yours,' said the judge, Sir Gerald Dodson. He'd given a good deal of thought to the case and decided that Lilian had 'followed a very natural womanly instinct in trying to succour and protect this man with whom you had intimate relations over a period of years'.

Lilian Goldstein had successfully convinced the judge that she was the victim of a dangerous man. Why Gerald Dodson changed his mind is unknown, but when he'd first been appointed judge at the Old Bailey in 1934, the Lord Chief Justice had given him a word of advice, 'Be merciful'. Since then, he had never passed a sentence 'without a feeling of reluctance', and he believed that leniency was more likely to reform an individual than prison. He also had an artistic side, having written the lyrics for a romantic light opera, *The Rebel Maid*, which premiered in Leicester Square, and was known as the 'wit of the Old Bailey'.

Ten officers were recommended for reward as a result of the arrests of the 'British Bonnie and Clyde'. It was described as outstanding police work and it gave all the officers 'an immense amount of satisfaction to take part in the capture of Sparks and Goldstein'. But the truth was that the Bobbed Haired Bandit had once again outwitted the police and evaded jail, just as she'd done during her criminal heyday.

Lilian Goldstein is one of very few female criminals to be recognised by some crime historians today, and most describe her as 'a middle-class Jewish girl from Wembley'. But, in fact, she wasn't Jewish or middle class, and she came from the other side of London.

Lilian Rose Kendall was born on 4 August 1902 in Tooting Bec. Her father, Henry, was a builder and housepainter, and her mother, Rosa Flint, had worked as a servant for Thomas and Alice Bowler, inventors of the bowler hat. Lilian's brother, Victor, joined the navy on his eighteenth birthday, but within a few years he was working as a housebreaker and smash-and-grab raider with Ruby Spark.

Ruby was a year younger than Lilian, born in Camberwell Green, and his mother was a member of the Forty Elephants. She was 'a very high-class buyer', he explained, and 'some of the best thieves in London' came to the family home to sell stolen silver and gold.

Lilian had her own links to the Forties and is believed to have joined the gang as a girl. At 14, she left school and worked in a dressmaker's shop. Two years later, she moved in with Henry Goldstein, a 24-year-old master jeweller. He coerced her into prostitution and, in July 1920, he was convicted of living on 'improper earnings'. The judge found it 'a most pathetic case as far as this unfortunate girl is concerned'.

Lilian explained she'd met Henry when he was working at Hatton Garden, but he fell out of work, had no money and 'suggested that she should go on the streets'. Detective Sergeant Frederick 'Nutty' Sharpe later described meeting Lilian's mother, 'a dapper, quiet-spoken little woman, the essence of respectability', when she came to the police for help. She explained her daughter had met a man at a funfair. He'd persuaded her to go up to the West End, taught her to dress smartly and 'give the glad eye to men'. Henry denied the charges, but the judge didn't believe him, and he was sentenced to three months of hard labour. When Henry came out of prison, however, the couple got married.

Henry – also known as Harry and Harris – was the eldest of eleven children, and Keith Greene, a distant relative, describes him as 'my not-so-great uncle. I remember my mother saying that many of the Goldsteins, apart from her father, were a bad lot. She would not provide any detail as she probably didn't know just how bad they were.' Keith Greene had no idea he was related to Lilian Goldstein until he started researching his family tree and a cousin alerted him. 'Her story is one of heroic daring,' he says admiringly. 'I'm really interested to know how the family got involved with the Bobbed Haired Bandit, it seems unusual for a woman to play such a role in a male gangster world.'

Henry's brother, Hyman, also had a sinister past. In 1928, he was sentenced to eighteen months of hard labour for 'carnal knowledge' of an underage girl, after a 15-year-old went missing from home. One of the Goldstein brothers is also believed to have owned a London club called the Miramar, possibly a strip club.

Lilian didn't stay too long with Henry Goldstein. She worked as a dressmaker and shop saleswoman, and also appears to have returned to prostitution. At the end of May 1926, she was bound over for soliciting under the name of Lilian Johnson. But by now, she was already working with Ruby Spark. He'd started out as a cat burglar, before deciding to try his hand at 'grab-and-run' raids, smashing bricks through shop windows and speeding off with the goods.

His first attempt failed. He wrapped a brick up in brown paper and threw it at a jewellery shop window, but the brick bounced back and whizzed past his ear. So he drove to the suburb of Lewisham to practise, putting two bricks in a parcel and taking a run from the middle of the road before throwing it. This time, the entire window fell to bits, and Ruby scooped up £700 worth of jewellery – equivalent to around £40,000 today. Next, he got a 14lb hammer, sawed off some of the handle and wrapped it like a parcel, and practised with this as well. Eventually, he could knock a hole in any thickness of glass, grab the goods and run. Ruby Spark was ready to become a professional smash-and-grab raider.

Smash-and-grab raiders were a new breed of criminal in the 1920s. 'If it was thrills you wanted,' explained Billy Hill, 'well, there aren't any better than doing a smash job.' A successful raider depended on speed. Every move was timed to the last second, and a robbery could be completed in under a minute. If a bystander did want to call the police, they had to find a phone box, ring Scotland Yard and wait up to fifteen minutes just to get an operator.

Cars were central to this new mode of crime, and the notion of using them for thieving was 'practically sacrilege', explained Billy Hill, 'as motor-cars were highly respectable things … anybody who could drive a car in 1920 was a rare bird, as is a jet pilot today'. Like the old highway robbers, motor bandits were exciting. Men like Ruby Spark had glamour – and so did his driver.

At 3 a.m. on the morning of 25 August 1926, a car carrying four men stopped a policeman in Merton, Surrey, and asked directions to a chemist shop. Shortly afterwards, local residents heard three bangs, followed by a crash and the sound of splintering glass. The gang drove off with an armful of stolen cameras, the police took chase, but the raiders escaped. However, most dramatic of all – the driver was a woman. 'A girl motor bandit with an Eton crop is setting Scotland Yard a big problem,' reported the *Leeds Mercury*.

The day before, a good-looking girl had made a daring daylight raid on a house a few miles away, along with a male companion, forcing entry with a jemmy and getting away with 'a small amount of booty'. According to other reports, the Eton-cropped girl had stayed in the car while two women ransacked the house.

More raids followed. At eleven o'clock one morning, Lilian drove along Bond Street towards Cartier jeweller's, suddenly blared her horn and swung the car onto the pavement. The door attendant jumped back, and Lilian slammed the car's nose straight against the door. Ruby Spark was in the car behind, along with a gangster called Golly-Eyes, who also swung his vehicle onto the pavement. Ruby appeared through a hole in the roof, which he'd cut open with a hacksaw, smashed the shop window, leaned over the grille and took £18,000 worth of jewellery and watches – equivalent to just over £1 million today. Lilian, meanwhile, had nipped out of the driving seat, edged her way through the crowd and was making her way home.

No one ever interfered with their raids, according to Ruby. Instead, passers-by stood dumbfounded, only jerking to life six seconds later, once the gang had sped away. Sometimes, however, onlookers threw umbrellas, briefcases and handbags at the escaping car. Flying glass became an occupational hazard, and Ruby began carrying bulldog clips to hold the gashes shut until Lilian could stich them up. It was her idea, he explained. She sterilised them in boiling water and then wrapped them in a handkerchief. She also suggested that Ruby disguise himself by putting pieces of rubber in his cheeks to make his face look different.

The couple usually had a buyer ready before the raid, who had viewed and valued the items in the shop window. Within an hour of the theft, the buyer had received the goods and handed over the cash.

Despite headline news reports on the Bobbed Haired Bandit, the police appeared to have great difficulty identifying Ruby's female accomplice. She usually drove a big Mercedes, according to Frederick 'Nutty' Sharpe of the Flying Squad, but eyewitnesses gave such vague descriptions, and there wasn't much to see of her under her close-fitting little black hat and a man's raincoat with the collar turned up. There was no doubt she could drive. 'She could whizz that great long tourer about with the skills of an artist' and she enjoyed taking women neighbours out for 'joy rides in her great big car'. Detectives were certain she was not a known criminal, but 'the educated type of crook, and belongs to a higher social elite'. She was 'a very spunky girl', admitted Nutty Sharpe, 'her trouble was that she ought to have been a boy.'

Cars were a symbol of twentieth-century masculinity, and many resented the idea of a woman behind the wheel. Towards the end of the nineteenth century, there had been just over a dozen cars on Britain's roads, but by 1930 there were 1 million, and while owners needed a licence, no driving test was required.

A coroner in Reading insisted that very few women drivers 'are fit to drive anything. They have no idea at all of driving, and they are most selfish.' A feature entitled *The Truth about Women Drivers* explained that women were 'usually inefficient and incompetent', while the Motor Cycling Club, Britain's oldest sporting motor club, overwhelmingly voted to keep women out. The problem was biological, women were naturally more timid, and it was also mechanical – they just didn't have the skills.

Joe Carstairs, however, had already established a car hire and chauffeuring business in South Kensington in 1920, along with three colleagues from the Women's Legion Mechanical Transport Section. It became known as 'X Garage', offering holiday tours in the UK and guided tours of war graves in France and Belgium, and ferrying guests from the Savoy Hotel in luxurious six-seater Daimlers.

Women would soon prove themselves in the sporting world as well. In 1931 Gwenda Stewart was declared the 'fastest woman motorist in the world today', breaking four international records in a single weekend. Three years later, Fay Taylour won the Leinster Trophy road race in Ireland, in which she was the only woman competitor. But in the mid-1920s, a woman behind the wheel was still viewed as an excitement-seeking rebel – and quite possibly a Bobbed Haired Bandit.

The title itself had been imported from the United States, where in 1924 Celia Cooney had become a criminal celebrity after robbing a string of grocery stores in New York, along with her husband, Edward. The couple taunted police and evaded capture for nearly four months, despite the largest 'manhunt' in the city's history. Press attention was extensive and 20-year-old Celia was portrayed as the criminal master-mind – a 'gun moll' who barked the orders, while her husband Ed was the weak-kneed accomplice. There was 'something abnormal, and not womanly about her actions', explained one police psychiatrist, although Celia insisted that she and Ed were equal partners.

The couple began their hold-ups in January 1924, when Celia was five months pregnant, and when the *Telegram* called her 'the Bob-Hair

Bandit', the name soon caught on. The press speculated feverishly on her identity. Was she 'a young woman of refinement' who wanted thrills, or was she 'the type to be found among habitués of cheap dance halls and cabarets'? Was she addicted to cocaine, or was she under the influence of the man she loved? According to one police source, Celia was a female Dr Jekyll and Mr Hyde. She worked by day as a stenographer, meekly taking dictation, while by night she gave orders with a pistol in her hand. In reality, however, Celia Cooney was a laundress at a city hospital and Ed was a mechanic.

Her usual method was to walk into a store and ask for eggs, pull out a gun and tell the clerk to 'Stick 'em up quick'. It was 'more exciting than anything I thought I'd ever do', she later explained, 'for once in my life I was boss'. Celia wore different outfits for these raids, but seemed to favour a pink turban hat, a heavy black veil, and a three-quarter-length sealskin coat.

When Ed shot a cashier after a struggle in a store, the couple fled to Florida, and shortly afterwards Celia gave birth. Two days later, their baby died in a dirty rooming house and the couple were caught. Again Celia was portrayed in two opposing roles – to some she was an uncaring mother who wasn't displaying sufficient grief, to others she was a bereaved mother who'd stolen for her baby. Was she sorry, asked one newspaper, or was she still 'SAUCY'? Celia later explained that her robberies weren't motivated by 'diamond earrings and gin and jazz and a good time', she just wanted money to look after her baby, so it 'won't have the rough time I had'.

The British press borrowed liberally from their American counterparts when it came to reporting on their own Bobbed Haired Bandit. Sometimes, she had an Eton crop and wore a man's trench coat, other times, she was 'the Girl in Red', her small innocent face peeping out from under a red beret. She too had a Jekyll and Hyde existence, one day motor bandit and the next, a young woman of fashion.

Criminal women were particularly skilled at transforming their appearance at a moment's notice in the 1920s. Blonde Alice Smith, often described as an American thief, was able to undergo 'a complete change of costume in a matter of minutes', from a hobbling 'old crone' to a tall, stately blonde. The American press gloated at her ability to elude the London 'Bobbies' and dubbed her the 'Chameleon Countess'. One newspaper provided a large illustration of Blonde Alice Smith making 'a lightning change' – having pulled off a wig, she appeared to be in the process of ripping off her clothes.

Blonde Alice worked with several leading male crooks in the early 1900s, including Joseph Grizzard, a fence who funded an international network of jewel thieves. Alice's role was reportedly one of lookout and decoy, surveying robbery targets and passing the tools.

In 1913, she took part in the Great Pearl Robbery, when a £150,000 pearl necklace was stolen near Hatton Garden, earning her the nickname 'Diamond Dolly'. In 1923, when she was convicted for stealing nine diamond rings from a jeweller's shop in Stockton-on-Tees, she was hailed as the 'Queen of Crooks'. She 'openly taunted that in crime she was the equal of any man', reported the *Belfast Telegraph*, 'no matter how daring the venture'.

But like Lilian Goldstein, her identity was confusing. Her 'real name' was reported to be Alice Mary Smith, but three years later, when she was convicted for stealing diamonds from a jeweller's shop in South Kensington, 'her real name' was Elizabeth Archer. She would later add to the confusion with a series of newspaper confessions in which she gave her birthplace as Manhattan and explained she'd eloped to England with a boyfriend.

But Blonde Alice Smith wasn't an American. She was born Elizabeth Mary Murray in Marylebone in 1880. Her parents were both tailors, and at the age of 19 she married Edward Pheney, with whom she had two children. She also had his name tattooed on her right arm, 'I LOVE TED PHENEY'. Elizabeth had several other loves, with four further tattoos on her arms: I.L.G.W, I.L.A.E. I.L.T.P. and I.L.J.W.

In 1928, she appeared in the *Police Gazette* as Elizabeth Archer, described as 4ft 11in with a fresh complexion, blue eyes and 'smart appearance, plausible'. She was a member of a gang of notorious expert and continental jewel thieves who frequented race meetings, good-class hotels and jeweller's shops. Her mugshot was said to be a fair likeness, but she looked nothing like the lithe Mayfair beauty portrayed by the

American press four years earlier. Blonde Alice was approaching 50, she'd spent years in and out of prison, and she looked dishevelled, her eyes slightly wild. According to American Queen of Crooks, Chicago May, Blonde Alice ended up in Chinatown 'smoking opium and sinking fast'.

Coverage of the mysterious Bobbed Haired Bandit, meanwhile, intensified and in September 1926 Lilian Goldstein was involved in more 'daring daylight raids' on country houses. According to Ruby Spark, she'd suggested some country air, packed a set of clothes and a thermos of tea, and off they went to tour the provinces.

The press reported that the Bobbed Haired Bandit was now the new Queen of the Forty Elephants, but this seems unlikely. Alice Diamond had been jailed after the Johanna Street riot of 1925, but that didn't mean she'd abdicated. Witnesses testified to seeing a woman at the wheel in burglaries all over the country, and in at least seven motor raids in London. She was 'as dashing and elusive as the Scarlet Pimpernel', commented *The People*, and 'able to be in at least three different places at once'. In September 1926, the *Illustrated Police News* carried a full-page illustration titled 'London's Female Bobbed Bandit Escapes Capture', showing a bobbed-haired young woman in fashionable flapper clothes clambering out of the back of a car.

The female bandit became a popular cinematic figure. *Silk Stocking Sal* told the story of a beautiful little bobbed-haired bandit from New York, while in *Honesty the Best Policy*, a gunman, detective and bobbed-haired bandit formed 'a triangle of thrilling intrigue'. The criminal title became so well known that an 86-year-old woman in Derby was arrested after she accused her 80-year-old neighbour of being a 'bobbed-haired bandit'. She was found guilty of using indecent language and bound over to keep the peace for six months.

Lilian Goldstein was never convicted for any of the smash-and-grab raids or country house robberies, although in 1927 she was arrested in Southport and charged with receiving stolen property. The case sparked huge press coverage, after police used a fire engine to block the getaway car, and Lilian Goldstein, 'a distinctly good-looking woman', was named as 'a suspected woman bandit'. She was not, however, identified as the Bobbed Haired Bandit, and the charges were dropped because Ruby took full responsibility, as he would after his prison escape in 1940. 'I pleaded guilty to everything they wanted,' he explained, 'to get the Bobbed-Hair Bandit in the clear, prison being harder on a woman's hands than it is on a man's, and their complexions suffer, too, which is bad for their pride.'

Lilian was also arrested in 1930, along with her brother, Victor, who received three years as a motor bandit, but she was released without charge. The following year, when a smash-and-grab gang raided a furrier shop in East Ham, the getaway car, driven by a 'bobbed-hair woman', was seen by a constable on duty 100 yards away, but before the alarm could be raised it had disappeared.

Still no one seemed to know who the Bobbed Haired Bandit actually was – or how many female bandits there were. Perhaps she was a society woman 'seeking a new thrill', suggested the press, or a former student 'at a London music college'.

In 1932, when Ruby Spark was convicted for his role in a riot at Dartmoor Prison, police described his partner as the bobbed-haired bandit, although again Lilian wasn't named. In 1933, she was arrested for stealing £104 worth of nightdresses and pyjamas from New Bond Street, and it was only at this point that the press specifically linked 30-year-old Lilian Goldstein to 'the woman described as the bobbed-haired bandit'. She had been 'put up for identification', explained the police, but was 'not picked out'.

According to Lilian's defence, she was separated from her husband and had one child, but there are no further references to a child, and neither the police nor Ruby Spark ever mentions Lilian being a mother. Lilian's defence attempted to portray her as an innocent middle-class shopper. She had simply seen 'these delicate pieces of lingerie' in the New Bond Street shop and 'was tempted'. But she was jailed for four months, in what appears to have been her only prison sentence.

The judge didn't believe she was suffering from kleptomania, and he was right, for Lilian Goldstein was now back working with the Forty Elephants. The following year, she was arrested with baby-faced Maggie Hughes after stealing grey squirrel fur coats from two shops in Carlisle.

The women's favourite barrister, Geoffrey Lancelot Hardy, convinced the court that on the day of the offence Maggie had been ill in bed, while Lilian had been busy in London where she worked as a canvasser for a hosiery firm. The case was dismissed for lack of evidence, and once again the Bobbed Haired Bandit was free to go.

Lilian Goldstein appears to have given up the criminal life in the early 1940s. According to Ruby, she refused to be involved in a £30,000 pay-roll snatch planned while he was on the run from Dartmoor. 'You can count me right out,' she told him, after learning the gang planned to throw a bucket of ammonia over the bank messenger. 'I wouldn't drive on a job that meant grievous bodily, Ruby, and you know it ... I've had this Bandit Queen lark. Crime is for kids ... not for grown-ups.' She was fed up of waiting for him to come out of prison.

In 1943, she divorced Henry Goldstein, and then changed her name back to Kendall, further disassociating herself from her former husband and her own criminal career. She settled down with a bookmaker called Charles Henry Beresford, and died in Brighton in December 1977.

Lilian never wrote her own story or published any confession, unlike Ruby Spark, who, in 1940, accepted £400 from the *Sunday Pictorial* for the tale of his escape from Dartmoor. It was accompanied by an 'exclusive' photograph of 'Mrs Lilian Goldstein, Spark's lover', a bobbed-haired woman in her early forties, with a string of pearls round her neck. But whether the photograph is actually Lilian is open to question, and if it is, then where did the paper get it from? Historian Alyson Brown believes the portrait looks remarkably like those that were used to accompany the 'confession' of Joyce Alexandra Powys-Wilson.

In 1938, Nutty Sharpe devoted an entire chapter to the Bobbed Haired Bandit in his memoirs, yet he referred to her only as 'Gloria'. His tone was admiring, 'Of all the characters hunted by the Flying Squad when smash-and-grab raiding was at its height the most romantic and highly publicised was a woman.' But he had no idea what happened to Gloria. She 'just faded away as mysteriously as she first appeared'. He was wrong, of course, for two years after he published his memoirs Lilian was on trial at the Old Bailey for harbouring an escaped convict.

The Bobbed Haired Bandit also appeared in two books in the 1960s. The first was Detective Inspector Edward Greeno's memoirs, *War on the Underworld*, in which he portrayed her as nowhere near as dangerous as she'd been two decades earlier. In the summer of 1940, he'd gone to great lengths to catch Lilian Goldstein, describing her as devious and cunning, and expressing immense satisfaction at her capture. Now he seemed to have changed his mind. Lilian had 'a romantic reputation', he wrote rather dismissively, 'most of which I did not believe, for the daring driving of getaway cars for smash and grab merchants'.

The following year, Ruby Spark published his ghost-written auto-biography, *Burglar to the Nobility*, in which Lilian was portrayed as a tough, 'game girl', who 'wore her silver fox like a duchess'. The couple worked as equals, plotting, planning and carrying out the smash-and-grab raids. She was 'afraid of nobody', had nerves like ice and was 'not the sort of girl to cry unless you stuck a finger in her eye'. But while Ruby named her as 'Lil' or 'Lily', he didn't describe her physically, or give any information about her background, or explain where she'd learned her driving skills.

By the time his memoirs were published, Ruby Spark had also gone straight, running the Penguin Club in Soho and then a newsagent's and tobacconist shop in Chalk Farm. He remained a dashing character, appearing in several histories of crime, even though he was accused of the hit-and-run murder of a young woman in Birmingham.

His getaway driver, on the other hand, was relegated to a minor role. According to *East End Gangland*, Ruby Spark carried out the robberies while Lilian just 'patched up his wounds'. So, was she a girlfriend who reluctantly became involved? Or was she an independent woman who made her own decisions? From an exploited teenager forced into prostitution by her first husband, she'd gone on to become the most daring female motor bandit of the day.

After her trial in 1940, the term Bobbed Haired Bandit went out of fashion. Lilian had come to represent all female motor bandits

– emancipated women who sought excitement by driving fast cars and who could change identity at a moment's notice. But at her trial she'd been revealed to be under the control of a dangerous man, and so the problem had been resolved. And now, according to Ruby Spark, she'd retired from crime to lead a domestic life, preferring 'a few honest quid a week and sweaty overalls to wash' to speeding around the streets of London in a Mercedes.

Lilian Goldstein may not have been Queen of the Forty Elephants, but she did work closely with the gang. And while her co-conspirators had been jailed after the Johanna Street riot of 1925, they had not hung up their hoisters' bloomers just yet. Instead, the moment they were out, they went straight back to work.

12

THE FORTY ELEPHANTS BAR

Two days before Christmas 1927, a fleet of fourteen cars set off from the Elephant and Castle to launch a massive shoplifting spree. Alice Diamond was out of prison, and she appeared to be making a point. Around forty women took part in the expedition, targeting shops on Oxford Street, Knightsbridge and Bayswater. Some stores were 'quietly taken apart', writes Brian McDonald, while others suffered wholesale disorder as the women crashed through the doors, snatched the goods and ran.

Police raided Alice's flat in Kennington but nothing was found, and while she spent the night in police cells, she was then released. Aside from a brief stay in Holloway in 1936, for allegedly managing a brothel in Lambeth, the Queen of the Forty Elephants evaded arrest for the rest of her life. Her lieutenant, Maggie Hughes, however, received several more convictions for assaulting police, drunkenness, prostitution and shoplifting. In 1932 she was back in the *Police Gazette*, her mugshot no longer the fresh-faced woman in a tam o' shanter hat. Her hair was bobbed with a stylish wave and her coat had a fur collar, but she was not as lavishly dressed as before. Maggie's eyes looked glazed, and her lips appeared lopsided, perhaps with a smirk.

Alice Diamond continued to oversee shoplifting raids throughout the 1930s, and her gang members included Sarah Carr, niece of the first queen, Mary Carr. Some of the women focused on coastal towns in the south, such as Brighton and Margate, posting the stolen goods back to 'a central receiving office'. Others headed north, and Detective Chief Superintendent John Capstick recalled waiting at Euston Station in the small hours of a Saturday morning, watching as half a dozen women came down the platform, returning home after a shoplifting expedition. It was a waste of time trying to search their bags – 'the swag had been sent ahead by parcel post or luggage in advance' – but occasionally police would grab 'a couple of the little dears' and ask, 'All right, girls, where have you been this time?'

He described Maggie Hughes as the leader and 'one of the slickest thieves I ever tried to follow … she knew every trick in the book'. Like other members of the Forty Elephants, she kept a large mirror in her handbag, holding it up like a periscope to keep watch through the car's rear window.

John Capstick once tailed Maggie over 10 miles to Kingston upon Thames, where she parked outside a department store and then marched up to his car and informed him, 'Well, now, *we're* going to a funeral, if you'd like to follow us!' Then she drove off, giving 'the Victory sign through the rear window. At least, it looked like the Victory sign.' If the Detective Chief Superintendent walked into a pub where the Forties were celebrating, they would throw him a smile – and sometimes send the barman over with a glass of milk.

By the end of the 1930s, shoplifting was so widespread that traders were once again urging drastic action. A 1938 Pathé film, *£100,000 Leak! Govt. to Tackle Shoplifting?* revealed that female shoplifters – rich and poor, young and old – were everywhere. The kleptomania defence had fallen out of favour; now the vast majority of shoplifters were regarded as plain criminals.

That same year, Maggie Hughes was sentenced to six months for stealing clothes in Portsmouth. Her last known offence, however, occurred during Derby Day at Epsom Downs, the same spot where

Mary Carr had allegedly kidnapped a boy in 1895 and lost her title as Queen of the Forty Thieves.

Once again, the incident occurred in a refreshment booth. Maggie Hughes made 'some nasty remarks' to a Mrs Louise Williams, then struck her in the face with a glass – or alternatively a hat pin. Louise was taken to hospital, and her left eye had to be removed. That evening, Maggie attacked one of Louise's daughters in a public house and she too ended up in hospital. The prosecution suggested it was a feud over a man; Maggie Hughes was 'a woman of the very worst type' and addicted to the use of weapons. She was sentenced to three years and during her final spell in Holloway, Maggie also lost an eye in a fight with another prisoner.

She was released in 1941 and lived her last years in a Soho flat provided by her brother, Billy, who had now established himself as 'Boss of the Underworld'. He boasted that his 200-strong gang, known as the Heavy Mob, were 'the toughest team of screwsmen ever to be formed in the United Kingdom' – although others would argue it was gangster Jack 'Spot' Comer who dominated London's underworld.

Maggie Hughes died in 1949 and, according to her brother, she'd spent so long in Holloway that the authorities planted a tree in her memory. She'd been a career criminal for nearly three decades, known for her violence as much as her shoplifting skills. She had been a victim of domestic abuse, her husband Alfred used to 'batter' her before Billy stepped in, and she had committed her fair share of violence as well, particularly against other women. But while Billy could brag openly about carving up his opponents, female aggression was another matter, and his sister has been largely side-lined from histories of crime.

When Australian Judy Spalding started researching her husband Brian's family, aware that he was related to the famous Billy Hill, she found plenty of books and articles on the Boss of the Underworld. But it was only when another descendant got in touch that Judy finally heard about his sister Maggie and her own life of crime. Since then, Judy has built up a wealth of documents relating to Maggie Hughes. 'I realise crime is wrong,' she says, 'but we didn't walk in their shoes in those times and life was very hard, so it seemed like the only way to obtain money to feed and clothe oneself.'

Alice Diamond stopped working with her lieutenant around the time of the Epsom assault, and apparently took a more backseat role in the underworld. By the late 1940s, she was ill, living in Walworth with two of her brothers and cared for by her sister, Louisa, a former member of the Forties, who lived next door.

Alice died in 1952 at Lambeth Hospital, at the age of 54. She 'seemed to have little to show for her life of plunder', writes Brian McDonald. 'Her money had run out, and whatever was left at her death went to Louisa.' Her death certificate named her as Alice Black, the surname her mother had used in the workhouse in 1896, and her occupation was 'spinster, a flower seller' – the same occupation as Mary Carr, the very first Queen of the Forty Thieves.

The Forty Elephants could trace their history back some seventy years, from Victorian pickpockets and blackmailers to twentieth-century housebreakers and hoisters. They had come of age in the roaring 1920s as the most successful female crime syndicate Britain had ever seen, but now their story was about to be rewritten.

In 1949, the year of Maggie's death, a new half-hour crime drama series launched on national radio, *Secrets of Scotland Yard*. It was a hugely popular programme, with dramatic re-enactments and gruesome titles such as 'Buckets of Blood' and 'Murder Without Motive'. One of the very few episodes to feature women was 'The Lady is a Crook', and it began with the Forty Elephants. It was 'an apt name', explained the narrator, 'for most of them were outsized women. One of them in fact was almost six feet high.' The gang 'went about doing a bit of well-planned shoplifting', but their specialisation was blackmail. Some were 'really attractive under the bright lights of London's nightlife', and they used their sexual wiles to entice men outside to be beaten and robbed.

This sounded more like the early days of the Forty Thieves than the modern operation run by Alice Diamond and, according to the *Secrets of*

Scotland Yard, the women were also killers. When one hapless man refused to hand over a share of stolen loot, they brazenly murdered him in the street. The whole resources of Scotland Yard were immediately mobilised and the Forty Elephants were 'hunted down one by one'. Today, the narrator assured his listeners, 'they are no more than a terrible memory'.

Yet Alice Diamond was still alive when the programme aired, and her gang had not disbanded. 'Mad' Frank Fraser described working for the Forties in the early 1950s, ensuring they got away after shoplifting raids on Harrods, by bumping 'into the guy who was going to give them a pull, or give him a right-hander if he got too clever'. Frank admired the women so much that he compared them to men, 'like fellas, they risked their liberty every day of the week to get a pound note'. In 1960, John Capstick described them as 'the cleverest gang of oysters' Britain had ever known, and 'some of them still operate today'.

But according to the *Secrets of Scotland Yard*, the gang had been wiped out, and in the decades after the deaths of Alice Diamond and Maggie Hughes, the women were largely ignored by historians and compendiums of crime. In the twenty-first century, however, there has been a sudden resurgence of interest in the women of the Forty Elephants and now, like seventeenth-century Moll Cutpurse, they are being rediscovered and celebrated again.

I'm leaning against a cocktail bar in what used to be the headquarters of the Metropolitan Police, a huge red-brick Edwardian building just off Whitehall in central London. It's 10 a.m. on a miserable February morning and I've chosen a non-alcoholic drink – a 'Lady Sherlock', a mix of Laphroaig vinegar, dates, peach and jasmine soda. The cocktail is named after Annie Betts, the twentieth-century store detective who used to hurry after the Forty Thieves as fast as she could go. It is just one of a dozen cocktails at the Forty Elephants Bar, on the ground floor of the new five-star Great Scotland Yard Hotel.

The bar is quite small, with a marble floor and plush deep red walls, and I'm the only visitor here. The hotel opened just a few weeks ago after a £50 million conversion. The bartender, Dan, hands me my drink and explains it's whisky with the alcohol burnt out. It has a rich, brown colour and a slightly vinegary taste – it would probably have given lady detective Annie Betts quite a kick.

'Cheers,' I say, and then I pick up my glass and realise there's a massive diamond-shaped piece of ice in the middle. Dan offers me a diamond-shaped piece of chocolate as well, and says the chocolate knuckledusters are particularly popular among customers. He is from Hungary and had never heard of the Forty Elephants until he started here. 'I'm very surprised that I didn't know them,' he says. 'It has such great potential as a story. I can't believe there hasn't been a movie. They were so successful.'

The Forty Elephants cocktail menu has been designed to 'reflect the women's personalities', he explains, and Mary Carr's is 'light, fragrant and fizzy', with bergamot liqueur and carbonated Victorian perfume. However, it's not just the drinks that celebrate the Forty Elephants. There's a high glass cabinet near the bar – an 'evidence table' full of loot – pearl necklaces and cash, purses, gloves and buttons, as well as an ivory knife and a pair of handcuffs. There are photos, too, including the mugshots of Alice Diamond and Maggie Hughes from the 1920s *Police Gazette*.

It's a little odd seeing their images under glass, I feel like I'm looking down on a coffin. But it's Lilian Goldstein – 'the Bobbed Haired Bandit' – who takes centre stage in the Forty Elephants Bar. Her luminous portrait is hanging above the fireplace, a colour silkscreen print embellished with diamond dust. It was created by artist Nicola Green, who found 'much more to Lillian than meets the eye' and 'an interesting interplay between masculinity and femininity; both brutal and tender at the same time'. Lilian's skin is alabaster white, her rosebud lips bright red and her eyes heavily lined with kohl. Her hair is bobbed, with a kiss curl in the middle of her forehead, and she's wrapped in an orange fur coat that seems to glow.

Lilian's cocktail reflects her driving skills. The Six Cylinders Martini is a £14 mix of vodka, vermouth and Mexican cedron-infused hemp oil. 'They used hemp oil for cars to make them run smoothly,' explains Dan, 'so we use it on the rim of the martini.'

I tell him that Lilian wasn't actually the Queen of the Forty Elephants and he nods, 'No, but she worked with them, she helped them out!' The press has also elevated Lilian's position. Both the *Daily Mail* and BBC's *The One Show* have cited her as Queen of the Forty Elephants, with the gang now described as Robin Hood figures who 'looted from the rich and wealthy', rather than from department stores.

Dan the bartender draws my attention to more images of the Forties, etched faintly around the top of the walls, then he points up to a 'smash-and-grab' chandelier that hangs from a skylight, designed to resemble shards of broken glass with a jewelled necklace in the middle. 'Diamond's Hostage' was designed by Czech company Lasvit and the central necklace has forty gems, 'each symbolising one woman of the gang'.

Dan asks if I want to see the whisky bar, which I hadn't noticed because it's concealed behind a fake bookshelf. It's like a speakeasy inside, with a long marble bar where guests are served rare and limited-edition whiskies, paired with three different types of chocolate. I think the Forty Elephants would have liked it in here, and they would have been amused by the ladies' toilets, where the old-fashioned wall cisterns are embossed with gold plaques announcing, 'Great Scotland Yard'.

The hotel appears to have brought women to the fore, and given them a room of their own, but much of that is down to the glamorous portrait of Lilian Goldstein. It would be hard to imagine the 1932 mug-shot of Maggie Hughes, with her glazed eyes and lopsided smirk, ever being put up on the wall. I can't decide if the five-star hotel is celebrating forgotten criminal women or – with its smash-and-grab chandelier and glamorous cocktails – glorifying theft and violence.

The Forty Elephants Bar is just one example of a significant revival in the reputation of Alice Diamond and her gang, but some of the portrayals are inaccurate, patronising and highly sexualised. Stephen Fry's audio series *Victorian Secrets* described the Forty Thieves as 'well known for attracting men and then turning what looked like seduction into extortion'. *Gangs of Britain*, a true crime series hosted by Gary and Martin Kemp, acknowledged the leadership of Alice Diamond and correctly gave her height as 5ft 8in. But the programme referred to her as the 'so-called Queen', and repeatedly showed shots of a woman lifting up her skirt to show her hoister's bloomers. It also presented the Forties as an appendage to men. They were 'a branch' of the Elephant and Castle Boys Gang, 'comprised of wives, daughters and girlfriends', and it was supposedly the boys who chose Alice Diamond 'as the perfect candidate to lead their female army of shoplifters'.

As with the eighteenth-century Black Boy Alley Ladies, the women's role and their relationship with male crooks had shifted, they had lost their independence and now they worked for men. Their apparent size continued to define them. They were 'beefy women', according to one modern historian, 'who relied more on fear than sleight of hand'. Frank Fraser described them as 'wild', and 'when they let their hair down, they were totally outrageous. Sexually, some of them were hot stuff.' Frank also insisted that Alice Diamond had a daughter who married gangster Billy Benstead, but there is no evidence that Alice either married or had a child.

Other modern portrayals, especially on the stage, are less stereotypical. Hiype Productions' *The Forty Elephants* aimed 'to bring awareness … about the seriousness behind girls in gangs' in south London, while the Forty Elephants Theatre Company was established to 'bring more tenacious female roles to the theatre'.

Some of the Forties have appeared in literature. Anna Freeman's gripping novel, *Five Days of Fog*, portrays a gang of female criminals in the early 1950s, while Jessica Fellowes' *Bright Young Dead*, set in the 1920s, features Alice Diamond as a towering figure who strides into a bar followed by other gang members, 'chosen courtiers with their monarch'.

This rediscovery of the Forties is mainly due to Brian McDonald's book, *Alice Diamond and the Forty Elephants*, published in 2015, which also inspired the creation of the cocktail bar at Great Scotland Yard Hotel. He isn't surprised by the surge in interest. 'It's a fascination with girl gangs,' he explains. 'Press coverage of girls joining gangs and carrying knives has people searching for comparisons in past years.

Inevitably, it focuses on the Forty Elephants. The brazenness of these women is particularly celebrated by women.' His book is now being developed as a TV series, billed as a 'female *Peaky Blinders*', the glamorously violent BBC drama based on a largely male gang in Birmingham.

Brian wrote the book because he has direct links to the Forties. It was his Uncle Bert who renamed them the Forty Elephants, after a brief affair with Alice Diamond. In the early 1950s, Brian himself was 'a member of a group who revelled in being Elephant Boys and got into all sorts of mischief'. He had other connections too. His aunt Ada Johnston was a fence for the Forties and her brothers ran the Elephant and Castle Gang. Ada had also briefly been a suffragette and in 1908 she attended a mass rally in Hyde Park with her sister Annie Burnup who, according to family lore, was jailed for four months after she 'biffed a copper' with a placard she'd picked up from the ground. The portrait of Lilian Goldstein in the Great Scotland Yard Hotel cocktail bar comes from the cover of Brian's book, and is based on a photo that was found among Ada Johnston's possessions when she died. It's believed to have been taken around 1926, and the name 'Lil' is inscribed on the back in ink.

Many of the stories in Brian's book came from conversations with his Aunt Ada, and when she told him about her brothers leading the Elephant and Castle Gang, 'my ears pricked up, and it prompted me to find out more'. Brian's father was 'tight-lipped about it when I asked him. My mother, Grace, who was entirely respectable, would frown if he got started on any criminal enterprise.' But Ada Johnston was a good talker, and Brian was an eager listener. 'She was in her seventies when I made prolonged visits to her home in Stead Street in Southwark,' he explains. 'My mother went shopping in East Street Market, dragging me along, and we finished with tea at Aunt Ada's. She was a generous lady, very fashionable, who still sold fashionable clothes from her home, at that time legally bought from the gigantic Houndsditch Warehouse in the City.'

But Brian had no idea that Alice Diamond, the Queen of the Forty Elephants, still lived close by at the time, and that he may have unwittingly sat side by side with her in an East Street Market pub. If Brian could meet Alice Diamond now and ask her a question, what would it be?

'Where did all the money go?' he asks, 'the furs, jewellery, etc. Did her sister Louisa have it?'

Alice Diamond had been a Queen of the Underworld for some thirty years, imposing order on crime, much as Moll Cutpurse had done in the seventeenth century. She introduced a hoisters' code, divided the gang into cells, collected subscriptions to hire defence lawyers and support families, and demanded loyalty and respect. She was a leader who kept her title, despite repeated imprisonment, and a savvy business-woman who regarded shoplifting as work.

The next Queen of the Forty Elephants would not emerge until the 1960s, but in the meantime, post-war Britain was about to witness a new type of female lawbreaker, and this one would crown herself queen of a whole new criminal enterprise.

MOLL CUT = PURSE.

Mary Frith, the seventeenth-century pickpocket and fence known as Moll Cutpurse, was famed for wearing breeches, smoking a pipe and carrying a sword, as seen in this eighteenth-century etching. (Unattributed engraving, Mary Evans Picture Library)

The den of thieves depicted in William Hogarth's *The Idle 'Prentice* is believed to feature the Black Boy Alley Gang. The most notorious female member was Ann Duck, arrested and acquitted nineteen times for highway robbery. (Wikimedia Commons)

The IDLE 'PRENTICE betrayed and taken in a Night- Cellar with his Accomplice.

Proverbs Chap: VI. Vc 26.
the Adulterefs will hunt for
the precious life

Shoplifting was portrayed as a peculiarly female crime, motivated by suppressed sexual desire. In this copy of a late eighteenth-century print, two male assistants apprehend a well-dressed young woman, while one pulls a length of lace from between her legs. (Classic Image/Alamy Stock Photo)

129S

American Queen of Crime Sophie Lyons visited London in the late 1880s for a two-week crook's tour of the West End, targeting jewellery shops and luxury dressmakers. (National Portrait Gallery, Smithsonian Institution; gift of Pinkerton's, Inc.)

SUPPLEMENT A

No. 14.   FRIDAY, JULY 8, 1921.   Vol. VIII.

Alice Diamond, Queen of the Forty Thieves, pictured in the *Police Gazette* of 1921. The year before, she'd been convicted of stealing fur coats from four West End establishments, and soon she was masterminding shoplifting raids all over England. (The National Archives)

SUPPLEMENT A

No. 2.   FRIDAY, JANUARY 21, 1921.   Vol. VIII.

'Baby-faced Thief' Maggie Hughes, pictured in the *Police Gazette* of 1921, was Alice Diamond's fearsome lieutenant and was known for her volatile temper. (The National Archives)

Ada Johnston worked as a fence for the Forty Elephants, whose members were celebrated for their 'good looks, fine stature, and smart clothing'. (Brian McDonald/Milo Books)

Alice Diamond died in 1952; her death certificate named her as Alice Black, the surname her mother had once used in the workhouse. Her official occupation was 'flower seller', just like her predecessor Mary Carr. (Author's own/Crown Copyright)

CERTIFIED COPY OF AN ENTRY OF DEATH

GIVEN AT THE GENERAL REGISTER OFFICE

Application Number 10585654-2

REGISTRATION DISTRICT					LAMBETH			
1952 DEATH in the Sub-district of	Prince's				in the	Metropolitan Borough of Lambeth		

Columns:-	1	2	3	4	5	6	7	8	9
No.	When and where died	Name and surname	Sex	Age	Occupation	Cause of death	Signature, description and residence of informant	When registered	Signature of registrar
293	First April 1952 Lambeth Hospital	Alice BLACK otherwise DIAMOND	Female	54 years	9 1 Barrett House Browning Street Southwark Spinster a Flower Seller Daughter of Thomas Diamond a Broome Maker Parks (deceased)	Acute suppurative broncho pneumonia certified by R.B Harvey Hyatt Coroner for London after postmortem without inquest	E. Lockwood Sister 17 Albany Road S.E.5	Fourth April 1952	[signature] Registrar

CERTIFIED to be a true copy of an entry in the certified copy of a Register of Deaths in the District above mentioned.

Given at the GENERAL REGISTER OFFICE, under the Seal of the said Office, the 16th day of December 2019

DYE 421008

See note overleaf

The inner gate of London's Holloway Prison, which first opened in 1852 as a 'terror to evil-doers'. It became home to many Queens of the Underworld, few of whom were deterred by their time inside. (Wandsworth Prison Museum)

Holloway's B wing. The prison became a female jail in 1903, and was soon known for its brutal regime, including the forcible feeding of suffragettes. (Wandsworth Prison Museum)

The grim interior of Holloway's DX wing. In the 1940s, it housed younger prisoners sentenced to borstal, while in 1960 it was home to the great escape artist Zoe Progl. (Wandsworth Prison Museum)

Elsie Florence Carey led a shop-breaking gang in the early 1930s and was described as a 'poker faced hard-bitten West End gangster'. Her portrait tells another story. (Photographer unknown/ Linda Sansum family collection)

Anne Barker met Elsie Carey while working as a welfare officer in Holloway Prison; she later became assistant director of social services in Kensington and Chelsea. (Photographer unknown/Linda Sansum family collection)

'They were always together': Elsie Carey (left) and Anne Barker, pictured outside their favourite holiday destination, the Hotel de la Plage in Jersey, in the 1950s. (Linda Sansum family collection)

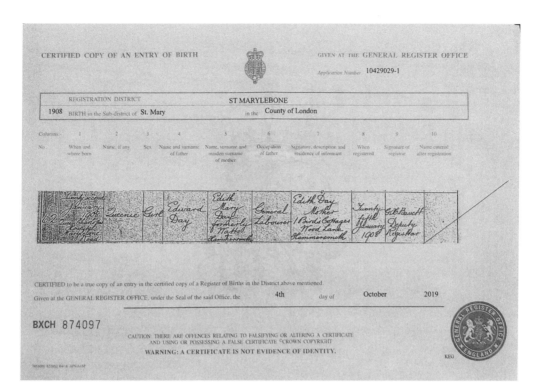

CERTIFIED COPY OF AN ENTRY OF BIRTH

GIVEN AT THE GENERAL REGISTER OFFICE

Application Number 10429029-1

REGISTRATION DISTRICT ST MARYLEBONE

1908 BIRTH in the Sub-district of St. Mary in the County of London

CERTIFIED to be a true copy of an entry in the certified copy of a Register of Births in the District above mentioned.

Given at the GENERAL REGISTER OFFICE, under the Seal of the said Office, the 4th day of October 2019

BXCH 874097

CAUTION: THERE ARE OFFENCES RELATING TO FALSIFYING OR ALTERING A CERTIFICATE AND USING OR POSSESSING A FALSE CERTIFICATE ©CROWN COPYRIGHT

WARNING: A CERTIFICATE IS NOT EVIDENCE OF IDENTITY.

Queenie Day was convicted of theft in 1918, and sent to a reformatory where she was trained for domestic service. Her birth certificate shows she was only 10 years old at the time. (Author's own/ Crown Copyright)

In 1922, Queenie was arrested for stealing fruit and sent to Aylesbury Borstal, where 'wayward' girls were handcuffed and put in solitary confinement. Conditions radically improved after the appointment of a new governor in 1923; here inmates are pictured working in the borstal kitchen. (Mary Evans Picture Library/Peter Higginbotham Collection)

From Prison Cell . . .

GANG QUEEN CALLS UP HOME

BY A SPECIAL CORRESPONDENT

GANG queen and motor bandit Elsie Florence Carey, Eton-cropped leader of criminals, forgot her masculine ways and dropped her tough guise for a few moments yesterday.

She went into a very feminine " huff " in her cell at Holloway Gaol, to which Mr. Justice Finlay sent her last Friday to begin her four years' penal servitude.

I was standing at the window of her flat in Carleton-road, Tufnell Park, with Queenie Day, her flat-mate. Over the week-end Elsie, the woman in man's clothes whose criminal career was cut short at Oxford Assizes, discovered that coincidence had given her an amazing last chance of communicating with the outside world before she goes to prison.

Her cell in Holloway faces her old flat, and over the 200 yards of gardens, walls and courtyard she was able to shout greetings and signal to Miss Day.

Repeated yells of Queenie brought no response at first yesterday morning. "They must have moved her to another block," said Miss Day. " She called this morning, but my curtains were drawn and I didn't reply. Maybe she has gone off in the huff."

Waving across to Elsie Florence Carey, in Holloway Gaol . . . Miss Queenie Day, the convicted woman's flat-mate.

Half-Hearted Wave

The dark-haired girl kept calling. Then we saw a handkerchief waved half-heartedly through the bars. "There she is," said my companion.

"They must have been making her do some work this morning. I saw her with a paint-brush in her hand through a chink in my curtains. But when I didn't reply she must have been fed-up."

I called across to the gaoled woman. She shouted that she expected to be in Holloway for a month—then Aylesbury.

" I am fine ! " floated across from the prison. " I hoped to be able to cheer her up a bit," said Miss Day, " but now I've learned that she won't be long there."

EDEN MAY CANCEL VOLUNTEERS PLAN

BY OUR POLITICAL CORRESPONDENT

TO-MORROW'S opening of Parliament by the King will be overshadowed by foreign affairs. When he has read his first Speech

Queenie Day at the window of her Tufnell Park flat in 1937, smiling and waving at her lover Elsie Carey inside Holloway Prison. The image only became available online during the final stages of writing this book. (Mirrorpix, 25 October 1937)

The enigmatic Bobbed Haired Bandit, smash-and-grab getaway driver Lilian Goldstein, outwitted police for over a decade. This glamorous portrait is believed to have been taken in 1926. (Brian McDonald/Milo Books)

Blonde Alice Smith 'openly taunted that in crime she was the equal of any man'. Her mugshot appeared in the *Police Gazette* in 1928, when she was identified as part of a gang of expert continental jewel thieves. (The National Archives)

The Forty Elephants Bar, situated in the five-star Great Scotland Yard Hotel, formerly the headquarters of the Metropolitan Police. Lilian Goldstein's portrait dominates the room, while a 'smash-and-grab' chandelier hangs from the ceiling. (Great Scotland Yard Hotel)

Noreen Harbord, former debutante and Queen of the Contraband Coast, attending her smuggling trial in Lewes in 1950. She denied any knowledge of the 8,000 Swiss watches found hidden in secret compartments inside her Chrysler. (Rex Features/ANL/Shutterstock)

DAILY MIRROR, Tuesday, October 15, 1963   PAGE 13

UNDERWORLD QUEEN SAYS 'I ABDICATE'

By TOM TULLETT

BLONDE "Zippy Zoe" Progl, the only woman to escape from Holloway Jail, walked out of the main gate there yesterday and said:

"They used to call me the Queen of the Underworld. Now I'm abdicating."

Now Zoe looks for a job

Zoe, 35-year-old mother of three, who is also known to Robert O'Leyland as "Blonde Mick," has just served three years.

Part of it was for theft and part for her latest escape.

She carried that out in broad daylight. She climbed up a home-made rope ladder to the top of the 20ft. wall—and down an ordinary wooden one the other side.

A waiting car whisked her away. But she was recaptured at Saffron Hill, West London, six weeks later.

Human

Yesterday, as she walked to freedom, she gave some conciliated views on prison affairs. She said:

The staff performance at the Governor, Mrs J. K. Kelley, were wonderful to me. They were really human.

Although I had escaped, they came to trust me. And I got so that I did not want to let them down.

I was let out on my own to attend my father's funeral, and I was allowed to go alone to hospital for an operation.

For her ambitions didn't extend to the prison service.

I am certain there is not enough aspiration of prisoners.

I found everyone around me together—people who are all people who are just plain criminals.

Some youngsters are keen enough to teach themselves tricks to learn themselves for the perfect crime.

And she has quite definite opinion as to how to reform.

I believe people who steal should be made to repay.

Future

My advice to those: "If it's not yours, don't take it."

If I had behaved that I wouldn't have been reared up for so many years.

And what of the future now that she has abdicated from her underworld "throne"? ...

I'm going to train for a job and ask where I've been.

If there are no jobs, outside an inside I reckon I ought be able to start work.

I would hate to see any young girl follow in my footsteps. Really life means enough at eighteen, and then prison and misery arrives.

GERMAN ATTACKED—10 YEARS FOR SOLDIER

TWO British soldiers were jailed yesterday for attacking a German civilian, they got SIX years, the other TEN.

A court martial at Minden, West Germany, imposed the ten-year sentence on Rifleman J. Williamson, 22, of Glasgow, who was charged with robbery and wounding with intent.

The other man, Rifleman F. Stafford, 21, of Widnes, Lanarkshire, was accused of robbery.

Both soldiers, stationed at Minden with the Cameronians, were ordered to be dishonourably discharged from the Army.

The findings and sentences are subject to confirmation.

It's a lot of fire for the money

AND THE GOOD DESIGN IS FREE

It's over 2 ft. wide and it's called the SOFONOFLAME

Zoe Progl outside the wall of Holloway Jail yesterday ... the 20ft. wall she scaled in her daylight break for freedom three years ago.   Picture by Mirror Cameraman JACK MAINWARING

'My advice to young girls is, if it's not yours, don't take it.' Zoe Progl, pictured by the perimeter wall of Holloway Prison, announces her intention to retire from crime. (Mirrorpix, 15 October 1963)

Britain's No. 1 Woman Burglar relaxing at home, with a 'well-earned drink' according to the *Mirror*, after her final release from Holloway Prison in 1963. (Jack Manwaring, Mirrorpix)

'Mum lived by her own rules. She always said she didn't regret anything.' Zoe Progl, pictured in her early sixties. (Tracy Bowman family collection)

Twenty-year-old Eileen Blackmore, holding a .22 Winchester rifle at the window of her flat in Muswell Hill, during the siege of 1965. (Rex Features/ANL/Shutterstock)

'Bonnie and Clyde': Chris Tchaikovsky and her partner Jenny (seated) in 1969. Four years later, Chris was convicted of fraud as the leader of the Happy Firm. (Photographer unknown/Ben's family collection)

When Chris was arrested in 1972, the police offered her a deal: if she made a confession, they would let Jenny go. The couple pictured together with their dog Charlie, in the late 1960s. (Ben's family collection)

'A woman who was gifted and deeply loving': Chris with her 2-year-old son Ben in 1974. (Ben's family collection)

'The police refused to believe that I as a woman could have masterminded this amazing theft.' In 2004, Joyti De-Laurey was convicted of stealing £4.3 million from her bosses at Goldman Sachs. (Kirsty Wigglesworth, PA Images/Alamy Stock Photo)

13

NOREEN HARBORD
QUEEN OF THE
CONTRABAND COAST

One late afternoon in 1949, a gang of smugglers were slowly making their way along the south-eastern coast of France towards the village of Bandol. They had set off from Genoa, Italy, and were travelling in an ex-Royal Navy launch. At the helm was an Englishwoman called Noreen Harbord. She was in her mid-thirties, wearing slacks and a jersey, and she had a .45 Colt revolver strapped to her waist. As the boat neared Bandol, a pirate ship came into view and Noreen ordered her crew to bring out their rifles and ammunition. 'If there was going to be any monkey business,' she later explained, 'I decided we would fight it out.'

But then there was a burst of machine-gunfire and a few moments later, the hull was hit. Noreen slowed the boat down and hoisted the Red Ensign flag to show the vessel was British, but the pirates pulled alongside, and a 'dark-skinned blackguard' leapt onto the deck. 'Don't you know we are a British ship?' Noreen yelled in Italian. 'What do you mean by firing at us?'

The pirate laughed, 'Yes, a British ship, a British *smuggling* ship. And you are the Queen of the Smugglers.' The pirates ransacked the boat and seized the usual contraband – strips of gold, cases of Scotch whisky,

American cigarettes and hundreds of pairs of nylons – then the 'black-guard' kissed the skipper's hand before he left.

Noreen Harbord had been Queen of the Contraband Coast for the past three years, travelling from Tangier in North Africa to European ports in Spain, Italy and France. As 'Admiral of the Fleet', she was apparently so well known that she was instantly recognisable, even by a pirate in the middle of the Mediterranean Sea. But even more exciting to the British press, Noreen was a former debutante and society hostess.

She was born Noreen Leonie Ross Rose in the British garrison town of Robert Heights in Pretoria, South Africa, on 16 October 1913. She described herself as 'not exactly a criminal born and bred. In fact, my family is quite a distinguished one.' Her mother was Agneta Wendela Elizabeth Van Citters, while her father was Major Launcelot St Vincent Rose, a member of the Royal Engineers. He was an accomplished rower, runner, polo player and big-game shooter, and was commended for his bravery on the Western Front, where he was killed in 1914.

At the age of 18, Noreen was presented at court, joining the other debutantes on the crimson carpet at Buckingham Palace, dressed in white gowns to curtsey before the king and queen. It was a glamorous, theatrical event, as was the social whirl that followed, and Noreen's photograph often decorated the pages of society magazines. She was a frequent visitor to the Royal Enclosure at Ascot, where well-connected ladies competed to gain access. 'Being in the Royal Enclosure at Ascot,' explained *Vogue*, 'is being on the inside looking out.'

In 1935, Noreen's engagement to Arthur Harold Bligh Harbord, a wealthy man about town and the son of a brigadier general, was announced in *The Bystander* magazine. It was accompanied by a glamor-ous photograph of Noreen looking a little like film star Mary Pickford, with a wavy bobbed hairstyle, pencil-thin eyebrows and cupid-bow lips. The couple married in Kensington the following year, but by 1939 Noreen was living without her husband in a flat at 61 Harrington Gardens, South Kensington, just a few doors down from the luxurious Bentley Hotel.

She threw herself into life as a society hostess. Her parties were 'popu-lar with nobility' and were said to be particularly 'wild' during the war.

She hosted gambling sessions for former military officers, but when the police 'put a stop to that', she had to look for another way of making money. 'Of course I had not been trained to do a job,' she explained. 'Debutantes in my day scorned such notions.' Instead, debutantes were trained to find suitable bachelors and then devote themselves to being a wife and mother.

'Girls of a certain background were not expected to be academic or career driven,' writes historian Lucinda Gosling. It 'simply wasn't done to be clever'. Most debutantes received 'a lacklustre education', although many were sent to finishing schools in Paris or Switzerland, where they learned to entertain, speak French and arrange flowers. By the time Noreen was 30, she'd apparently been divorced three times and had two children.

Unlike the women of the Forty Elephants, Noreen Harbord didn't come from a background of workhouse poverty or struggle in a poorly paid job. Her initial motivation for crime may have been to pay off gambling debts, although she later argued it was to pay her children's boarding school fees and fund her own love of luxury.

After the war was over, she became a bookmaker, and then her ability to speak 'several' foreign languages led to a job as an interpreter with a British firm in Milan. But this wasn't enough to indulge her expensive tastes, so she decided to find a new way to make money.

In the years after the Second World War, Europe was 'cursed by complicated currency regulations', and the rules varied from country to country. The Swiss authorities, keen to attract British tourists, were offering a good exchange rate on travellers' cheques, a form of payment that had been used since Victorian times. £1 worth of travellers' cheques could be cashed in for 17 Swiss francs, whereas the British pound in cash was worth only 10 francs. Italy offered no similar incentives, and Noreen realised there was a handsome profit to be made by changing British travellers' cheques in Switzerland and taking the francs back to Italy.

She scoured Milan for fellow Britons on holiday, bought their travellers' cheques at the official rate and when she'd collected several hundred pounds' worth, she crossed into Switzerland to exchange them for cash. 'Somehow I never thought of it as smuggling,' she explained, and it was easy to 'gaily deny' to police and customs officers that there was anything in her bag beyond a pound or two for shopping.

In the summer of 1946, Noreen made the bus journey across the border fifty-seven times and not once was she asked to open her bag. Her net profit totalled more than £8,000 – equivalent to around £250,000 today. But eventually the border officials grew suspicious – her face was becoming too familiar.

There was a further problem. A new regulation meant that travellers' cheques could only be cashed in the presence of the person named on the cheques, and they had to sign each cheque in front of a bank or travel agency official. So Noreen decided to take a holiday and set off for Gibraltar to see an ex-officer friend called Johnnie. Together they bought a twin-screw harbour defence launch, a former Royal Navy vessel. The idea was to cruise for a few weeks under the Mediterranean sun, sail to Britain and then sell the boat.

Noreen intended to use the £8,000 she'd made on the travellers' cheques to buy into a small business in London and then 'settle down to a normal family life with my son and daughter'. But this was not to be, because when Noreen and Johnnie docked in Seville in Spain, they were surrounded by people begging for tobacco, coffee and whisky. They'd been mistaken for smugglers, and Noreen Harbord had stumbled upon an ideal way to make her fortune.

The couple sailed to London, docked on the River Thames, and went to see a man named Freddy – a Polish ex-RAF pilot who controlled a smuggling gang. There were half a dozen members, all men, and most were ex-officers with a 'taste for adventure'. A conference was held in Noreen's flat, and she agreed to buy a quarter share in 'a gigantic smuggling organisation'. Freddy was commander-in-chief, while she would run two smuggling boats along the Contraband Coast. But when Noreen asked Freddy for 'a machine gun or two for defence', he was against it, fearing she might start firing not just on pirates, but on the customs officers' revenue boats as well.

In early 1947, Noreen and Johnnie sailed from Gibraltar to Tangier, an international zone and free port where there was no duty on tobacco and no currency restrictions. Billy Hill, who arrived in Tangier a few years later, described the port as full of 'desperadoes and villains of all shades'.

Noreen and Johnnie bribed a customs official and bought cigarettes from a duty-free warehouse, before sailing on to Seville. Freddy kept in touch via a portable transmitter in London, sending coded messages to the wireless set on the launch. That summer, their two boats made eleven crossings and Noreen Harbord bought herself a mink coat, dined and danced at the most exclusive night clubs, and paid her children's boarding school fees.

But then one night, while sailing in open sea, a big black shape loomed up out of the water and Noreen was frightened out of her wits. It turned out to be a submarine, which drew up alongside and swivelled its gun in her direction. She stopped the engines and dropped her revolver into the sea, 'then out stepped the commander to board us. When he saw me, he smiled and saluted. "Aha," he said, "the Queen of the Contraband Coast".' Noreen felt 'quite flattered' but denied she was a smuggler, and happily showed him around the boat, its illegal cargo having already been safely delivered in Spain. But she was arrested and taken to prison, and while Johnnie and the crew were soon freed, it took a month before Freddy 'fixed' her release through bribery.

Numerous British-based smuggling gangs were at work in the late 1940s, and Noreen saw 'nothing morally wrong' with slipping cigarettes, nylons or liquor past customs. Rationing was still in place, luxury items were scarce, and most British holidaymakers smuggled in a little something as they came home through customs. One gang, run by a former submarine commander, brought in wine and spirits from France, which were sold on the black market in the West End. Others smuggled in cash, gold jewellery, diamonds, cameras from Germany and bulbs from Holland. British, Canadian and American pilots had been known to smuggle silk stockings and perfume in the wings of their planes. Almost everything was in short supply, explained Billy Hill, and these were 'the halcyon days of loot'.

At some point, Noreen also started transporting expensive drugs such as penicillin and streptomycin, again bought in Tangier, using the name Mrs Harry Lime. It was an unsubtle choice of alias, considering that

Harry Lime was a villainous character in the hugely successful 1949 film *The Third Man*. When Noreen discovered that the drugs were being diluted and the results could be fatal, she wired Freddy in London to say she would never do it again.

He suggested taking a new type of cargo and so Noreen started transporting gold strips from Genoa to Bandol on the French coast. Her crew consisted of Johnnie and two engineers from Gibraltar, and they had a high-ranking customs officer on their payroll. The gang travelled at night and once they neared Bandol, under the cover of darkness, they transferred their cargo to small local fishing vessels, which were less likely to be searched. Then they waited for daylight before sailing in, 'just as if we were on a holiday cruise'.

There were plenty of holiday cruisers on the Riviera at the time. It had been a luxury resort for British aristocracy since the mid-nineteenth century and in the years after the Second World War it became an increasingly glamorous destination. Resorts like St Tropez were popular with the international jet set and, with the launch of the Cannes Film Festival, Bandol was attracting Hollywood stars like Marlon Brando.

Noreen delivered contraband whisky to a local café owner, who conveniently also had a 'small smelting plant' in his shed, where the gold strips were melted down into smaller sizes before being shipped to Paris. Once the smuggled goods were disposed of, Noreen and Johnnie went on a spree for a few days. She rented a villa and bought a 40-horsepower car and 'as far as the Bandol people were concerned, I was a wealthy English woman enjoying the pleasures of life on the Riviera'.

The gold smuggling came to an end in 1949, after the pirates opened fire, and Freddy suggested they turn their hands to smuggling Swiss watches. Noreen returned to England and converted a flat in Chelsea into a black-market warehouse. Her 30ft lounge was filled with thousands of watches, taken from Switzerland to France and then through customs in England. A number of London businessmen were 'willing to buy Custom-free goods', she explained, and she put on this 'show' eight times a year, selling £8 watches for under £2 and making £1 profit on each one. Noreen personally smuggled more than 30,000 watches through customs, making the equivalent of over £1 million today.

◆

Female smugglers posed a particular problem for customs officials. They had to be searched by a woman officer and several English ports had to 'borrow' a policewoman from a local police station. By the time the officer arrived, the contraband goods had often been passed on to someone else. Smuggling was seen as a crime well suited to a woman, just like shoplifting because, as one journalist explained, they 'can conceal things better on their bodies'.

When a Swiss woman was arrested at London Airport, 380 watches were found sewn into the pockets of a body belt, while a woman from Londonderry had 1,400 cigarettes concealed in her 'smuggler's pockets' under a skirt. Another woman arrived in New York with £176,427 worth of diamonds secreted in the hollow heels of her platform shoes. She said she'd been a dupe for strangers, who had 'persuaded' her to wear the shoes.

Some women may well have been threatened and coerced into smuggling, but Noreen Harbord had a major share in her operation, and she was apparently working on an industrial scale. She took a flat in Paris, which served as the gang's continental headquarters, and hired a nearby underground garage. Cars were turned into smuggling vehicles, with special metal trays welded under the silencer boxes, liquid-proof compartments inserted inside petrol tanks, and cupboards for watches concealed in spare tyre containers. Freddy, the ex-RAF pilot, bought the watches in Geneva, while Noreen drove to Switzerland to collect them and returned to France, 'to all appearances as if I had been on a Swiss holiday'. But the car was 'no joke to steer', seeing as it contained up to 14,000 watches.

Once she was stopped by a policeman, who pointed out her lights were off, and when he failed to mend them he chivalrously drove the car himself, right through the customs barrier to a garage. On another occasion, her petrol tank started to leak, and customs officials made a thorough search of the car, 'looking for minor items of contraband like bottles of scent'. Eventually an official fixed the leak with a piece of chewing gum and waved her on. On a third occasion, she took her children on a smuggling trip in an old family car with 10,000 watches hidden inside.

Noreen Harbord didn't look like a criminal; she was a former debutante who might slip a bottle of scent into her glove department, but certainly not 14,000 Swiss watches. When she arrived in Paris, the mechanics set to work, burning out the numbers stamped into the steel engine blocks and chassis and stamping new ones, and changing the number plates. The gang also had a small printing press in the garage, where they produced false travelling documents for the cars.

But in July 1950, when Noreen arrived at the British port of Newhaven on the Sussex coast, she was in for a shock. Customs officers found 7,742 watches hidden in secret compartments inside her Chrysler. Despite being caught red-handed, she insisted she knew nothing about it and was 'absolutely horrified'. She also said, 'I am going to marry the Governor of Tangier next week, then you will not be able to search my belongings as I will have a diplomatic passport.' She mixed with 'the best people', she explained, 'and when I go racing at Ascot and places I am photographed'. She had 'my position in Society to consider' and would 'never be mixed up with smuggling'.

What happened next is a little unclear. The haul of Swiss watches was found at around 5 p.m., and an hour and a half later Noreen Harbord and the customs officers retired to a public house where they drank 'for some time'. Noreen enjoyed several gins, and then drove them all some 50 miles to Croydon, where the formal interview began at 11 p.m. and lasted until 3 the next morning.

According to Noreen, once in Croydon, the group shared four bottles of wine, but the customs officers denied they'd partaken of alcohol and said she'd finished two bottles herself. But why had the customs officers gone to a pub with a suspected smuggler in the first place? Were they hoping she'd get drunk and confess? Or did they see an opportunity to strike a deal?

The press explained that Noreen had come to England 'after being up all night and going to a night club' in Paris, and by the end of the formal interview she was drunk and 'in hysterics'. 'I think I behaved badly,' she admitted. 'I spat like an alley cat. I felt as if I had a pack of hounds after me.' She denied saying 'I hate you and I hate this country', but she threatened one officer, 'if you twist anything I said the other night, when I was drunk, I'll get one of my boys to give you the biggest ***** hiding yet.' Noreen had dropped her mask – she wasn't an innocent lady traveller, but the leader of an international smuggling gang.

In December 1950, she was charged with attempting to smuggle the 7,742 watches, valued at around £30,000. She was also charged with attempting to import nearly 11,000 watches, along with John Stapleton Gordon, a well-known racing driver, ex-public schoolboy and former tank commander, and Guy Jason-Henry, a car dealer. Noreen's gang had recently been sending sportscars over to the Continent, to take part in road races and then smuggle back watches, and that year John Stapleton Gordon had raced a Delahaye DUV 870 sportscar in the Le Mans 24 Hours as part of the Aston Martin team. It was in this car that Guy Jason-Henry arrived at Newhaven, with thousands of watches hidden inside a fake petrol tank.

The seven-day trial in Lewes drew widespread coverage and the courtroom was packed. Newspapers printed photographs of customs officials examining Noreen's Chrysler and dismantling the racing car so the petrol tank could be carried into court. Noreen, 'an attractive titian-haired woman', was pictured striding into court in a tailored suit with pearls around her neck, gloves and handbag in one hand and a cigarette in the other. It was a modern tale of two cities, explained the press: a story of intrigue and smuggling between London and Paris, and the jury were marched 300yds under police escort to examine the cars at a local garage.

Noreen's lawyer pleaded the usual defence. His client was an inno-cent woman and, just like Lilian Goldstein the Bobbed Haired Bandit, she'd been used unwittingly by men. Some of Noreen's boyfriends might have been engaged in smuggling without her knowledge and 'there's no doubt that she was in touch with an international collec-tion of boyfriends, Italians, Poles, French and Spanish'. But she was not on trial for her morals, and 'She is a woman who talks. Do you think anyone would take her into a conspiracy and tell her all about it?' Noreen had been duped into working for the gang and who in their right mind would trust a woman with the intricacies of an international smuggling plot? She also had a 14-year-old daughter and an aged mother to care for. She was a society lady who'd never been involved in criminal proceedings.

This wasn't quite true, however, because in March 1941, Noreen Harbord of Harrington Gardens, Kensington, had been charged with stealing a £100 fur coat from a Regent Street restaurant. She hadn't realised the coat wasn't hers until she wore it some time later and found an envelope in the pocket. 'I don't think the evidence satisfies quite that you knew you had another person's coat,' agreed the magistrate, and Noreen was found not guilty and discharged.

The police admitted they knew very little about Noreen Harbord. She'd been a FANY, a member of the First Aid Nursing Yeomanry, during the war, when she'd driven lorries. She'd also been 'a monitor on the BBC listening to Dutch broadcasts'. Other than that, the Queen of the Contraband Coast seemed to be a bit of a mystery.

Noreen appeared in court, 'pale but otherwise unmoved', as she waited to hear her fate. The judge was certain 'there are others behind you who deserve more severe punishment', and he found it 'painful to see a woman like you in this position'. The Queen of the Smugglers was sentenced to twelve months in prison, racing driver John Stapleton Gordon to two years, and Guy Jason-Henry was fined for trying to import a pistol. The gang's 'king-pin', Freddy, however, was never caught.

According to the Australian press, Noreen was unfazed by the sentence. 'I am just one of those people who do the most outrageous things,' she said, and then she asked, 'Which is the best women's prison – Aylesbury or Holloway?' But while the judge appeared to believe that Noreen had been duped into smuggling and had only played a minor role, the prosecutor took another view. Derek Curtis-Bennett described her as 'a woman of skill and intelligence – far more intelligence than her two compatriots in the dock'. Less than eighteen months later, it turned out he was right.

In April 1952, *The People* breathlessly announced a new serialisation, 'Former debutante confesses: I was the queen of the smugglers'. The series ran for five weeks and was accompanied by photographs of 'Norah Price', as well as the smuggling cars, the Rock of Gibraltar, a fishing vessel and a map showing the location of Tangier.

This 'placid-looking' woman was once a respected figure in London society, explained *The People*, but her lust for money had taken her 'from the top of the social ladder to its very bottom'. She had defied the customs and police of 'every country' in a criminal career that had made her Public Enemy No. 1. Noreen had now left England, 'to live on her ill-gotten gains abroad', but before she went, she'd written a 'full confession of her astonishing exploits'. It would tell the whole truth and put on record the facts about her contraband gang.

'A few weeks ago I came out of Askham Grange Prison, Yorkshire,' began Noreen:

> I had completed a twelve months sentence for smuggling 8,000 Swiss watches into Britain. Frankly, I got off more lightly than I deserved. If the judge at Lewes Assizes had known what I had been up to ever since the end of the war, he would have put me away for a good long stretch.

Less than two years earlier, Noreen had pleaded ignorance. Now she was openly boasting; she'd made a fortune that would 'keep me in luxury for the rest of my days'. But while crime had 'paid off for me in a big way', the strain on the nerves had been deadly – especially for a woman. So Noreen had decided, while lying in her prison cell, to 'abdicate as queen of the smugglers'. All she wanted was to 'live down the past and forget both the excitement and the terrible fears that made up my life for six long years'. Smuggling, she had realised, was 'no way of life for a woman and a mother'.

Noreen's confession was very thin on facts and clearly written by a journalist. The male members of the smuggling gang, including Freddy, the commander-in-chief, were referred to only by their first names, and her own changes of name weren't explained – how had Noreen Harbord become Norah Price? There was little information on her family background, aside from her society connections, no mention of her place of birth and very few dates for any of the crimes. I also can't find concrete evidence that she was presented at Court at 18, or that she'd been divorced by the time of her arrest.

The real purpose of the 'confession' was to entertain readers with a tale of a greedy, immoral, society hostess. She was 'hardly the respectable type', noted the press, and even her own lawyer had emphasised her loose morals and collection of international boyfriends. Noreen might have sounded regretful, but she was still an unnatural mother, travelling the high seas as 'Admiral of the Fleet' and taking her children on a family holiday in a car full of stolen watches.

Noreen's story fitted the period perfectly, for in 1950s Britain, women were once again being accused of aping men, just as they had in the 1920s. Their roles may have changed during the war, when 'courageous women' had been actively recruited to drive ambulances and army lorries and praised for 'doing a man's job', but ultimately, they were supposed to be homemakers. The traditional family unit was breaking apart, and women like Noreen Harbord, with their lust for money, lack of sexual morals and habit of wearing slacks, were to blame.

Female criminality was again said to be on the rise in the 1950s, and the statistics were alarming. The number of women and girls found guilty of serious offences had increased by 63 per cent between 1938 and 1948. It was no longer a sensation to read of a female criminal. Instead it was the age of 'she-crime'. 'Women are beginning to present a crime problem of their own,' warned the journal *Britannia and Eve*, and those who wore trousers were 'mentally conditioned into committing acts and crimes which would appear to them in a different light if they stuck to their normal women's clothes'.

The image of the female criminal in popular culture was becoming increasingly dangerous. Women were gang leaders in Hollywood films such as *Lady Scarface* and *The Story of Molly X*, or they persuaded men into a life of crime in *Queen of the Mob* and *Gun Crazy*. In *The Bonnie Parker Story* of 1958, loosely based on the career of the 1930s American bank robber, the female criminal was a cigar-smoking killer with a machine gun.

Alongside this apparent rise in 'she-crime' came new theories of female criminality. In 1950, Otto Pollak, an American professor of sociology, published *The Criminality of Women*, in which he argued that women committed far more crime than anyone had yet realised. Their crimes were more easily hidden because they occurred in the domestic sphere, and were less likely to be reported, especially thefts by prostitutes. If women were caught, then they were supposedly treated more leniently. Otto Pollak's overall theories weren't new, and he drew on a dubious 'wide range of sources', including the former Victorian prison governor, Arthur Griffiths, author of *A Prison Princess*, and Harry Ashton-Wolfe, the 'true crime adventure' writer of the 1920s.

Once again, biological theories took centre place, just as they had in Victorian times. Menstruation, pregnancy and menopause made women impulsive and irrational and led to public order offences, arson and murder. Otto also explained that women were naturally deceitful because, while a man must 'achieve an erection in order to perform the sex act' and could not 'hide his failure', women could 'pretend' to be aroused when they weren't. Otto Pollak added a psychosexual dimension as well, building on Sigmund Freud's 'envy for the penis'. Girls saw menstruation as a punishment. 'It destroys their hope ever to become a man', intensified their feelings of inferiority and aroused their desire for revenge.

But as misogynistic as some of his theories were, Otto's conclusions could be startlingly apt. 'In our male-dominated culture,' he wrote, 'women have always been considered as strange, secretive and sometimes dangerous.' Men weren't comfortable with their apparent superiority and were worried about the possibility of rebellion or revenge. They tried to deny women the ability to do the things that men do, and either idealised or maligned them, in order to condemn them. As a result, he argued, crime became a form of rebellion – a way for women to revolt against the burden of discrimination – and a demonstration of pent-up resentment. Women were making deceptive use of the feminine role and abusing it for criminal purposes.

Reactions to *The Criminality of Women* were mixed. One fellow academic called it 'the first significant and emotionally uncomplicated statement in the literature relative to the criminality of women' and advised law enforcement officials to 'reexamine and reevaluate their own thinking'. But Frank Hartung, a professor of sociology, asked the following question: If women were basically deceitful, and if their crimes were characterised by deception, did this mean 'that we men commit our crimes honestly and openly?'

Noreen Harbord, meanwhile, settled in Spain, where she ran the Hotel Costa Brava in Puerto De Soller, on the north-west coast of Majorca. The hotel became one of the first destinations for British package holidaymakers when, in 1952, Horizon Travel was granted a seven-year licence to fly to airports in Corsica and Majorca. The company's co-founder, Vladimir Raitz, had already made a quick trip to Majorca to look at Noreen's hotel, which had been recommended to him. He found 'a colourful and highly unconventional' woman, who 'worked hard, but played and drank even harder'.

Not all of Horizon's clients liked her 'exuberance and salty language', but most enjoyed their holidays. Noreen referred to her guests as 'the Horizontals' and regaled them with tales of her 'amorous experiences' and of the time she'd spent in prison after being caught with an ex-lover racing driver smuggling watches from Switzerland into the UK.

In 1954, the author Alan Sillitoe, who would become famous for his novel *Saturday Night and Sunday Morning*, also came across Noreen in Gibraltar. She wanted to buy a Ford Popular car and take it back to the hotel she owned, but as a resident in Spain, she would have to pay substantial tax to get it over the border. So Noreen suggested that Alan bought it in his name, and she would obtain 'notarised permission' from him to use it. He didn't explain if he knew who Noreen was, but seemed happy for her to drive him back to Soller, where he was 'generously provided with free board and lodging for a fortnight'.

Noreen was still running her hotel until at least 1970, and Horizon was still sending its guests there. But eventually she returned to England and, in 1994, at the age of 81, she remarried in Kingston upon Thames. 'I have lived and loved vividly,' she declared during her trial in 1950. 'I have had a number of boyfriends in a number of countries. Why not?'

The Queen of the Contraband Coast died in Hounslow in 2002. She appeared to have enjoyed her notoriety as a post-war smuggler – driving her own boat, carrying a gun, fleeing from pirates and submarines. And while she might have abdicated in 1952, her assertion that crime was no way of life for a woman was unconvincing. Crime had freed her from the role of debutante and society wife, and replaced a life of domesticity, however privileged, with one of adventure. She'd swapped Ascot dresses and chaperoned dances for life on the open seas, with a cargo of gold strips and a .45 Colt revolver. Noreen Harbord had taken full advantage of the criminal opportunities available after the Second World War, and she would not be the only female crook to succeed in a 'male' branch of crime.

14

ZOE PROGL
NO. 1 WOMAN BURGLAR

The 1950s was a prime time for British criminals. Less than a quarter of crimes in London were being detected, the police were understaffed, and the courts were overcrowded. Lorryloads of tea, sugar, butter, clothes, cigarettes and whisky were disappearing nearly every night, according to Detective Superintendent John Gosling, while thieves who 'worked like phantoms' were stealing jewellery and cash from private houses all across the capital.

Seventy-five per cent of reported crimes were thefts and break-ins, but burglary by a woman remained rare. Housebreaking was considered a skill, a 'science' that required specially made instruments, and female offenders who did appear in the press tended to take small items – a purse with a few coins or an umbrella – usually from someone they knew. But one woman possessed far more expertise, and for Zoe Progl, post-war Britain provided the perfect climate for success. London thieves had 'never had it so good', she explained in her autobiography *Woman of the Underworld*, it was 'easier to succeed in crime ... than ever before'.

Zoe was born Zoie Tyldesley in Lambeth Hospital on 28 March 1928. She was the third child of a 'long-suffering' mother, Marjorie Gainey, and a lorry-driving father, Arthur, the son of a fishmonger from Lancaster. Arthur was often 'fighting drunk', his 'second home was Arbour Square nick' and visits from the police were so frequent that Zoe began to look at them 'in the same way as relatives'. In one case, her father was arrested for exceeding the 20mph speed limit, ejected from a police court, charged with assaulting two officers on the way to the cells, and then refused to pay a fine. 'I will take fourteen days or a month and have a rest at your leisure,' he told the judge. 'It will do me the world of good as well as you.'

Zoe had two older brothers, one of whom was a merchant seaman who died at 18 when his boat was torpedoed by a German submarine. The family lived in a bug-ridden basement flat in Limehouse, near the north bank of the Thames, an area known for its opium dens and where the police patrolled in pairs.

Zoe's first thefts were motivated by hunger – swimming the Thames to raid barges and filling her haversack with bananas, nuts and tins of fruit. At school she rifled through other girls' coat pockets and when she realised that she had stolen and got away with it, it marked the beginning of a new philosophy: 'It's smart to get what you want without being detected.'

In September 1940, amid wide-scale bombing of the London Docks, Zoe was evacuated to the countryside where she discovered newfound luxury with a foster family. She was given a room of her own, a wardrobe full of flowered cotton dresses and a hot bath every night. When Zoe returned to London, she vowed that 'the better-life would one day be mine – somehow!'

At the age of 13, she broke into her first house, stealing coins and selling them to a dealer. She then used the proceeds to 'have some Polyphoto pictures taken of myself … I suppose I could interpret this as the first sign of my vanity – a vanity which has, in a way, contributed to my downfall.'

Zoe's autobiography has many similarities with Moll Cutpurse's seventeenth-century diary. There are times when her sense of fun comes through, but the overriding voice is that of a disapproving man, in this case, a *News of the World* journalist eager to explore his subject's downfall and 'sex' up her confessions. After leaving school at 14, Zoe worked at Woolworths, where she apparently decided to 'specialise in being sexually provocative' while hiding cosmetics in her stockings. Next, she discovered Maxie's Café in Gerrard Street, Soho – a rendezvous of villains and thugs, 'deserters, ponces, pimps, prostitutes, drug addicts, lesbians and homosexuals'. Soon she was working as a nightclub 'come-on girl', encouraging male customers to buy overpriced, watered-down drinks while avoiding clients who had 'as many hands as an octopus has tentacles'.

Zoe clearly moved in a world of constant sexual harassment, and she had been sexually assaulted by a cinema projectionist as a child. Yet, she is portrayed as insatiable, even as a teenager. Her autobiography was published in 1964, against a backdrop of sexual 'permissiveness' and when, once again, there were fears that women were abandoning their roles as homemakers, and turning to sex, drugs and crime.

At 18, Zoe married Joe Progl, a master sergeant in the US Army. But, while she tried her best to 'play the part of the happy little domesticated wife, I was a flop. Cooking for a husband was just not for me … it was all a big bore.' So, she took up with Johnny Gelley, a Canadian gunman known as 'Johnny the Junkie', and together they embarked on a life of crime.

Her first raid was a mansion in Potters Bar, where she kept watch in a stolen Jaguar as Johnny and a friend emerged with £7,000 worth of furs. Overcome with excitement, Zoe promised herself that next time she would go in with them. More robberies followed, including a sub-post office in Surrey, where the gang broke in with a crowbar and stole a safe with £12,000 in cash and savings certificates, equal to around £500,000 today.

Then, in February 1947, Zoe was arrested for using forged cheques and a stolen Post Office Savings book, along with Johnny Gelley and another man. Zoe believed she'd be dealt with leniently – she was only 18, it was her first offence and she was also three months pregnant. The Old Bailey judge was Sir Gerald Dodson who, seven years earlier, had 'cancelled' Lilian Goldstein's prison sentence because he'd sympathised with her 'womanly instinct'. He didn't think Zoe Progl was 'guilty of anything but mixing with the wrong kind of society', but he still sent her to borstal for three years. This, he explained, was 'for your own protection in the hope that you will realise the harm you have done … and straighten out your life'. Gerald Dodson believed that borstals could reclaim delinquent girls and, as he explained in his memoir, 'the most wonderful efforts are made to restore the feminine dignity of the inmates, and to lead them back to moral living, honest labour'.

Zoe was taken to Aylesbury, where Queenie Day had been held in the 1920s, and she saw herself as 'the big daring criminal' – until the 'bad girls' filed into the dining hall, 'the toughest assortment of cookies I had ever encountered'. Post-war borstal girls generally came from backgrounds of domestic service or factory work, and their initial crimes were minor, spending an employer's milk money or failing to show an ID card. They frequently had an 'illegitimate' child, and like Zoe Progl, many had had relationships with men in the armed forces. They were so 'disturbed that they behave in a way of which the community disapproves', explained one leading psychiatrist, and while delinquent boys might steal cars and break into shops, delinquent girls became 'sexually promiscuous'.

Aylesbury Borstal was full of 'bad girls', just as the Kent House of Mercy had been in Victorian times. Inmates had often run away from home or approved schools or both, and many had been physically assaulted by a father or boyfriend. There were also cases of sexual abuse, which the authorities listed under 'criminal background' – as if it were the girl to blame. Borstal girls were the fallen women of the mid-twentieth century.

Zoe Progl's stay at Aylesbury simply educated her further into a life of crime, and she took down shoplifting tips, 'never knowing what branch of crime I might have to take up on my release'. She also learned how to pose as a wealthy young woman while 'kiting' or 'kite-flying' – buying goods with stolen cheques. In the summer of 1947, Zoe gave birth to her son, Tony, inside borstal, and after her release she was soon pregnant again, after an affair with Tommy 'Scarface' Smithson, whose gang included the young Ronnie and Reggie Kray.

After the birth of her second son, Paul, Zoe Progl started to shoplift, using the techniques she'd learned at borstal. She entered a jewellery shop, put on a 'County accent' and asked to see expensive rings. Then a friend came in and asked to see watchstraps, while Zoe fixed a diamond solitaire to a piece of chewing gum under the counter. When the assistant grew suspicious, Zoe acted affronted – 'I have never been so insulted in my life' – and swept through the door like a Victorian lady thief, while her friend made off with the ring. The women were using the same methods that penny weighter Annie Grant had deployed in West End jewellers' shops some forty years earlier. Soon Zoe was running a mail-order shoplifting business, 'hoisting' goods to order.

She branched into 'jump ups', stealing lorries around the London Docks and selling their contents, along with a crook called Ches, in Tufnell Park. The theft of loaded lorries had become endemic by the 1950s, according to detectives, with vehicles taken from car parks and rest stops, driven to secluded barns, unloaded and abandoned. Two million Player's cigarettes were found inside one farm building near Southend, as well as a ton and a half of sweets. Zoe also teamed up with two north-country screwsmen and broke into a mansion in Oxfordshire, using a set of 'twirls', similar to toasting forks, to gain entry and then escaping in a stolen Jaguar.

Before long, Zoe Progl was back in Holloway, sentenced to three months for robbing an American soldier with a friend, Rosina. The two women had enticed him with their 'come on' smiles, but when he suggested one of them go to a hotel for the night, 'Coyly, we told him that neither of us was that type of girl.' Just like eighteenth-century street robber Ann Duck, and American 'badger' Chicago May, Zoe had embarked on 'rolling' – acting as a prostitute in order to steal from potential clients. She felt relieved when 'the Yank' passed out on the bed, stole his money and escaped to Brighton for two weeks, before being caught.

On her release from prison, Zoe moved to a twenty-roomed house in Warwick Square, Pimlico, known to the Flying Squad as the 'Thieves Retreat'. It was home to hoisters, cat burglars and thieves, who used a dumb waiter to move stolen goods between floors during police raids.

But one night, a gang staggered home with a 5-hundredweight safe. A few hours later, seven officers from the Flying Squad burst in and

Zoe was taken to the police station. She rang a local solicitor's firm for help and told a Mr Piper about her troubles. There was a brief pause, and he replied, 'My dear young lady, I would love to help you but I'm afraid that were I to do so, I would be guilty of unprofessional conduct, because I have a personal interest in the case – you see, it's *my* safe you've stolen!' The police had followed the scratch marks on the pavement leading to Zoe's flat. She was taken back to Holloway for the third time, having been sentenced to fifteen months.

According to her autobiography, as soon as she was released, she threw herself into the London drug scene, smoking marijuana at orgies where couples 'fornicat[ed] on the floor' and injecting herself with speedballs – a mixture of cocaine and heroin. But when a lover cheated on her, she felt 'overcome with everything I had done that was rotten and sinful'. Her mind and body were 'soiled', and she tried to kill herself with an overdose of phenobarbitone tablets. Just like Moll Cutpurse, Zoe was apparently disgusted with the criminal life and her own immorality.

But she continued with her career, moving to Clapham where her flat became known to 'all the best thieves in the underworld'. In January 1957, she gave birth to her daughter, Tracy, and a few weeks later she returned to jump ups. Her reputation grew. So many buyers came to her flat that she had to rent a garage, known as 'The Shop'. 'If ever one of my cronies ran short of an item,' she explained, 'it was a fair chance that we had what he or she wanted.'

Not all jobs were lucrative, however. On one occasion, Zoe joined a gang on a wage snatch, anticipating £7,000 in cash. They ended up with £26, a cauliflower and ½lb of cheese.

She continued to break into houses, either alone or with an accomplice, stealing jewellery, furs and blank chequebooks. But when she realised that a fence near Hatton Garden wasn't giving her a fair price and had paid her £500 for a set of jewellery that was worth several thousand, she decided to educate herself. She bought a bottle of aqua fortis (nitric acid) – a few drops on an item of jewellery was enough to tell if it was solid gold – as well as a pair of scales and a spyglass. She borrowed books from the library and began studying the nature, weight and value of precious stones and metals. Soon, she developed a second sense and could pick up a ring and tell at once, by its colour, sparkle and weight, if the diamonds were genuine and how much they were worth. Now she could cut out the middleman and sell direct to 'bent' jewellers.

To test out her newfound knowledge, Zoe broke into a Mayfair apartment and took a diamond ring to 'one of the most reputable firms of jewellers' in London. She explained she was being kept by a wealthy man, had fallen into debt and needed to sell the ring as discreetly as possible. Zoe signed the relevant paperwork, giving a false name and address, and received the price she wanted.

Spurred on by her success, she embarked on a whole series of house-breakings, spending days in a neighbourhood casing joints, using an array of disguises. She could make herself look twenty years older by growing her eyebrows and wearing old-fashioned horn-rimmed glasses and a bucket hat, or a decade younger by dressing in teenage clothes, with her hair in a ponytail. Sometimes, she adopted a 'harmless school marm' look, especially when using forged cheques, which called for 'unwavering nerve and audacity'. She put false moles on her face and filled the gap between her teeth with dental latex. Like Blonde Alice Smith in the 1920s, she had become a chameleon countess, and like Victorian jewel thief Emily Lawrence, she knew how to 'come the lady'. One day, Zoe went to 'a famous Knightsbridge store' in a hired Rolls-Royce and selected goods worth over £300. Then she signed a cheque with a phony double-barrelled name, instructed the sales assistant to take the goods to the car, and drove off.

But then Zoe was caught after breaking into a Regency house in Brighton on Easter Monday 1960, leaving a fingerprint after tearing her nylon glove. She was already on bail, and now she knew she was heading to Holloway once more.

On 27 June 1960, she was sentenced to two and a half years for housebreaking and larceny. Her occupation was noted as 'housewife', and the authorities didn't seem aware of her previous spells in Holloway, which weren't recorded.

Conditions had improved since the post-war years. The prison's first woman governor, Charity Taylor, had introduced classes in typing, first aid, art and current affairs, while prison-issue clothing had become more 'feminine', with coloured frocks and cardigans. Joanna Kelley, appointed governor in 1959, also set about creating a more 'homely' environment and encouraging friendship between staff and prisoners. But Zoe Progl didn't plan on staying inside Holloway. Instead, she vowed to 'make criminal history by being the first woman to get over the wall'.

15

THE GREAT ESCAPE

On the morning of 24 July 1960, Barry Harris, a 'good-looking ex-sailor full of guts' and one of Zoe's 'newest boyfriends', stood outside the 25ft wall that encircled Holloway Prison. He was in an area known as prison-lane, to the east of the jail and next to a bombed-out building site. It was 7.30 on a Sunday morning and Barry was impatient. He was waiting for Zoe Progl to appear on the other side of the wall.

She'd been a model prisoner during the few weeks she'd spent inside, and as a result she'd been assigned a 'soft job', cleaning offices. One morning, she'd accidentally knocked over the phone in the senior medical officer's room and realised she had a direct line to the outside world. Zoe called Barry Harris, and after a few more conversations they agreed on the details of her escape.

Zoe's cell was on DX wing, which lay near prison-lane, and at 7 a.m. each day she crossed a quadrangle to the hospital wing, where she served breakfast to the patients. On the morning of 24 July, however, instead of returning to her cellblock, she ran across the quadrangle to a 5ft-high pile of coke, which had been carelessly left against the prison's 7ft-high inner wall. She climbed to the top, slipping three times in her ill-fitting prison-issue shoes, and ripping her bloomers in the process. Then she jumped down and stood by the outer wall, waiting for a sign.

A few moments later, someone called her name, and this was followed by a clang as an extending ladder was thrown against the wall. Barry's head appeared and a rope ladder was dropped down. Zoe clawed her way to the top and, terrified by the sheer drop below, called out, 'I don't think I can make it …' But Barry urged her down, frantic because Bryanna O'Malley, a friend who'd been released from Holloway the day before, was pinned in a phone box 100yds away with two prison officers stationed outside.

Bryanna's job had been to occupy the phone box so it couldn't be used to raise the alarm, but unbeknown to Zoe, two of her friends had decided to come and watch the fun and had parked outside the prison gates in a pink Ford Zephyr with leopard-skin seat covers. This had naturally aroused the suspicion of prison officers, who'd recognised Bryanna standing in the phone box and had gone to investigate. In a panic, Zoe jumped 25ft to the ground and ran with Barry to the getaway car, soon followed by Bryanna and another friend, Bernard. They were joined by the final member of the gang, Adelaide De Boer, also an ex-Holloway prisoner. Then Zoe Progl sped away, roaring through the backstreets of Holloway in a stolen car.

By lunchtime, the BBC had reported the escape, and the next day it was front-page news. The Victorian jail was supposed to be impenetrable, a fortress from which few prisoners ever escaped, and those who had were quickly caught. The public was warned to be on the lookout for '"Zippy Zoe" Progl, the blonde housebreaker', 5ft 1in, with a fresh complexion, oval face, brown hair dyed blonde and a scar under the left eye. Detectives and plain-clothes officers were posted at the Liverpool Docks, while the Flying Squad swooped on underworld haunts in south London and the West End.

Zoe hid at a friend's flat, then collected her daughter Tracy from another friend, and Barry Harris drove them to a caravan site in south Devon, along with Bryanna O'Malley. Here, Zoe enjoyed 'an idyllic fortnight' where, instead of feeling 'like a woman on the run from the police I was carefree and happy'. According to her autobiography, she also found 'something that had been denied me for years – the joy of motherhood, just looking after Tracy, washing her, dressing her'. But after two weeks, the money ran out and Zoe, Barry and Bryanna set off on 'a crook's tour of seaside towns'. They would later be convicted of five charges of housebreaking and six charges of using stolen cheques in Southampton.

On the night of 10 August, police received a 999 phone call. 'Zippy Zoe' had been spotted in a Chelsea hotel in London, wearing slacks, her hair dyed red and sitting at the bar drinking gin and bitter lemon. The Flying Squad rushed at once to the hotel, but Zoe had already left. Detectives suspected the call had been 'arranged with Mickie's knowledge and certainly came in AFTER she had left the bar. We are not amused by this show of bravado. Not at all.'

Zoe had left behind a letter addressed to the Home Secretary, urging that her sentence be reviewed. If he reduced it by twelve months, she would give herself up. 'The letter is being considered,' a government spokesman told the press, 'but the Home Secretary is not in a position to bargain with escaped prisoners.' Finally, on 2 September, the Flying Squad caught up with Zoe Progl when Detective Inspector Leonard Mountford burst into a flat at Notting Hill Gate at 4.30 a.m. and found her in bed with her boyfriend.

When Zoe appeared at Bow Street court, extra police were drafted in and there were 'special anti-escape precautions' as she was taken from the ground-floor cells up to Court No. 3. Barry Harris, her 'broad-shouldered lover', was said to be infatuated with Zoe, whom the press noted was eleven years his senior. The judge appeared sympathetic. 'You have got embroiled with this woman of thirty-two and I know that toils of this sort are the very devil to get out of. Your heart overcomes your common sense.' He would deal with Barry leniently in the hope he would go straight, and sentenced him to nine months.

Adelaide de Boer was found guilty of harbouring Zoe after her escape. She already had eighty-three convictions for soliciting, but police described her as 'not all bad' – she was a kind, helpful woman with 'really good qualities'. Bryanna O'Malley, on the other hand, was 'a girl who had everything' – good looks, intelligence, a public school education and wealthy foster parents. But her motto was 'anything for kicks', and she craved excitement. 'It is a terrible thing to see a young woman of your age and education standing where you are,' said the judge. 'You have gone steadily downhill from the time you left school.' Adelaide and Bryanna were each sentenced to nine months.

As for Zoe, she told the court that she'd only escaped because she was desperate to see her daughter, as well as her lover, Barry. She wept when the judge sentenced her to a further eighteen months, and she wept again when he told her that she was responsible for the jail sentences passed on her friends. 'You heap troubles on your own head and the heads of your poor little children,' he warned. 'Your children are all with foster parents. The amount of consideration you show them is negligible.' Zoe was led from the dock with tears streaming down her cheeks – she had been publicly castigated as an unfit mother.

Attitudes towards unmarried mothers were hardening in the 1960s. Marriage was said to be on the decline, although around 95 per cent of people under 45 were married, while the birth control pill was promising a 'sexual revolution', although it was only available to married women. The rising rate of 'illegitimate births' – one in twelve in England and Wales – was also blamed for the rise in juvenile delinquency. Unmarried mothers were 'treated as scapegoats', explained Baroness Edith Summerskill. A child's father had few obligations while the mother was blamed for the new 'permissiveness in sexual behaviour which characterises our time … society feels that the mother must be punished'.

According to Zoe's autobiography, it was her maternal instinct and guilt over her children that finally made her turn her back on crime. One morning, she was summoned into Holloway's visitors' room to find her son Paul and 'darling daughter', Tracy, who'd saved her pocket money to buy a tiny bottle of Woolworth's perfume. While Zoe was allowed to take the gift, it was later removed. 'When are you coming out of hospital, Mummy?' asked Tracy, and 'as she was gently led away, the tears streamed down my cheeks. I never felt less like a Queen of the Underworld.'

Zoe's autobiography ended with an emphasis on her badness, just like Moll Cutpurse's diary. 'For years, I had been everything that was rotten,' she wrote. 'I had swum in a pool of scum.' Now, like Noreen

Harbord, the Queen of the Contraband Coast, she had realised that crime was no way of life for a woman.

Zoe settled down in Holloway Prison to serve her time and didn't try to escape again, but she did manage to 'find a laugh or two'. She helped a fellow prisoner with an illicit still, stole milk and tinned salmon intended for the prison cats, and formed Zoe Progl Cosmetics Unlimited, producing face cream made from shoe polish, powdered red paint and a sprinkling of talcum powder, which she sold for five cigarettes a pot. At Christmas, Zoe helped decorate the prison with angels made from sanitary towels.

At the end of that year, Pathé News recorded a four-minute film entitled *Hope for these Women*, shot inside Holloway and shown at a cinema in Trafalgar Square. Inmates were seen queuing to buy Christmas cards from the prison canteen with their 1s festive bonus, visiting nurses sang carols and officers served Christmas puddings and handed out free cigarettes. A group of prisoners also performed a pantomime, 'King Arthur', and sitting on a throne on the makeshift stage was Zoe Progl, dressed as the Fairy Queen, with a cardboard crown on her head.

A year later, she sued the police for the return of a £400 diamond ring, which she'd been given by gangster Tommy Smithson. The police had confiscated the ring some two years earlier, and now she wanted it back. Zoe was taken from Holloway Prison to Marylebone court to hear her claim under the Police Property Act, and she was triumphant when the police were ordered to return the ring.

On her release, Zoe immediately sold her story to the tabloid press, following in the footsteps of Noreen Harbord. The *News of the World* photographed Zoe outside Holloway, wearing a fur-rimmed cape and holding a large white handbag, pointing up to the spot where she'd escaped over the wall. The *News of the World* could afford to pay handsomely: it was selling up to 8 million copies every Sunday and had recently paid Christine Keeler £23,000 for her 'confession' over the Profumo Affair.

Zoe took full advantage of the press interest by striking a deal with the *Daily Mirror* as well, and she was pictured at her flat 'on her first morning of freedom', dressed in a flimsy negligee and golden slippers.

Presumably, she was asked to try on different outfits, as she was also pictured in a patterned dress, holding a cocktail and sitting on the headrest of an armchair, looking slightly nonplussed.

Not long afterwards, Zoe married Roy Bowman and the couple opened a cab firm in South Norwood, where their daughter was born. Zoe continued to attract media attention, appearing on BBC's *Whicker's World* and *Late Night Line-Up*. In October 1965, she contributed to a Granada TV series, *Crime and the Bent Society*, in which 'professional practitioners of crime set out to justify their vocation', including 'Zippy' Zoe Progl, who appeared wearing a long, black wig.

She was one of the 'Golden Girls of Crime', explained Detective Superintendent John Gosling, and if a panel of gangsters were asked to select the winner of a Miss Underworld competition, 'they would surely have to crown Zoe'. She had a dynamic personality, was attractive to many men, beautifully dressed, and was 'able to pack a solid punch in both hands'. But the majority of women in 1960s Britain were still 'minor players' in the world of crime, their main role was creating 'a feminine diversion – such as throwing a faint'.

Zippy Zoe soon retired from the limelight. She'd learned the error of her ways and, as she explained in her autobiography, instead of gambling with her children's future, she was going straight.

It's the autumn of 2019 and I'm back in south London to visit Tracy Bowman again. I haven't seen her since last summer, when she first told me about her mother, and I set out to try and find other queens of the underworld. Tracy explained that a journalist had rewritten parts of her mother's autobiography, and now I've come back to learn more. 'Which parts of this are true,' I ask, putting my copy of *Woman of the Underworld* on the table, 'and which are made up?'

Tracy sighs. It hasn't been easy rereading her mother's memoir. The process has been confusing and upsetting, and it also makes her angry. 'Mum was embarrassed by that book,' she says. 'Some of it was complete fiction made up by the journalist. His name was Norman Lucas.

She didn't want me to read it, I remember her moaning, saying, "This isn't right, it wasn't like this".'

Tracy objects to the portrait of her grandfather as violent and fighting drunk. 'Mum adored him,' she explains. 'He was a softy and he was kind. Mum wasn't the victim of a violent father and a victim of circumstances, she made her own decisions.'

But what angers Tracy the most is the way her mother is portrayed as a 'sexually provocative' teenager and a woman who went to sex parties and took lots of drugs. 'All the bad, seedy sides in the book are wrong,' she says. 'The orgies and the heroin – these are the things that Norman Lucas wanted her to put in, because he said otherwise it would be too boring. Mum did lots of things, but heroin and hard drugs were not her thing.'

Tracy was also shocked to read about her mother's attempt to take her own life. 'Mum was very open. She was a straightforward person and she would have told us. She didn't tell fibs; well, she did to the police, obviously, but not to us.'

The theme of regret is also nonsense. 'It's not true,' says Tracy, 'because she loved it all. She wasn't "floating in scum", she was having the time of her life.' And as for the nickname 'Zippy Zoe', it was invented by the press, although her mother was called Mickie, 'probably because she loved Mickey Mouse'.

When it comes to Zoe's criminal skills, however, then the book is accurate. She did teach herself to become an expert at identifying jewels, and Tracy still has one of her mother's old shopping lists that includes aqua fortis. 'She passed the skill on to me,' she laughs. 'Mum was always coming home with big bags of tom and going through it and giving me the rubbish. If I pick up a ring, I know if it's genuine. I've been handling jewels all my life.'

It's also true that Zoe loved to wear disguises. 'Mum was an actress,' says Tracy. 'When she was casing a joint, which took weeks, even months, she dressed up so she was not out of place.' *Woman of the Underworld* includes photos of Zoe in various disguises, although they all look a bit similar to me – so did she look like a different person to her daughter?

Tracy laughs, 'She just looked like mum with different hats on to me. She had a box of velvet moles for her face and one time it went missing. I had put on all her jewellery and stuck the moles all over my cheeks and set off down Clapham High Street!'

Tracy believes her mother probably did leave a letter to the Home Secretary while on the run from Holloway Prison. 'She was clever, and she liked to provoke the police. One time she opened the window and sprayed them all with a hosepipe.' She also thinks Zoe may have represented herself when she sued the police for the return of Tommy Smithson's diamond ring. 'She always said she would have liked to be a lawyer; she wasn't silly by any means. She was very clever, but she went down the wrong path, or she went down a different path. She thought she was a Robin Hood character, robbing from the rich to give to the poor.'

But, I say, what about the times she wasn't stealing from the rich, like the night she helped Tommy Smithson take a safe containing staff wages from a children's shoe factory? Tracy agrees, 'She glorified it a bit, I've thought of things she did that worry me now, she made it so glamorous.'

When it comes to the theme of motherhood, it's much harder deciding on the truth. Tracy isn't convinced by her mother's insistence that all she wanted was the chance to be a mother, or the idea that she escaped in order to be with her daughter. 'It doesn't ring true,' she says. 'Mum was playing happy families at the caravan park in Devon.' And after all, Zoe hadn't gone away with her daughter alone, instead she was with her boyfriend Barry and friend Bryanna, and together they were about to embark on a series of raids in Southampton. But the autobiography of a criminal woman had to follow convention: if Zoe was going to be redeemed then she needed to show regret, abdicate from crime and become a proper wife and mother.

After Zoe Progl's final prison sentence in the early 1970s, she settled in Streatham. 'I went to see her every day,' remembers Tracy fondly. 'She was still shoplifting. She'd ring me and say, "There's a lot of fish and meat in the bath, babe".' When Tracy went out with her mum, 'I knew she was shoplifting from the way she sniffed. If we were in a shop and I heard that sound' – Tracy gives a sharp sniff – 'then I knew what was up. I'd say, "Put it back!" And tell her off.'

Tracy only once followed in her mother's footsteps, 'When I was around 13, I pinched something from Boots and was caught. The store detective said I had to tell my parents, or she would call the police. So I told mum and she went mad, she kept crying, it was very dramatic. Then she didn't talk to me for a week, and she threatened to tell Roy, that's what scared me. Maybe she didn't want me to be like her. I never did it again.'

Instead, Tracy became a barrister's clerk, then worked at a women's refuge, and today she is a youth worker. 'It's child focused,' she explains, 'perhaps because of the way I was brought up. I have great empathy for kids brought up in care.'

In the early 1980s, Zoe Progl had a brief and successful change of career when she became wardrobe assistant to theatrical producer Harold Fielding. She worked on his musical *Barnum*, based on the life of the Victorian showman, which made its West End debut with Michael Crawford in the title role. 'She loved the job,' says Tracy. 'I'm not sure if Mr Fielding was aware of mum's past, but they became friends. It was a lovely job.' Zoe had finally found a way to put her knowledge of fashion, disguise and performance to good use. When she died on 26 August 1995, in Streatham, her occupation was given as 'wardrobe assistant (retired)'.

Zoe Progl had first started stealing as a young child, and for fifty years she'd honed her skills, from kiting and rolling, to jump ups and burglary. She'd mixed with the leading male gangsters of the day and, in the summer of 1960, she'd made criminal history by escaping over the wall of Holloway Prison. But still no one has written her full story, or brought her to life on the screen, although Tracy would love to see a film or play based on her mother's career.

The few modern references to Zoe Progl are dismissive. *The Guardian* describes her as 'a fraudster, thief, and general good time girl', while

London Gangs at War identifies her as Tommy Smithson's girlfriend and 'highly sexed'. A recent blog portrays her as a vain woman, who was 'arrested stark naked in the middle of the night', while *Brewer's Rogues*, published in 2002, describes her as a gangster's moll known as 'Blonde Mick'.

But within the family, Zoe Progl is remembered with love and pride. Tracy has two daughters, Ellie and Emma, and both are fascinated by their grandmother's story. When Ellie auditioned for the BRIT School, the performing arts school in Croydon, 'she had to tell a story about someone she admired,' explains Tracy. 'She chose Mum. Ellie had read her autobiography and she showed pictures of Mum and told her story. And she got in!'

'Why did Ellie admire her?' I ask.

'Because she was exciting,' says Tracy. 'Mum lived by her own rules.'

Zoe Progl wasn't the only underworld queen to live by her own rules in the swinging '60s. The Forty Elephants had a new leader now, a glamorous south Londoner and protégée of Alice Diamond, and soon she was organising shoplifting raids the likes of which had not been seen since the 1930s.

16

SHIRLEY PITTS QUEEN OF THE SHOPLIFTERS

I'm standing outside a research centre called Design Against Crime, on the first floor of Central Saint Martin's Art School in north London, about to meet Professor Lorraine Gamman. She founded the centre in 1999 and one of its aims is to develop fittings, products and packaging that help to stop crime, including shoplifting.

Every year in the UK there are around 374,000 incidents of shoplifting reported to the police, and retailers estimate the actual figures are twenty times higher. The most popular items tend to be small and expensive, easily stolen and easily resold, including alcohol, cosmetics, perfume, packaged meat and clothing accessories. For students at the Design Against Crime Research Centre, the challenge is to balance design, business and crime prevention, to enable sales while at the same time reducing theft. Recent examples of their work include LinkCuffs, a silicone loop which links together bottles of spirits to prevent theft from small off-licences, and a perfume station with pump dispensers to stop people stealing tester bottles from department stores.

The door to the research centre opens and Professor Lorraine Gamman comes hurrying out, carrying lunch for us to share. She's in her early sixties, dressed all in black except for a large, bright bead necklace, and she strikes me as the sort of person who will get straight to the point. It's taken weeks to set up this appointment because Lorraine is frequently involved in projects outside the office, such as Makeright, a prison design course, on which HMP Thameside inmates have recently created an anti-theft bag range.

But the roots of the research centre lie in shoplifting, and one shoplifter in particular – Shirley Pitts. She was the biggest hoisting queen since Alice Diamond and, like seventeenth-century outlaw Moll Cutpurse, her career lasted fifty years, including fraud, jewellery theft, burglary, bank robbery and running an escort business.

Lorraine knew Shirley Pitts well, through family connections. In the early 1960s, Lorraine's father ran the Regency Club in Stoke Newington, which was later taken over by the Kray twins, and Shirley was a regular visitor. Lorraine's mother had a wool shop near Hoxton Market in the East End, where Shirley Pitts lived with her husband Chris Hawkins, who ran a fruit and veg stall. Lorraine remembers Shirley arriving at the market in the mid-1960s. 'She'd been in mum's shop and she was wearing a fox fur hat and a fox fur coat, almost like Julie Christie in the 1960s film *Dr Zhivago*. She was *so* glamorous.' Lorraine laughs and throws open her hands, 'She had a Marilyn Monroe quality; as a woman, she was all that you're supposed to be. She had it, whatever it is, beauty, charisma, star quality – she had it. She could throw a silk scarf around her neck and look like a film star.'

When Lorraine decided to focus on shoplifting for her PhD at Middlesex University, Shirley Pitts was the ideal person to interview. The collection of oral recordings led to a biography, *Gone Shopping: The Story of Shirley Pitts, Queen of Thieves*, first published in 1996. Lorraine had already co-written two academic books, *The Female Gaze* and *Female Fetishism*, 'but my large East End family couldn't understand or relate to them,' she says, 'nor my feminist lifestyle. I wanted to do something that focused on a powerful woman involved in crime, but written in a non-academic way, so my family could understand and enjoy it. I wanted to write a life story from my mum's world, something she could relate to. Shirley was from home and I just loved her.'

The process of writing *Gone Shopping* had a profound influence on Lorraine's life, and on what she would do next. Having gained a better understanding of Shirley's shoplifting techniques, she went on to launch the Design Against Crime Research Centre.

Gone Shopping is narrated in the first person, based on years of oral recordings, as well as stories from Shirley's community. 'She was dying,' explains Lorraine. 'That's why she eventually told her story. She wasn't frightened, she had nothing to lose, and she enjoyed talking about the past – it was a much nicer place for her reliving exciting times than dying of cancer in the present.' But Lorraine felt there were parts of herself that Shirley held back. 'She was an enigma that I couldn't ever get to the bottom of; I couldn't ever really understand what made her tick. She wasn't ever really in one place. She was funny, a proper story-teller, daring and never scared. She was also unreliable. She would tell a story ten different ways.'

To begin with, Shirley told the stories that she thought Lorraine wanted to hear, 'but I wasn't interested in male figures like the Krays. I was much more interested in how Shirley kept herself and her kids together when she was working, and the love she had for them, that was clearly more important to her than anything else in the world.'

The book took years to write and could be frustrating. 'Shirley would just change her mind,' Lorraine laughs. 'She'd throw away a tape, or just fuck off somewhere, on more than one occasion with the tape recorder for a year.'

The process was also emotional. Shirley Pitts was her friend and had been diagnosed with breast cancer during the writing of the book. Lorraine admired her. She wanted to help tell her story and leave a legacy, and today she speaks about Shirley Pitts like an advocate and defender. 'Like a lot of people who earn their living from crime, she was extremely creative,' says Lorraine. 'If she had different educational opportunities, a different background perhaps, she could have used her creative talents very differently.'

Gone Shopping is an unusual book. Stories of professional thieving by women are rare, especially first-hand accounts, and Shirley had far more control over the way her story was told than underworld queens Moll Cutpurse and Zoe Progl. There were no anonymous male dia-rists making up events or tabloid journalists inventing salacious tales to suit their own purposes. 'I loved Shirley's fighting spirit and her non-conformity,' says Lorraine. 'She was a woman in a man's world who succeeded. She was not a victim, she had agency, she wanted more.'

Shirley Sally Pitts was born in Lambeth on 24 November 1934, one of six children. She was a breach birth and coming out feet first meant she was 'born to run'. Her mother, Nelly Taylor, 'a big baby herself', was just 16 years old, while her father, Harry, was a cat burglar, bringing home hauls of Chippendale furniture, fur coats and oil paintings.

Shirley idolised her father, who'd named her after a male friend. 'A boy's name was just right for me … I was always with the boys.' When Shirley was around 7 years old, her mother told her and a younger brother, Adgie, to take milk from neighbours' doorsteps. Then they stole bread, the milkman's petty cash tin and items from the grocery shop, with Shirley hiding a knuckle of bacon or a big lump of cheese under her coat. 'I thought we were doing good getting the food,' she explained, 'because when we got home my mum started to show affection to me and Adgie. Adgie would get a cuddle, and then I think I thought I could make her love me too if I got things for her.' Shirley started stealing, not just out of necessity and because she was told to, but as a way to get her mother's love and attention.

One day, her father asked Alice Diamond, a regular visitor to the family home, to get the children some clothes. The Queen of the Forty Elephants was in her mid-forties by then, and apparently keeping a low profile, living with her brother Harry and giving her official occupation as 'unpaid domestic duties'.

Shirley was impressed by Alice Diamond. 'She was the biggest woman you ever did see, with diamond rings on her fingers and fox furs around her neck. I thought she looked the business.' Alice took Shirley to a store on the Cut in Lambeth, to pick out clothing for the family. 'Will this fit your brother?' she asked as they moved around the shop, and when Shirley said yes, the item was put into a holdall bag. Shirley was nervous and excited. How would the Queen of the Forty Elephants get out of the shop with the bag?

As they queued at the counter, she was told what to do. 'When I give you the nod,' said Alice, 'I want you to take this bag and walk out of the door.' Shirley was scared, but thought she should do as she was told, and the moment the shop assistant was distracted, she was instructed to leave the shop. Eventually, Alice Diamond came out, having bought a pair of socks and a handkerchief with half a clothing coupon. She pinched Shirley's cheek and said, 'I'm going to treat you, darling, for being such a good girl.' She was given 30s and 'I was in heaven'. Once again, Shirley was being rewarded for theft, but now she was also being paid for it. At school the next day she bought everyone ice creams and was 'big bananas' in the playground for a week.

Shoplifting had brought her popularity and given her the opportunity to be generous. Not surprisingly, she couldn't wait to go out with Alice Diamond again – she was being initiated into the powerful, glamorous world of the Forty Elephants. The women were like film stars, with furs and beautiful make-up, and they picked her up in a Chrysler to go to the West End. They worked in groups of up to eight, and 'sometimes they just belted the shops. They would take everything in sight and have you working until nine o'clock at night.' Shirley would stroll in with an empty bag, exactly the same as the bag carried by Alice Diamond. Once Alice's bag was full, they swapped, and Shirley walked out. It was 'child's play, and such a good technique' that, forty years later, Shirley Pitts was still using the same method in Kensington shops such as Louis Vuitton.

By the age of 13, she was a fully fledged shoplifter, earning around £20–30 a job when a London shop girl could expect just £3 basic wages a week. The Forty Elephants taught Shirley about fashion and classic clothing and trained her in different shoplifting techniques. She knew 'how to roll the gear as well as carry it out' and she had her own set of hoisting drawers. Her first were a pair of big old bloomers, which were made of silk, 'You can get more stuff down, because it slips around you.'

To begin with, she walked like a duck, uncomfortable with all the clothing down her drawers. But she soon learned to hide larger, heavier items like leather, suede and mink. The Forty Elephants showed her how to roll clothing from the bottom to the top of a hanger, drop it off a rail and into her bloomers, using 'a red-herring item' to cover the action of the rolling. They took a teenage Shirley to luxury department stores and posh hotels, and dressed her up in a stolen 'college girl uniform' for a shopping spree at Harrods, where she was told not to open her mouth – 'I was so Cockney then.'

When Shirley saw the department store toilets at Harvey Nichols and Debenhams it was like 'visiting a palace'. Like Zoe Progl during her wartime evacuation, she had been introduced to a different lifestyle and it 'made me think that one day I wanted to live like this at home'. Shirley also wanted to look after her family, and the Forty Elephants had shown her a way to do it. 'She was forced into shoplifting,' says Lorraine, 'and she was very good at it. Her criminal inspiration was simple necessity.'

One day when her sister Peggy needed shoes, Shirley took a friend along to steal from Bon Marché in Brixton. They were spotted and fled, but when Shirley got home the police were waiting. She was sentenced to nine months at Stamford House Remand Home in Shepherd's Bush.

The home was for boys and girls. It had a high staff turnover, and its residents were known for absconding. One 13-year-old had covered himself with an overcoat and jumped head first through a window.

On her release, Shirley returned to shoplifting, but again she was caught in Brixton, and 'inadvertently' knocked a store detective through the shop window. She was sent to a reform school for three years for causing grievous bodily harm. One Sunday, as the girls were being led back from church, Shirley and a friend 'just legged it over the wall' and hid in an allotment shed. She managed to stay on the run for nearly two years, and her father built a false panel in a bedroom to hide her at home. When Shirley did go out, she wore disguises, and like Zoe Progl she became expert at 'playing with clothes and make-up to change myself'.

Eventually Shirley was rearrested, and then in September 1953 she was convicted of housebreaking at a farmhouse in East Sussex, along with two young men. Shirley insisted she was innocent, and the police believed others had been involved, but she was sentenced to three years at Aylesbury. Shirley was 19 years old, pregnant and facing three years behind bars.

One morning in January 1954, Shirley was taken to London, where she'd been summoned to give evidence against a south London gang at the Old Bailey. According to Shirley, when they arrived at Euston Station, she asked a prison officer if she could go to the toilet. Once inside, she managed to climb through a tiny window, land on a platform, outrun two prison officers, jump in a cab and escape. But according to reports of the time, she escaped from Marylebone Station, out of a van. The press explained she'd been threatened with the 'chiv' – a razor-slashing attack – if she gave evidence against the members of the 'cosh gang'. The *South London Advertiser* described her as 'a gunman's moll' and part of a housebreaking gang, which Shirley later dismissed as 'just bloody stupid'.

She went to hide out with friends, desperate to a find a way to 'get hold of the sort of money I needed'. Two sisters, one of whom she knew from borstal, took her out to teach her the game of rolling. They set off to Wardour Street, where they started 'just selling me on the street', asking men for £10 'key money' as a deposit for a room, then running off with the money.

Shirley and her friends earned up to £300 a week, less the cost of paying minders to look out for them. But it could be dangerous. One of the sisters had already had her nose broken, and they all drank brandy to get up courage before they went on the street. If any trouble started, a 'minder' would pretend to be a plain-clothes policeman and invite the man to come to the station to press charges.

The women were using methods that were as old as the Black Boy Alley Ladies and the Forty Thieves. In the 1740s, Ann Duck had pretended to be a prostitute to assault and rob potential clients, occasionally making use of male bullies as back-up. Victorian Mary Carr had refined the process by waylaying gentlemen and blackmailing them with accusations of indecent behaviour. Now Shirley Pitts was avoiding physical contact altogether, by demanding money from the men upfront.

Shirley used her profits from rolling to finance shoplifting trips in the West End, hiring a driver and car for the day. She also travelled with other hoisters to Manchester, Liverpool and Blackpool, accompanied by her brother, Eddie. By day, they shoplifted – furs, jewellery and shoes – and by night, they went rolling.

'We just went mad wherever we went,' remembered Shirley. 'Scotland, Devon, Manchester – we weren't prejudiced, we would shoplift anywhere.' Their job was 'getting money and spending it, getting clothes and wearing them, getting dressed up to go out and having a good time … We were on the road and out to enjoy ourselves.' Like Alice Diamond and Maggie Hughes, Shirley wanted the latest clothes and jewellery, and she'd found a way to get them.

In the summer of 1954, Shirley's first child, Joanne, was born prematurely at St Thomas's Hospital, and kept in an incubator for a month. Shirley was afraid the police would find her, so she left the hospital and crept in and out in disguises to visit her baby. Then, after eight months on the run, the police finally caught Shirley at her mother's house, where she was hiding behind a sofa. One of the officers said he would let her go, 'if you let me get behind the settee with you and have a quickie'. When Shirley told him to 'piss off', he called his colleague, and she knew her next stop was Holloway Prison.

The *Daily Herald* described detectives standing on doorways and landings as the 'weeping blonde girl' was led out of a tenement house in Southwark and returned to borstal. Shirley's mother pleaded for leniency – her daughter had escaped because she didn't want her baby born in prison. Did this make her 'bad at heart?' asked *The People*. 'Would not love for her child do more to reform than prison?' During her months on the run, Shirley had knitted baby clothes, bought a pram, cot, baby bath and layette 'of which any mother would have been proud'. Her mother argued that if Shirley were freed 'on condition that she looked after the baby', she would be reformed. But instead she was sent to back to Aylesbury.

Shirley was released in 1956, and immediately went back to rolling. She worked with her sister, Peggy, around Park Lane and Bond Street, and 'we turned it into an art form the way we used to run off with their money'. The sisters got into a car, told the client the price, and then left their handbags while they went into a private block of flats to check a room was free. While the man waited for the signal, Shirley and Peggy ran off, leaving the empty handbags, which they'd shoplifted earlier. The sisters also started hoisting again, selling some of the clothes to Violet Kray, who dressed 'high-class smart and liked classic makes'. Violet's sons, Ronnie and Reggie, were just a year older than Shirley, born in Haggerston in east London, and they were beginning to establish a reputation as violent gangsters. Their gang, 'The Firm', dominated organised crime reports into the 1960s, including murder, armed robbery, fraud, arson, protection rackets and assaults.

Shirley and her sister, meanwhile, became the leaders of the 'Happy Hoisters', famed for 'hoodwinking detectives who tried to trail them on their shoplifting trips throughout the south of England'. The *Mirror* reported thefts in Bournemouth, Folkestone, Woking, Maldon and St Ives, with the police attempting to track the women using sports cars, a taxi, a station wagon, a small bus and on one occasion a fruit van.

The 'Happy Hoisters' reportedly stole more than £5,000 in two years, but while shopkeepers identified both Shirley and Peggy, not once were they caught in the act. Just like their teachers, the Forty Elephants, they were able to move with lightning speed and had the miraculous ability to avoid getting caught on the job.

The two sisters also appeared to be enjoying themselves. When they were stopped by police, they got out of their car and held out their hands to show they were empty 'and they laughed'. Another time, they led detectives up a blind alley and again 'they laughed'. Then Peggy was arrested and admitted stealing a Persian lamb coat from a Knightsbridge store, 126 gramophone records and a wireless set, and was jailed for twenty-one months. But 24-year-old Shirley Pitts, the gang's ringleader, according to the Flying Squad, had 'not been found'. She would successfully escape conviction for the rest of her career and, when it came to shoplifting, she was only just getting started.

17

THE CRIMINAL MASQUERADE

Britain's retail landscape had changed quite a bit since a young Shirley Pitts had first been taken hoisting by Alice Diamond, and by the late 1950s there was a new form of shopping – the self-service store. No longer did a customer choose an item from a window display as they'd done in Victorian times or take it to separate counters as they had in the 1940s; now they were being invited to take what they wanted themselves.

Self-service stores were slow to catch on and existed mostly in the grocery sector, but right from the start there were concerns about theft. Once again, the weaker sex was unable to resist an impulse to steal, this time for psychological reasons. Dr Gibbens, a lecturer at Maudsley Hospital, found a quarter of female shoplifters were 'ill in various ways', both mentally and physically. 'They are in fact neurotic women,' he explained. 'They feel that their husband and children are taking them for granted.'

One woman went on an orgy of shoplifting so that she could get caught and 'draw a little attention to herself', and the actions of female shoplifters apparently resembled a 'miniature attempted suicide'.

The idea that women who committed crime were ill wasn't new, it had been around ever since the kleptomania defence of Victorian times, but now it was really taking hold. Soon female criminals as a whole were pathologised, their actions defined as 'mad' rather than 'bad'. Prisoners at Holloway were 'all, in one way or another ... mentally disturbed and deviant from the norm', explained Governor Joanna Kelley.

But Shirley Pitts didn't fit the medical profile: she wasn't shoplifting to get caught. Instead, she was working hard not to. And while she might have started stealing as a way to get her mother's attention, it was not a cry for help from a neurotic woman. It had become a way to earn a good living.

By the early 1960s, Britain's retail sector had finally recovered from the effects of war and the nation embarked on a 'consumer revolution'. Self-service supermarkets were growing, as were new boutiques and department stores. In some shops, women could help themselves to clothing and footwear, try them on in fitting rooms and then take them to a counter for wrapping and payment. Furs and suits were lined up on racks, security devices were 'quite pathetic', according to Shirley Pitts, CCTV was restricted to car parks and, as usual, shop assistants didn't expect respectable-looking customers to steal. A shoplifter could just throw things over her arm, or pick up an entire tray of rings, and walk out of the shop.

Shirley Pitts worked with her sister Peggy and other young women from Hoxton, wearing their trusty hoisters' bloomers, long johns with elastic sewn around the bottom of the legs. 'You could pack things down to your knees,' explained Shirley, and when it came to a fur coat, 'you tuck it right under your fanny and push and push until it goes upside down and hardly notices under a smart flared coat'. Shirley went hoisting at the Yves Saint Laurent shop in Knightsbridge 'because his designs were the best', and then sold the clothes to 'lords, ladies and even film stars'. Shot-silk eveningwear was particularly in demand, as was Christian Dior velvet.

When Shirley's brother Adgie bought a betting shop on Jermyn Street, not far from the Ritz, she used it as a base in which to dress up. 'I'd make myself look like a different girl,' she explained, 'so I could go back and rob the same shops over and over again.' Adgie's betting shop became 'the biggest crooks den in the West End', reminiscent of Moll Cutpurse's Fleet Street brokerage, and Zoe Progl's The Shop. Burglars and hoisters came to sell their goods and the betting shop began to resemble a wholesalers, with minks, jewellery, carpets and 'whatever lorry load had gone that week – all the corners in the place were piled up with gear'. One hostess at the Embassy Club recalled giving her 'sugar daddy', a top QC who later became a judge, hoisted clothes, including cashmere jackets and silk ties that had come from Jermyn Street.

Shirley Pitts dressed so stylishly that people wanted what she wore, and she became a walking advertisement for quality clothing. She also redesigned stolen clothes, employing a seamstress to move a pocket or alter a detail on outfits from Yves Saint Laurent or Dior. Shirley assumed the role of the middle-class shopper in order to shoplift, just as Emily Lawrence and Alice Diamond had done, then she used the profits to *become* the middle-class shopper, whether browsing for furs at Harvey Nichols or lunching in Knightsbridge.

She also developed new methods in response to increased security – wrapping a box in quality paper from Selfridges, so it looked like an expensive present, then lining it with foil. She could get three mink coats inside the box, and the foil prevented the alarm going off when she left the shop. In some cases, she could just pull the alarms off clothes, or put her bag high up on her shoulder and walk out, undetected by door alarms that were only waist high.

But then, in 1967, Shirley Pitts stopped hoisting. Her beloved brother Adgie died in a car accident and she 'went off my head' with grief. 'Money just flew out of my hands,' she explained. 'I even started buying things from the shops, that's how bad I was.' For a year she was inconsolable, but eventually she went out hoisting again and 'managed to get a little gang together who were pretty good'.

Shirley began to work internationally, raiding shops in Amsterdam, Paris and Geneva. She was earning a fortune, 'slaughtering the same shops', and no longer cared if she got caught. 'I just couldn't stop and

I would take anything I could get my hands on.' Her shoplifting began to sound obsessive; she bathed 'compulsively' afterwards, and never washed her 'big old girdle bloomers' in case it brought her bad luck.

In the mid-1970s, Shirley grew fed up with hoisting. She'd walked around Selfridges once too often. There were more obstacles to shoplifting now, and it was getting harder for her drivers to find a parking space. Some days, she 'just wanted to be an ordinary wife and mother', but like burglar Zoe Progl, she knew 'I probably wouldn't have enjoyed the quiet life being at home every day.'

Yet Shirley Pitts did devote herself to being mother to her seven children. 'She always provided for her kids,' says Lorraine Gamman. 'She didn't want them to follow her, she wanted them to be designers, architects, film stars, she wanted more for them. Being a mother was sacred to Shirley.'

She also financially supported her long-term partner, Chrissie Hawkins. They'd met in the early 1960s and were together for over twenty years, but Shirley described him as jealous and violent, once smashing a bone through her nose and breaking her teeth, and only stopping after a warning from the Krays. Chrissie's friends have objected to the way he was portrayed in *Gone Shopping*, but like many underworld queens, Shirley wasn't a stranger to domestic violence: another partner had broken her jaw shortly after she'd given birth.

By the time Shirley Pitts was 40, she'd been hoisting for nearly thirty years. She'd been 'in all the shops you could go into, visited different countries, taken everything you could think of – the hoisting job lacked satisfaction'. So, she set up an escort agency, working with her brother Eddie and hiring both female and male escorts. She distributed business cards in the West End, set up a twenty-four-hour phone service, and while her Berkeley Square agency was 'not completely legal', it ran smoothly to begin with.

Then she received warnings from 'cardboard gangsters', and the police threatened to arrest her for prostitution and give the story to the *News of the World.* Shirley didn't want to be represented 'as a hooker when actually I was primarily a thief' and, worried about the impact on her children, she closed the business down. She became involved in a 'beef swindle', shipping meat from Ireland to Iran, which turned out to be a cover for an international arms fraud. She also took part in an identification parade, after a woman 'matching her description' collected £1 million from a bank in Geneva – but Shirley Pitts wasn't picked out.

She was still operating as a hoister in the late 1980s, wearing disguises and her shoplifting bloomers, and had further refined her techniques. Instead of a box, she used a quality leather bag or a smart carrier bag 'from somewhere posh', layered inside with thick foil. But now she had modern alarms to contend with, not just at waist level but placed all over shop doors and on ceilings.

Alarms on clothing came in different forms – magnet, ink, chains, stick-on, and buzzer alarms that went off in car parks. Shirley was particularly annoyed by security buzzers with ink, 'They are disgusting – who invented them, I don't know! Some people do get covered in ink and ruin the clothes even after they have got them out of the shops.' This waste of stolen clothes was 'a real crime', but she found a solution when a friend who worked in a store gave her 'a tool' which saved her from wasting a fortune.

One of Shirley's favourite tricks was to snap buzzers off clothes, creep up behind the most respectable-looking customer and drop the tags in their carrier bags. As the person tried to leave, the alarms went off and Shirley took advantage of the general commotion to load up with goods. The ideal target was posh, because they always made the most fuss when stopped by security.

Shirley wasn't the only woman running a shoplifting gang in the 1980s, and Kim Farry, who grew up in Kingston upon Thames, similarly saw it as her job. She'd started stealing sweets as a child and by the time she was a teenager, she was hoisting clothes and returning them for cash refunds. Shoplifting became 'the entire focus of my existence', she explained, and at 9 a.m. every day, she went off to work, seven days a week. Her customers ordered goods, whether designer clothes, prams or furniture, and she delivered them within twenty-four hours, 'a bit like Amazon Prime'.

Kim then started returning stolen goods for vouchers, receiving orders from lawyers, teachers, fitness instructors and well-off mothers. She was brazen, walking into Hennes and leaving with bin liners stuffed full of clothes, carrying nail clippers and plyers to remove alarms, and lining empty store logo bags with tin foil.

Kim treated shoplifting 'like any other person would treat their own company'. Her employees received on-the-job training and worked for a trial period. They had to be loyal and follow a dress code, and in return she paid their fines if they were caught. Kim's career lasted forty-six years, during which she was jailed five times. 'Shopping ruled my life,' she later wrote, 'and gave me the feeling of security, power, happiness and love. I felt invincible and in control of all the shops, hundreds of them. I was my own boss. The Boss.'

Shirley Pitts, meanwhile, often had fun shoplifting, and Lorraine describes her story as 'daring, exciting and psychologically compelling'. But her criminal career 'hardly offered a story of hope, or how to live'. Shirley enjoyed the adrenaline rush of thieving, but also complained it could be hard work, repetitive and boring. She once told Lorraine that she could have been 'so much more than a professional thief, but by the time she realised this it was too late'.

When Shirley died in 1992, she was nearly broke, just like Alice Diamond, aside from some jewellery and furs, and a small house in Chigwell co-owned with a son. One day, not long before she died, Lorraine asked Shirley if crime really *didn't* pay, considering the prison sentences, constant aggravation and messed-up relationships. Shirley Pitts became exasperated. 'Of course crime pays,' she retorted. 'It's getting caught that's the fucking problem!'

On 25 March 1992, Shirley Pitts was buried at Lambeth Cemetery, with twenty-one black Daimlers following the hearse along the 20-mile route from her home in Essex. She was laid to rest in a stolen £5,000 Zandra Rhodes dress, while wreaths from her friends in Hoxton included a huge display of white and yellow carnations spelling 'Gone Shopping', as well as a floral Harrods carrier bag. Her son Harry praised her courage, 'She was more of a man than most men', and the Krays sent their condolences with the message 'one of the best'. It was a royal funeral, explained Duncan Campbell in *The Guardian*, a tribute to a woman whose life had been 'as much Dickens as Dickins and Jones'. He described her as 'something of a pioneer', and 'one of the few women to escape from a British jail, slipping out of Holloway when pregnant with one of her seven children'. Perhaps he had mixed her up with Zoe Progl, for Shirley hadn't ever escaped from Holloway. But both women were south Londoners whose first thefts were motivated by hunger, who came of age in the emerging consumer culture of post-war Britain and made a career for themselves in the '60s. Shirley and Zoe were creative and entrepreneurial, they were experts at the criminal masquerade and they used the mask of femininity – created with clothing, make-up and hairstyles – as a cover for crime.

Shirley did not offer any apology for her career, and some disapproved of *Gone Shopping* because she didn't show enough remorse. 'She expressed regret only when she felt she had cheated a decent person who it hurt,' explains Lorraine. 'She rarely expressed any concern for the stores or institutions she stole from.' Some reviews of the book were spiteful, and Lorraine was angered by those who compared Shirley's story to that of Daniel Defoe's Moll Flanders, as if her life was fiction rather than fact.

The *Evening Standard* made sneering remarks about the book's launch, describing it as one of those 'all-too-rare literary parties where more people were dropping aitches than names'. It quoted Lorraine as 'shrieking, "Oi, 'ave you bought those books?"' to an 'astonished guest', while another guest set off the shop's alarm as she left. Lorraine laughs when I tell her this, explaining that the book launch was held at Murder One, a crime bookshop, and the staff had turned on the alarm as a joke.

Reviewers on Amazon had mixed reactions to *Gone Shopping*. 'Takes you back to the extreme poverty of those times of which I lived through,' wrote one. 'Shirley was a very kind lady. She stayed with us when she was on the run from police. I never knew who she was, she spent days cutting out pictures from an old Rupert the Bear book and making a flour and water paste to stick them on the wall of our grotty flat to make our life a less bit grim! Often think of her with love.' Another described Shirley as 'one of this world's great mothers', while a third asked why her story had never had the Hollywood treatment, was 'seeing women as anything other than clichéd powerless victims or predatory femme fatales too much of a stretch'? Shirley Pitts was 'a refreshingly feminist anti-hero'.

Other reviews were more critical. 'What a load of rubbish, most of it lies as we knew the family. I suppose they had to earn money somehow,' wrote one. Another was offended by the 'sordid goings-on' and argued that Shirley 'chose a criminal lifestyle not out of necessity but choice', and her apologists should ask themselves 'how they would feel if they'd been one of her victims'.

But contemporaries still revered her. She was 'the best hoister of my generation', writes Marilyn Wisbey, daughter of train robber Tommy Wisbey. 'She got me my dress for my twenty-first' – an oyster-pink ball gown. Shirley's exploits have gone down in shoplifting history, such as the day she stole a £15,000 fur coat from a dummy in the window of Harrods and replaced it with a mackintosh, stolen from somewhere else.

Like Zoe Progl, Shirley Pitt's life and career have not made it onto the screen, unlike her contemporaries, the Krays, who knew how to create a myth and build a brand. In 1969, they were convicted for the murders of George Cornell and Jack 'The Hat' McVitie, and successfully promoted their image as gangland stars for the next twenty years, making money from newspaper and magazine articles, biographies, films and merchandise. Over fifty books have been written about Ronnie and Reggie Kray so far, with their first biography published just three years after they were jailed for life. *Gone Shopping* has been optioned for a film several times, but the story of Shirley Pitts has yet to be made. She has inspired novels, however, including Jill Dawson's *Lucky Bunny* and David Wharton's *Finer Things*, and she's also inspired two £14 cocktails at the new Forty Elephants Bar at the Great Scotland Yard Hotel. 'On the Run' is an 'easy-drinking' tequila, while 'The Forger' is 'sweet, creamy, refined' and comes with an edible mini £50 note floating on the top.

Shirley Pitts was primarily a shoplifter, not a forger, but unlike other queens of the underworld, her story has stayed alive and she collaborated in telling it her own way. Shirley Pitts was the very last Queen of the Forty Elephants, but even in the 1960s, when she was at the height of her powers, the criminal landscape was changing. The new face of the female criminal would not be a glamorous shoplifter; instead she was violent and armed.

18

LIBERATION OF THE FEMALE CRIMINAL

I'm climbing up a long, steep hill of terraced houses in Muswell Hill, one of north London's most expensive suburbs. It's peaceful here, perched so high above the capital. Below me, the London skyline is draped in hazy blue. I pass Edwardian houses of clean, orange brick, with well-tended rose bushes in front gardens. The only sound is the rumble and slam as a man opens the door of his organic food delivery van.

I stop at a house on Woodland Rise, with a ground-floor bay window and a smaller window directly above the front door. Its walls are white and look newly painted, but all the shutters are closed, and when I ring the bell no one answers.

On 6 June 1965, three police officers arrived at this house looking for an escaped convict, and when they knocked, two bullets ripped through the door. Then Eileen Blackmore came to a first-floor window, with a .22 Winchester rifle in one hand and twelve rounds of ammunition in the other.

Eileen was 20 years old and on the run. In February that year she'd been convicted for possessing an offensive weapon, and not long afterwards, she'd escaped from Holloway Prison hospital. When an officer tried to reach her with a ladder, she put the rifle to her shoulder and shouted, 'F*** off now or you are dead!' Detective Lewis told her to throw the gun down before she hurt someone, at which she turned and pointed it at him, 'F*** off or it will be you.'

Eileen said she'd rather kill herself than be taken by the police, and she would 'take quite a few of you coppers with me. I know how to use this thing.' Then she pushed the rifle through the window, took steady aim and fired.

PC Thomas White, who was standing on the opposite side of the road, took cover behind a tree. 'But it was a rather inadequate tree,' explained the press, and he was hit in the back. The constable was taken to hospital, where his condition was said to be satisfactory, and he was later discharged.

Inspector Edward Welch also attempted to reach Eileen. He'd gained access to an adjoining flat and was leaning out of a window, but he was nearly shot as well. So Steve Davis, a 63-year-old press photographer from the *London Evening News*, decided he would try his luck. 'How about a picture?' he called up to Eileen. 'You are very good looking, and *Evening News* readers would like to see a close-up picture of you with the rifle.'

She refused – if she let him into her flat then the police would follow. So Steve said he'd join Inspector Welch, and take a photo by leaning out of the window next door. But when he asked Eileen to move forward for 'a close-up', he suddenly grabbed at the rifle and during the ensuing struggle the gun went off again.

The press photographer managed to disarm Eileen, by which time he'd presumably taken several photos. Steve Davis was hailed as a hero, and later awarded the George Medal for bravery. The ninety-minute 'siege of Muswell Hill' was over, and Eileen Blackmore was back in police hands.

The image of an armed 20-year-old woman single-handedly keeping police at bay in a wealthy London suburb would be dramatic enough today, but back in 1965 it was truly shocking. While there had been fears about increasing female violence in the 1920s and 1950s, women were still considered conservative and natural law-abiders. They lacked ambition when it came to crime and confined their activities to shop-lifting or acting as decoys and backstage accomplices.

Eileen Blackmore, with her 'Beatles-style hair do' and mini dress, was immediately portrayed as dangerously promiscuous. The fact that her first arrest had been at the age of 14 for stealing a jumper, and that at 16 she'd married an older man with a criminal record, appeared to be of little interest. Instead she had 'captivated' her 19-year-old boyfriend, Raymond Mindel, with whom she lived on Woodland Rise, and according to his defence, she was known for 'dominating' men. Eileen was his 'secret love', explained the *Mirror*, 'dark, petite and pretty ... and a woman with a past'. Raymond was fined £50, while Eileen was sentenced to five years in prison.

'Blackmore is a woman who is obviously vain,' declared the judge – a description that delighted the *Daily Mirror*. It provided a large photo of Eileen, sitting on a window ledge and smoking a cigarette, the rifle resting on one thigh, with the headline 'Vanity of the Gun-Siege Girl'. Eileen's 'vanity' was so extreme that the newspaper managed to use the word eight times in a half-page news report. It was a useful way to dismiss her. She was not defiant and armed, she was 'the tiny girl who liked to play the role of underworld queen'. Like burglar Zoe Progl, who'd bought Polyphoto pictures of herself with stolen coins, Eileen's alleged vanity had led to her downfall.

She was taken back to Holloway but it wasn't long before she was on the run again. In June 1966, she escaped from Styal Prison with two other women, 'a murderess and a trickster'. Press reports were confusing. The women appeared to have broken through a 10ft-high wire fence while being taken from their cellblock to the prison library. Seven hours later, Eileen was discovered under a hedge in an allotment. Presumably the press had been tipped off, for the *Mirror* published a photo showing Eileen Blackmore smiling as she was ushered into a police car, after a 'terrific struggle', during which she'd apparently bitten an officer's hand.

Eileen disappeared from news reports after this, but her armed siege marked a shift in the image of the female criminal, and by the mid-1970s, the 'gun girl' would become all too familiar. The gentle sex had turned vicious, explained the *Liverpool Echo*. They were resorting to violent acts to vent boredom and frustration. Women had more financial freedom and 'an urge to trample over long credited social conventions and justice'.

Headlines warned of girl gangs organising housebreaking and luring men out of pubs and schoolgirls mugging grannies on the streets. Offences involving violence had risen by 16 per cent among women, according to the authors of *Crime in Britain Today*, and many more were being cautioned and released. Various racist and homophobic theories were offered for the increase. One psychiatrist blamed 'West Indian girls', who were 'sexually mature at an earlier age and bigger physically than their white school friends'. Another medical expert attributed the rise to 'lesbian girls', who often showed 'dramatic violent tendencies', and 'more of them' were being sent to remand homes than ever before.

This apparent rise in criminal aggression didn't come in a vacuum, however. It coincided with the burgeoning Women's Liberation Movement (WLM).

The UK's first WLM conference was held in 1970, demanding equal pay, educational and job opportunities, free contraception and abortion on demand, and free twenty-four-hour nurseries. That same year, the Equal Pay Act was passed, followed by the Sex Discrimination Act, the Employment Protection Act and the Domestic Violence Act. There were strikes, marches to Take Back the Night, the launch of feminist magazines such as *Spare Rib*, and the formation of crisis centres and women's groups. The United Nations declared 1975 International Women's Year, to raise global awareness of women's rights, and International Women's Day became an annual event.

But as far as many journalists, criminologists and medical experts were concerned, there was a direct link between social, legal and political improvement for women and their willingness to commit crime. Girls from the age of 14 were 'seeing themselves as partners in crime with men', explained the *Newcastle Chronicle*. It was 'the in thing to be violent' and to 'act as tough and drink as much as the fellows'. A senior lecturer at the Institute of Psychiatry offered a note of reassurance – physically, women were not capable of being as violent as men, but then he added a disclaimer, 'unless there's a revolution and women take over'.

This, then, was the fear. A revolution wouldn't bring social justice, it would unleash a terrifying new generation of women who wanted to oppress men. Ever since Moll Cutpurse in the seventeenth century, women had been stepping out of their assigned place and encroaching on the world of men. Now, according to American criminologist Freda Adler, we were witnessing the 'liberation of the female criminal' and the result could be 'fateful for all of us'.

In 1975 she published *Sisters in Crime: The Rise of the New Female Criminal*, in which she debunked some long-held myths. Women did not have a totally separate psychology from men; there was no such thing as a masculine or feminine crime; and the scientific community and news media were dominated by men. But Freda also insisted that women were 'committing more crimes than ever before', just as Otto Pollack had argued in 1950, and now they even appeared on the FBI's Ten Most Wanted list.

Women had gained more freedom, and therefore had far more opportunity to commit crime. Technology also played a part, and the gun in particular had 'equalised the capacity for male crimes, including violence'. Young girls were roaming city streets like boys and taking part in gangs on equal terms. Prostitutes, who used to be 'docile body-peddlers', were mugging clients on the sidewalk. In London, dozens of 'granny-bashing' young girls, armed with switchblades, razors, clubs and fists, were attacking elderly women late at night. But according to Freda Adler, no one was acknowledging this rise in female crime, let alone its connection to the Women's Liberation Movement.

The British press, however, was full of it, and 1975 was dubbed 'the year of violent women'. The weaker sex had 'learned that guns and bombs could make them more than equal', explained journalist Paula James. She cited IRA members such as Marion Coyle, awaiting trial for kidnapping, and Rose Dugdale, convicted for robbery and hijacking, as well as Sara Jane Moore, who'd attempted to assassinate American President Gerald Ford. Dangerous women, armed with guns and bombs, appeared to be everywhere.

But one sociologist was sceptical of statistics that showed a dramatic upsurge in female crime. In 1977, Carol Smart published her ground-breaking book, *Women, Crime and Criminology*, providing a feminist critique of the figures and theories so far. She pointed out numerous problems with official statistics, questioned the idea that emancipation led to crime, and refuted the 'chivalry' myth – that women and girls were treated more leniently, when instead they were actively discriminated against.

Carol Smart wasn't the first to challenge the stereotypes that had underpinned theories of female criminality for over 100 years, but her book marked a new direction in criminology, and she systematically took the official statistics apart. While women made up a tiny minority of convicted criminals, often first offenders charged with trivial thefts, they appeared to dominate in two areas – prostitution and shoplifting. Yet Home Office statistics excluded male prostitutes from the category 'offence by prostitute', instead they appeared under 'homosexuality offences', so only women appeared to be prostitutes. And while women apparently excelled at stealing from shops, the number of men and women convicted for shoplifting remained very similar, as it had done in Victorian times. In 1974, there were 28,636 men convicted for shoplifting, and 28,019 women.

Home Office statistics also suggested a massive surge in violence by women, yet over 90 per cent of violent crimes were still committed by men. Officially, there had been a 300 per cent increase in women convicted for murder between 1969 and 1974 in England and Wales, but in real terms, this was just an increase of three women.

It was true that more women were being convicted of crimes such as burglary, fraud and handling stolen goods. Yet Carol Smart questioned whether women were committing more offences, or if they were being apprehended, charged and convicted more frequently. Police and social workers were more ready to define deviant behaviour by women and girls as violent, because women's position in society was changing.

Female delinquents were punished for being 'promiscuous' and 'ungovernable' in a way that did not apply to boys. Young women like Zoe Progl, Shirley Pitts and Eileen Blackmore were more likely to be institutionalised and sent to a remand home or borstal, even for a first offence.

The rate of male crime, meanwhile, was also rising. So where was the outcry about violent men? Offences by women and girls were being turned into a social problem. Female criminals were presented as 'sick', their behaviour irrational and illogical. Yet, as numerous queens of the underworld had already proved, they knew exactly what they were doing, and for one gang leader of the 1970s, crime was the purest form of rebellion and the most obvious way to reject the feminine role.

19

CHRIS TCHAIKOVSKY
QUEEN OF CHARISMA

On 22 October 1973, a young woman called Chris Tchaikovsky stood in the dock at the Old Bailey, waiting to hear her fate. The dock was particularly crowded that day. Alongside Chris were ten members of the Happy Firm, an international fraud gang that she had led for the past four years. The case was so complex that a specialist company fraud judge had been appointed. The trial lasted for five days and the prosecution called a staggering 115 witnesses.

Chris Tchaikovsky found the proceedings boring, so she focused on completing the *Times* crossword puzzle to stop herself from falling asleep. She knew she was facing up to five years in prison, but she was philosophical. She'd enjoyed the dangers and rewards of crime, travelled as much as she'd wanted and experienced more excitement than most. 'My criminality was the result of a rational choice,' she later explained. 'Nobody had coerced or cajoled me into it.' There were no 'psychological reasons' behind her career. It was neither 'environmentally determined or born of mental disorder'. Instead, as she explained in her autobiographical essay, 'Looking for Trouble', Chris Tchaikovsky became a criminal as a way to establish her own identity. She didn't want to be part of the system, and by committing fraud she was 'taking it on'.

Chris was born Christine Patricia Francis Ryder on 28 May 1944 in Newquay, Cornwall. She was one of six sisters, raised in a family described as 'affluent, loving, middle class'. But Chris was a rebel, like Moll Cutpurse had been, and refused 'to do what was required'. She was expelled from Falmouth High after hanging a pair of long johns on a flagpole, and then expelled from two further schools, before being sent to a child guidance clinic.

At the age of 15, Chris left for London with £4 in her pocket, in search of the bohemian lifestyle she'd read about in books. Like Jack Kerouac and other 'beatniks', she was on the road and out for adventure. Beat culture, originating in the States in the late 1940s, appealed to Chris. She liked its non-conformity, its rejection of materialism and rebellion against conservative middle-class values.

Once in London, she headed for the Café French in Soho, which 'smacked of Hemingway and Steinbeck' and where she felt at home among the thick Gauloises smoke and whispered conversations. She fell in with a limbo dancer who offered her a place to live, but then one of his friends raped her.

Chris didn't write about the impact of this, but after a week in London she returned home and got a job as a civil servant on a hospital board. However, she soon felt that her life was ebbing away and she was in danger of 'turning into a filing cabinet'. Then one day, she met three ex-borstal girls at Dirty Dot's, a café in Exeter. Pam, a 'man-loathing lesbian', had just had sex with a lorry driver for £2, and the girls were spending it on fried egg sandwiches.

Chris was fascinated, 'They did not fit into any group that I had ventured upon. They were outlaws. Rough, tough, loud, funny and, most importantly, completely different to the feminine women I had known.' The ex-borstal girls were not mindless office workers who talked of nothing but Twink perms and boyfriends. They didn't cake themselves in Panstick make-up and read romance weeklies like *Romeo* and *Valentine*. Instead, they were villains – wild, free, and scared of no one; even the men in Dot's café treated them with respect. Chris's years of provincial boredom had come to an end.

Together, they raided a newsagent's owned by a friend of Chris's mother, armed with duffle bags, a scarf, screwdriver and gloves. Later that night, high on her first break-in, Chris wrote a poem, 'I've broken your laws and entered my freedom. / I'm in front. I'm out there and I'm all on my own.'

Chris was arrested and charged with breaking and entering but, unlike the ex-borstal girls, her respectable background saved her, and her father had already hired 'the best brief he could find'. Chris paints an affectionate portrait of her father, who often took 'vicarious pleasure' in her misdeeds, but she refused bail and pleaded guilty. 'All I wanted to do was to go to Borstal or Holloway … and serve my time along with my sister villains.' But unlike her working-class predecessors Queenie Day, Zoe Progl and Shirley Pitts, Chris wasn't sent to borstal. A psychiatrist explained her IQ was too high – she'd be corrupted.

She became involved in active politics, joining the Youth Campaign for Nuclear Disarmament and taking part in an Aldermaston march. But once again, she didn't fit in – the marchers were too pretentious.

So she headed to St Ives to work in a harbour café, where she provided her beatnik friends with stolen crab, clotted cream, beef and pears. Residents of the Cornish town didn't seem too keen on the 'invasion' of beatniks in the early 1960s and the hordes of 'unwashed girls in tight black pants'. The council encouraged a 'Beat the Beatnik' week, with 'Beatniks not served' signs in pubs, coffee bars and ice cream parlours, and 'no jobs for Beatniks' hung at staff entrances to hotels and stores. The response from the beatniks was to establish a 'secret' headquarters in nearby woods, which they kept guarded day and night.

Chris didn't stay long in St Ives. She had fallen in love with a woman, Jan, 'a well-off postgraduate student', and moved with her to Bristol. But Chris was still intent on crime, buying and selling hash at the docks and teaching herself to make false half-crowns with solder, flux, plaster of Paris and matches, which she used to steal the contents of cigarette machines.

Then she bought stolen chequebooks from a ship's steward and headed to London, buying tape recorders, shoes and gold chains that she sold to a fence at half-price. Crime became her 'secret life', quite separate from her relationship with Jan, and after working non-stop for just a week, Chris Tchaikovsky had enough money to buy a car.

However, less than a year later, she was arrested. Friends had raided a deli – they were hungry and 'Capitalism sucked' – and when the police arrived at their flat, Chris was caught in the process of running out. A social worker informed her father that he was to blame, because 'girls must not be brought up like boys'. Finally, Chris got what she wanted: she was sent to Holloway Prison for six months for psychiatric treatment.

Chris was shocked by the prison environment. The Victorian jail was a Fagin's kitchen, according to one government official, 'a devilish hole, derelict, rundown, dirty'. But she was even more shocked by her fellow prisoners, women incarcerated for petty crimes, often with mental health problems and desperate after losing their children. Chris felt she deserved to be in Holloway – she had broken the law – but she was angry and appalled by the stories of those around her, women whose only 'crimes' were 'for the most part, poverty and ignorance'. Her time in jail also taught her new methods of crime, and on release she began forging post office books.

Chris returned to Devon, where she met another woman, 'middle-class again, a teacher and definitely a "good girl"'. The couple took a cottage on Dartmoor, but Chris couldn't resist the lure of crime and when she was invited to meet Mike, the King of the Mods, to 'do a little job', she was 'there faster than you could whistle Wordsworth'.

Together, they raided a garage in Plymouth. Chris drove the car and acted as decoy, while Mike ran into the kiosk to get the till. But when Mike pulled a gun, the terrified attendant dashed into the road and was nearly run over by another gang member just pulling into the garage. Chris was arrested and sentenced to six months for attempted robbery.

This time, she spent the first six weeks locked up on an empty wing in Holloway for twenty-three hours a day, haunted by the idea that the garage attendant could have died, although she knew by now it had been a toy gun. Chris swore she wouldn't work with other villains again. She'd only gone on the job to be 'one of the boys' and to keep up her reputation.

On her release, she settled in Notting Hill with her partner, the 'good girl', and found office work on a salary of £16 a week. But when a man called Alan offered her £200 to store a case of Georgian silver, she quickly agreed. Soon she was kiting again and selling the goods to Alan, who also bought stolen passenger suitcases from coaches at Heathrow and bribed the Flying Squad with regular briefcases of cash.

Chris continued to travel up and down England using stolen cheques, but it wasn't as easy as it had been. Fraud was on the increase. Shopkeepers were beginning to keep a list of stolen chequebooks and were asking for ID, while anyone withdrawing large amounts created suspicion. So Chris and Alan moved into travellers' cheque fraud instead. They bought the cheques 'from the boys at Heathrow', then travelled abroad, buying expensive perfume and Cartier lighters and selling the goods to French or Belgian fences.

During a trip to Brussels, Chris realised she could cash travellers' cheques directly at Bureau de Changes, and in two days she had £12,000 – the equivalent of around £170,000 today. She had become the modern version of the 1940s Queen of the Contraband Coast, earning a fortune through travellers' cheque fraud.

Soon Chris was running two flats in London, driving a finely tuned sportscar and had a reserved table at Gateways in Chelsea, the 'best gay club in town'. But while she had 'the status and kudos of being a villain', most of the profits were still going to Alan.

She wanted to be taken seriously by the male criminal fraternity, who could be 'even more paternalistic than their straight counterparts'. She had the money and was game enough, but 'I was still a woman and women were not really trusted'. Leading a secret life was also taking its toll. 'My teacher friend and I had a great relationship,' she explained, but 'the divide between my criminal allies and my straight friends widened'.

Finally, Chris established her own gang, hiring two men, Adrian and Gary, and buying travellers' cheques from 'a West Kent villain'. When Alan agreed to sell her travellers' cheques as well, she was jubilant. 'I had retired as a worker and I had, at last, made my way from being just another face to running my own little firm.'

Soon they were flying out of England three times a week, cashing travellers' cheques and returning the same day 'with nary a victim in sight other than the ledgers in the banks'. Chris bought a printing machine, which she used to make false driving licences – 'merely a green slip stuck into a red booklet'. Like Zoe Progl, she was learning new skills and refining her methods, and, like Noreen Harbord, she was operating on an international level and keeping a close watch on financial developments.

When Chris read an article in *The Times* about the Eurocheque system, she came up with a new plan. In 1970, for the first time since the outbreak of the Second World War, British travellers could cash cheques overseas by using their banker's card. 'Sign now, but you must still pay – later!' ran a headline in *The People*. Cheques under £30 could be cashed at any bank and no other ID was needed. A chequebook contained thirty cheques, so the potential profit with each book was £900. Chris and her gang immediately applied for chequebooks and cards, then set off to Paris where the banks had no list of stolen chequebooks and asked for no ID, other than the banker's card. They cashed up to four cheques at each bank and returned to England with up to £10,000 in cash.

But ID was still a concern, so Chris applied for a British Visitor's Passport, a single-page cardboard document introduced in the 1960s and intended for holidays and short trips. It was valid in most west European countries and was easily obtained from a post office.

Applicants had to produce a medical card, which consisted of black text on ordinary white card, without any watermarks or embossing. So Chris paid a contact to make fifty blank medical cards, and her workers were then able to acquire up to five separate passports on a single day. The firm began to grow. Chris hired four women as part-timers and another, Dolly, full time. They were known as the 'Happy Firm', because 'we laughed at and about everything'.

Like Shirley Pitts and the Happy Hoisters, they were having fun, and like the Forty Elephants, they were well organised, with an unwritten code of conduct. The cheque books and cards had to be fresh and not more than five days old, and only Chris was to 'carry the works' out of Heathrow and bring back the money. Her job was to destroy all the evidence – the passports, cheque stubs and receipts – straight after a book was cashed. The Happy Firm workers stayed at the best five-star hotels because 'they afforded the most anonymity and also put one in the right frame of mind for working'. But no one was to go out or drink the night before a job, they were to return home the minute it was over, and if arrested they were only to confess to their own role in the gang.

Chris had now successfully established herself in the London under-world. 'I mixed with villains because I enjoyed their company,' she explained, they were fun and generous, looked after their family and friends, and had a healthy contempt for money. The criminal life suited her. 'Camus had written that "in every act of rebellion one is being true to a part of oneself" … I was and had always been an "outsider" and I liked it that way.'

Chris acted as a receiver for a painting by French artist, Maurice Utrillo, as well as an II carat diamond, which was sold over tea in Fortnum's to 'a household name actress who had a penchant for fabulous, if bent, jewellery'.

Two years passed and the Happy Firm was still flying out of England two or three times a week. But the stress was wearing her down and Chris was constantly 'ducking and diving and buying and flying'. Then she met an actress, 'a member of a far left political party', who introduced her to *The Communist Manifesto*. Chris resumed work with a vengeance, and donated money to 'the party'. But again she grew disillusioned, convinced 'the capitalists keep the greater spoils, but the working classes shore up the system by their acquiescence'.

Like Shirley Pitts, who grew bored of going round Selfridges, Chris lost the excitement of trips abroad and never wanted to see the inside of another Hilton. 'I had got all that I had thought I wanted,' she wrote. 'Money, success and credibility with professional male villains. But why I had wanted it quite so much was not clear at all.' She had gone to great lengths 'to escape from all things feminine', but, while crime had given her independence and wealth, she needed to 'find the woman I was'. Her criminal work had started to appear futile. It would only end up with her returning to prison.

One day, while driving down the New Kings Road in Fulham, having picked up three chequebooks and cards, Chris was aware she was being followed. Ten minutes after she arrived home, her flat was full of the Flying Squad. She was arrested, along with six other members of the Happy Firm, and felt relief that it was all over. In the police cells, two of the men 'moaned like professional wailers rather than professional villains', but Chris and Dolly were stoical.

Then the police 'produced their trump card', and brought Chris's heavily pregnant teacher friend, the 'good girl', to the station. The police offered a deal: if she made a confession, they wouldn't charge her friend. Chris agreed, but she wouldn't try to defend or excuse herself, 'Mercy indeed! Who needs it, I asked the others? We had done it, we had known what we were doing, we had had a ball. If you can't do the time, don't do the crime, etc.'

The Happy Firm was given bail and a year later the trial began, although Gary and Adrian, the first two members of the gang, failed to show up. Eleven people stood accused of conspiracy to cheat and defraud, and some were also charged with handling stolen goods, including an emerald and diamond gold bracelet, a mink jacket and two gold medals that belonged to the cricketer Kenneth Carlisle. On 22 October 1973, Chris was sentenced to two years, and Alan to two and a half. Dolly was sent to borstal, although it was her first offence, while two of the part-timers received twelve and eighteen months each. Chris was also charged with possessing 'a quantity of cannabis resin', for which she pleaded guilty and received one month.

Yet, despite the number of people accused and the number of prosecution witnesses, I can't find a single press report on the trial of the Happy Firm. Perhaps fraud had become too common, or perhaps the press didn't realise the travellers' cheques gang had been run by a woman.

In 1976, Jenny Hicks was similarly surprised to find so little coverage of her trial, after defrauding the Post Office of £250,000 by 'fixing' a franking machine at her duplicating and mail order business. The case was described as the biggest postage swindle ever known in Britain, but the press downplayed the fraud, with one headline reading, 'Redhead Licks the Post Office'.

Chris Tchaikovsky, meanwhile, was sent to Holloway Prison. It was her final time inside and it would eventually alter the course of her life. In the early 1970s, Holloway was undergoing a major transformation. The Victorian 'terror to evil doers' was being torn down and in its place would be a secure hospital, including a new psychiatric unit, C1. The old Holloway had been built to intimidate and punish but now, according to Home Secretary James Callaghan, female prisoners needed 'medical, psychiatric or remedial treatment'.

The rebuild took far longer than intended, and as the female prison population increased, Holloway became overcrowded and understaffed once again. Relations between staff and inmates deteriorated, and there was a growing number of 'disturbed' inmates, some of whom were given 'calming injections' and put in Victorian-style straitjackets.

In March 1974, a few months after Chris's arrival, 20-year-old Patricia Cummings burned to death in her cell after her alarm bell had reportedly been disconnected because officers didn't want their sleep disturbed. Fellow prisoners 'shouted, barricaded, went on strike', and formed the Prisoners' Action Group. In response, the women were split up, threatened with loss of parole and not allowed to associate with each other. The roots of Chris's activism had begun.

After her release, she worked as a London ambulance driver, and set up Ryder Cars, an all-women mini cab company in Devon. But Chris's dream was to establish a Women's City, a space for all women to come together in London, with a crèche, launderette, courses in computer literacy and a theatre. To raise the funds, Chris opened the Women's City Disco, a lesbian disco in King's Cross, at The Bell on Pentonville Road. The club held benefit nights for Lesbians and Gays Support the Miners and the Lesbian and Gay Switchboard, and during Gay Pride there were 4,000 revellers, when capacity was just 400. 'It was an amazing atmosphere,' recalls Steve Rayner, who worked as a bartender. 'Occasionally it got a bit rough, what with the women attacking one another with pool cues. I'd get in between them and then they'd start on me.'

The plan for Women's City was vetoed by the council, so Chris decided to use the money to form a new organisation, Women in

Prison (WIP), along with criminologist, Pat Carlen. The need for WIP was acute, as there had been more deaths inside Holloway, and an article in *Spare Rib* made it crystal clear what the group was concerned with: 'What the fuck is going on in the new Holloway? Death from burns, or death by sexism?'

In 1981, Julie Potter died after a fire in her cell. The following year, Christine Scott died after injuries sustained from 'throwing herself around a cell' for up to twenty-four hours, and an unnamed woman died after she was refused an asthma spray or medication for a heart condition. Conditions in the C1 unit were degrading and barbaric, the majority of Holloway's prisoners were sedated – and nearly 70 per cent of the women inside had been convicted for stealing less than £100. In 1983, Women in Prison was launched, and the former criminal was about to become one of the nation's leading penal reform campaigners.

Chris Tchaikovsky worked tirelessly throughout the 1980s and 1990s, establishing Education Training Connection, a charity offering education and training opportunities to women in jail. She helped set up the Holloway Remand Scheme, with community-based programmes and practical support, and the charity Wish, originally named Women in Special Hospitals. She served on the Holloway Health Advisory Board, wrote academic papers, gave lectures and interviews, pressured policy-makers and contributed to academic conferences.

'She was an unbelievable character,' remembers writer and campaigner Melissa Benn, who met her in the early 1980s. 'She was physically striking and powerful. Her standard uniform was grey flannel shirt and trousers. You couldn't *not* take note of her, she was very charming.' Melissa was aware that Chris had been in Holloway. 'She didn't hide it. Her credibility came from her knowledge of prison. She was neither proud nor particularly embarrassed.'

But Chris didn't discuss her own career in crime, and while she was clever and ambitious, 'she could also be a loner'. Author and journalist Barney Bardsley met Chris while researching *Flowers in Hell: An Investigation into Women and Crime* in the mid-1980s. Barney's book confronted several long-held myths about crime, particularly the idea that crime was 'male' and a demonstration of machismo. She wanted to look at women who had 'the nerve to commit crime, to transgress those unspoken barriers of saintly femininity, and be *bad*'. She wanted to see 'if women too, could be criminal rebels', and so she interviewed Chris Tchaikovsky. She found the ex-leader of the Happy Firm articulate and political, but although Chris had plenty to say about women, crime and prison, she didn't speak much about her own criminal career.

Chris enrolled on a philosophy degree, and in 1997 she became a Cropwood fellow, spending a year at Cambridge University's Institute of Criminology, where she produced a study of 100 women on the Holloway Remand Scheme. The following year, the *Evening Standard* nominated her as one of the capital's top 100 women because of her influence on conditions in Holloway Prison.

Chris also supplied storylines for a new ITV prison drama, *Bad Girls*, which first aired in 1999, based on incidents she'd witnessed in jail. Episode one opened with a pregnant woman screaming in her cell, calling for a doctor and being dismissed by staff as 'attention-seeking'. By the time she was unlocked in the morning, she had miscarried and was lying unconscious and covered in blood. The scene was brutal, as was much of the TV series, which presented a new look at women in prison. It won several awards and at its peak attracted over 9 million viewers.

Just three years after *Bad Girls* aired, Chris Tchaikovsky died at the age of 57. Crime had not given her freedom, but it had given her insight into women in prison, and she had spent twenty years fighting for change. She was the 'queen of charisma', according to her friend and colleague, journalist Yvonne Roberts. 'She had a high IQ, and a huge appetite for learning. People from all walks of life were drawn to her.' As the boss of the Happy Firm, Chris had 'believed both in laughs and equal pay' and she'd spent 'bad money' on the 'finer things in life, and shared it generously with others'.

When Chris Tchaikovsky wrote her essay, 'Looking for Trouble', in 1985, she was responding to dominant theories of the time – that female criminals were maladjusted to their 'natural' roles or mentally ill. But she argued that 'women aren't in prison for what they've done, but for rebelling against their femininity'.

She wasn't a victim of biology or circumstances. She'd proved that women could turn to crime in order to be successful. Law breaking, while it lasted, had given her immense satisfaction, just as it had for the pickpocketing, shoplifting, smuggling, bandit and burglar queens before her. As a criminal, Chris had been a leader, financier and businesswoman.

'Looking for Trouble' is written in a witty, angry style. Her voice is clear and, unlike some underworld queens, no one is telling her what to say. But there are serious gaps. The chronology is confusing and important dates are missing. I can't find any reports on the garage robbery in Plymouth, or anyone called Alan or Dolly on trial at the Old Bailey in October 1973. There's no explanation as to why Chris changed her surname, and she seems to have used pseudonyms for everyone else.

Chris Tchaikovsky is still well known as a penal reformer, and Women in Prison continues to be the leading organisation for women affected by the criminal justice system, but her own career as a criminal has still not been documented. There are very few sources to draw on, and Holloway's criminal registers for the early 1970s have disappeared. Chris wrote 'Looking for Trouble' in her forties, and portrayed her younger self as a romantic rebel who had no regrets, and I can't help wondering if this was completely true. Who was the real person behind the youthful bravado? Was crime always as much fun as she made out? And had she really taken on the system with 'nary a victim in sight'?

20

LOOKING FOR TROUBLE

I push open the revolving doors of the Duke of Cornwall Hotel in Plymouth, a splendid gothic Victorian building and once the city's first luxury hotel. There's an impressive Christmas tree in the lobby, but it feels a little tired inside. The lifts aren't working, the dining room is closed because of a wedding, and a member of staff is trudging down a huge flight of stairs with a plate of half-eaten fish and chips. I turn left and into the lounge, a businesslike space with wood-panelled walls, and there at a corner table is Chris Tchaikovsky's sister.

Kay Thompson is in her late seventies, with a youthful face, pale green eyes and an open, friendly smile. She wears a soft white jumper and her nails are painted sparkly silver. Kay leaps up to order tea and we move to a table by the bar, so we can talk in private about her sister. She's with her daughter Tracey today, a hypnotherapist who has her mother's smile, as well as a very calm, measured gaze.

It's strange meeting Chris Tchaikovsky's relatives when I've spent so long trying to research her career. A year ago, I heard that Kay had contacted Women in Prison, the charity her sister founded in 1983. She'd discovered that her grandmother had once been in prison and wanted to find out more, and eventually we were put in touch.

I expect her to be wary today. Chris was her sister, not a distant relative from another generation. But Kay and Tracey clearly adored Chris and are happy to talk. 'She was an extrovert and very charismatic,' says Kay. 'She would never hurt someone, and she would always take the rap for someone else.'

'She always made you smile,' adds Tracey. 'She was hilarious. And she was kind.'

Kay was two years older than Chris, and she describes the family as 'reasonably well off'. Their parents were respected and they ran several businesses, first in Newquay and then in Falmouth, including a post office and a hotel. Their father was a Freemason, and friends' parents were happy for their children to stay over in the Ryder home, unaware that the children were out alone building bonfires on the beach. Kay describes a happy childhood, but her daughter thinks the girls' childhoods weren't as idyllic as they've been portrayed. Their parents fought and their mother was largely absent. 'You were running wild!' she says.

'No we weren't!' objects Kay.

'You were selling newspapers at the docks at the age of 4.'

Kay shrugs and raps her finger on the table. 'Our parents worked hard. We waited tables at the hotel and put on plays to entertain people. We were salespeople and performers from a young age.'

Their father was strict and didn't believe in education for girls. 'He was Victorian,' says Kay, 'and he had five daughters who were very outgoing. But Daddy adored Chris, he had been married before and had two children and she looked like the son from his first marriage. His name was Bernard and he died young. Daddy took Chris to climb trees, he treated her like a boy, she was a tomboy.'

She remembers Chris as a leader, always with a troupe of boys in a line behind her, ready to do whatever she asked. It was Kay who helped her sister put the long johns on the flagpole at Falmouth High, 'but I wasn't expelled, I don't know why.'

She laughs when she remembers something else Chris got up to. 'One summer, she had found a very sexy book, it was a Naval book, and when we got back to school, she had to write about what she'd done in the holidays. She was about 11 years old, and she wrote about the book. She got expelled! Then the next year, Chris stole money from the family's shop and gave it to the poor.'

'She did?' I ask, because there's no mention of stealing from her parents' shop in her autobiographical essay.

Kay nods, 'She went around giving it to tramps. Daddy was very upset and he beat her.'

'Oh,' I say, because Chris didn't mention this either. Instead, she portrayed her father as her defender.

'He gave me a hiding once as well,' adds Kay, 'and I never stole anything again.'

'But it didn't stop Chris?'

'No,' Kay says. 'I think that was really the start of all the crime.'

When Chris was around 14, the family moved to Exeter, where their father ran a pie shop. Soon the girls started travelling further afield, hitchhiking 200 miles to London to take part in CND marches. 'We told Daddy we were going to friends for the weekend,' explains Kay, 'then we went and sat outside Whitehall.' One day, their father opened his newspaper to find a huge photo of his daughter protesting in Trafalgar Square. 'The square was flooded and Chris was paddling across it,' explains Kay. 'Our father had seen us on TV, just a glimpse, and he thought it was us, but he wasn't sure. Then he saw the photo of Chris right in the middle of the newspaper!'

I ask if she knows the Café French in Soho, where Chris headed when she first left home. Was this the café frequented by artists, writers and actors like Francis Bacon, Lucien Freud and Quentin Crisp?

'I do remember going to a café in Soho,' says Kay, thoughtfully. 'It had disgustingly bad coffee. There was nothing very French about it.'

What about Dirty Dot's in Exeter, where Chris met the three ex-borstal girls?

'It wasn't the nicest place,' laughs Kay. 'It was slummy. But Chris liked it.'

She's not sure if her sister did break into a newsagent's belonging to their mother's friend – she believes it was a tailor's shop. But 'it was awful for Daddy, he adored her. He would have been very upset.'

Suddenly, there's a burst of noise from behind and I turn to see a crowd of people coming into the hotel bar, all dressed up and eager for drinks. I lower my voice a little and ask if Kay remembers her sister's Happy Firm days.

'Yes,' she says. 'I knew what she was doing, but I didn't know how big it was.'

She also didn't know anything about the Old Bailey fraud trial of 1973. 'Chris was very intelligent and had lots of friends,' says Kay. 'I never understood why she turned to crime. She could have started her own business, she was persuasive, she had charm. She would have made a good politician.'

'So why did she turn to crime?'

'I think it was the excitement,' says Kay, 'and the buzz. It gave her authority. It wasn't the money, because she never wanted things for herself. She had this big house in London, and she swapped it with a friend because the friend only had a tiny flat.'

'So she wasn't materialistic?'

'No!' Kay cries and shakes her head.

'She liked good clothes, though,' says Tracey. 'She was 6ft tall and very suave. She liked smart men's clothes like chino trousers, jackets and shirts.'

'She started wearing men's clothes when she left school,' explains Kay. 'She did stick out. She had lots of girlfriends too, but Daddy didn't know. It wasn't easy for two women as a couple in those days, that's why Chris and Jenny moved to London in the sixties, they were freer there.'

'Jenny?' I ask, 'Who was she?'

'Her girlfriend, they met in Plymouth.'

'Is that the woman she calls "Jan" in her essay?'

Kay shrugs, 'I don't think so.'

I ask where Chris got the surname Tchaikovsky.

'She married a Russian,' says Kay.

'She married a man?' I'm shocked. 'Why would she do that?'

'It was so he could stay in England.'

'Did she get paid? Is that why she married him?'

Kay shrugs again – she doesn't know. I later find that the marriage took place in Kensington in the summer of 1975, just after Chris's release from Holloway, and she was paid around £600.

Tracey is also surprised to hear of her aunt's marriage. 'Chris told me that she and her girlfriends all took composers' names, and she chose Tchaikovsky!'

As we continue to talk about Chris's life, I get the sense that mother and daughter are trying to piece things together, as any family does when talking about the past. But when it comes to trying to understand a family member with a criminal record, facts can be even harder to come by.

Tracey didn't see Chris much as a child, but in her early twenties, she too studied philosophy, and when *Criminal Women* was published in 1985, she went out and bought a copy. 'I read it and I almost felt pride. She was a bit notorious, but she'd pulled herself around. She told me she hadn't been a very nice person when she was younger.' Tracey stops and plays with her necklace for a moment. 'She said I wouldn't have liked her then. But we absolutely loved her. There is no stigma about her now in the family, we all adored her. But,' Tracey pauses again, 'when I asked her about the essay "Looking for Trouble", she told me it was a load of tosh.'

'She did?' I sit back, feeling alarmed. Have I been chasing after stories that weren't true in the first place? 'What did she mean?' I ask, 'Did she make some of it up?'

'I'm not sure,' says Tracey. 'Maybe she was embarrassed.'

We're silent for a while, thinking about this. Then Kay brightens up, 'Did you know Chris had a women's fashion shop? It was not far from Shepherd's Bush. It sold expensive things from Bali; Chris went to Bali a lot. The shop got robbed,' Kay chuckles. 'It was judgement on her. She had no insurance, so she closed the shop.'

'Do you think your sister gave up crime after her last time in Holloway?'

'Oh yes,' says Kay firmly, 'but she continued to feel guilty.'

'She did?'

Kay sighs, 'Yes. She felt guilty towards our parents and the people she'd stolen from.'

'So it wasn't true,' I say, 'what she wrote in her essay – that she didn't feel remorse?'

Tracey nods. 'She had a painting of Dartmoor on her wall, and she told me, "That's the last thing I ever bought with a stolen cheque". The woman at the art gallery had been lovely and very friendly and Chris felt so guilty. She'd kept the painting as a reminder that she would never do it again.'

When Chris fell ill with respiratory problems in the late 1990s, she returned to the south-west, moving to a village outside Plymouth. 'Her partner Jutta was there,' explains Kay, 'and Jenny moved into the cottage next door, their son was at university at the time.'

'Their *son*?' I ask.

'Yes,' says Kay. 'Chris and Jenny had a son, Ben. His father was one of their gay friends. Soon after he was born, Chris was in prison again. It was all too chaotic for Jenny.'

'Oh,' I say, because Chris didn't mention her son in her essay. There is no reference to Ben in anything I've read, not even her obituary. 'Do you think he would speak to me?' I ask.

'He might do,' says Kay.

Chris Tchaikovsky died on 19 May 2002 and was buried with her father in Buckland Monachorum village cemetery on Dartmoor. 'The funeral was packed,' remembers Kay. 'There were beautiful white flowers on the grave. And all the bad girls came.'

'The bad girls?' I ask.

Kay laughs, 'The actresses from *Bad Girls*, the TV show.'

The funeral was attended by a cross-section of those whose lives Chris had affected, including ex-prisoners, former police officers, probation workers, criminologists and social workers. There was also a memorial in London, and Shed Productions, who produced *Bad Girls*, arranged it at the BAFTA headquarters in Piccadilly. There were speeches by Pat Carlen, Helena Kennedy QC, and a former Holloway governor, Colin Allen.

'It was huge,' says Kay, 'and I so wished my mother was alive, to hear what people said about Chris.'

I look around and realise the Duke of Cornwall's bar is totally empty now. We've been talking for over three hours, the wind is whipping up outside and it's beginning to get dark. I thank Kay for trusting me.

'I was worried,' she admits. 'I'm very open and I was warned about speaking to you, that you might twist what I say.'

She hasn't told many people that her sister was in Holloway Prison. 'It doesn't really come up. I don't hide it; I just don't say it. But I'm proud of her charity and I tell people about that.'

I ask what her sister would have thought of my book. Mother and daughter look at each other. 'Chris would have wanted the truth told,' says Tracey firmly, 'and if she knew she was going to be in a book about being notorious, then she would have loved it!'

On the train back to London, I think about Chris Tchaikovsky and the reasons she turned to crime. If she hadn't grown up in the 1950s – if she could have been herself from the start – then would she have rebelled in the same way? Would she have ended up in prison? But she'd always seen herself as an outsider and as naturally disobedient, so perhaps she would have broken the law anyway. I wonder if she would have been surprised to learn that another relative had once been in prison. Kay has now discovered that their maternal grandmother, Ceridwen Harris, was jailed for bigamy in the 1930s, after she walked out on her first husband whom she'd accused of cruelty.

The summer after meeting Kay in Plymouth, she sends me an email. Chris's son has agreed to speak to me. I'm anxious about ringing him and worried about being intrusive. I'm not sure how to explain that, until last December, I didn't even know Chris Tchaikovsky had a son.

But Ben is cheerful on the phone, and like his aunt, he has a friendly manner and an easy laugh. 'There was a deal,' he explains, 'between my mum, Jenny, and Chris. It was don't tell anyone about being lesbian because if they did, then mum would definitely have lost her job in a posh school in Sloane Square.'

Discrimination against lesbians was still widespread in Britain, and Jenny wouldn't have been the first teacher, childcare officer or social worker to lose her job. 'She also would have lost it if anyone knew she lived with a criminal,' adds Ben. 'My mum was very, very shy; she just wanted a quiet life. When Chris was arrested in 1972, mum was arrested as well and taken to a police cell. She was pregnant with me, and to keep her out of it, Chris took the rap. That was the agreement.'

'Oh,' I say, finally realising. 'So Jenny is the middle-class "good girl", who the police released in exchange for Chris's confession?'

'Yes,' says Ben, 'but she wasn't that middle class. She was partially raised in a pub on the Plymouth Docks. Mum vetoed me from that essay, if you can put it like that. There was only so much she would allow in "Looking for Trouble" and she didn't want me mentioned.'

The women separated when he was 6 years old, although Chris later moved in with them, and then left again. 'She needed to be with lots of women,' says Ben. 'She fell in love with everyone, whether they were married, heterosexual, whatever. My mum, and lots of other women, were in *love* with Chris. I think mum couldn't share her, as much as she may have thought she could.'

Like Tracy Bowman, daughter of 1960s burglar Zoe Progl, Ben loved and admired Chris, but he also wants to present a balanced picture. 'So many people adored her,' he says. 'There were lots of hangers-on. People are keen to protect and promote her legacy; it's a tough balancing act. She had a public persona and a private one, and she kept her different worlds completely separate. As a child I would think, where's she gone? Why is she not even in my life? I have lots of photos of Chris and me, then there are gaps, and then there are photos again.'

Ben paints a picture of a complex figure; a woman who was gifted and deeply loving, who took people under her wing, and was generous and helpful. But he also describes her as problematic, narcissistic and someone who liked 'living on the edge of being caught out'.

I think of the secret life she wrote about when she first started in crime, and the widening gulf between the worlds of villains and 'straights'. Chris Tchaikovsky adopted a role depending on the circumstances and, like other underworld queens, such as Shirley Pitts, she tried to keep the two selves separate.

Ben only read 'Looking for Trouble' after Chris had died, and his mother, Jenny, passed away in 2010. 'When people are alive, we don't ask the right questions,' he says sadly, 'and it's only when they die, we get interested in their histories. I didn't ask Chris what I should have. But everyone has such different histories. Where do you start?'

Chris did tell Ben stories about the old days of the Happy Firm, however, and the crimes they'd committed, 'some of which I think was bullshit'. She told him she met the artist Salvador Dalí in a hotel bar in Paris, when he tried to pick her up because he thought she was a young boy. 'Whether or not that's true,' says Ben, 'it was a great piece of gossip. As a kid, I was really into Dalí and she told me this story, over and over.'

He doesn't agree that Chris didn't want to talk about the past, 'I just think maybe she knew that her intriguing past opened the door for her to talk about what was really important – women in prison. No one wants to glorify her criminal career, and it can sit uneasily with the work of Women in Prison. You have to strike a balance.'

A few days later, Ben sends me some photos, and as I scroll down the images on my phone it's like looking at snapshots from a life: Chris as an awkward young girl in a frilly top, walking the wilds of Dartmoor as a young adult, posing like a fugitive outside a city block of flats, on holiday with Jenny and Ben as a baby, and in a temple in Bali with Ben in 1996, when she looks immensely proud but also frail. Ben's favourite photo is one he calls 'Bonnie and Clyde', taken in Earls Court in 1969. His mother Jenny sits on a park bench, a glamorously beautiful woman in a summer dress and thigh-length boots, while Chris stands on the ground, one leg firmly planted on the bench, her hands on her hips. The photo is professionally taken, but Ben doesn't know by whom, or why. 'Mum looks like a gangster's moll,' he laughs. 'She wasn't in the gang, but I think she was a bit turned on by being the girlfriend.'

Today, Ben lives with his family in Derbyshire, where he makes handmade sneakers. Like other relatives of underworld queens, he has also worked with people affected by the criminal justice system. Elsie Carey's niece, Linda Sansum, became a children's guardian; Zoe Progl's daughter, Tracy Bowman, works with children in care; while Ben initially went to art college and trained as a primary school teacher. He then worked with a charity in Oxfordshire that supports children at risk, and taught music technology at Huntercombe, a young offenders' institution and now a prison for adult men. He also taught art to Category A prisoners in another prison and has worked with asylum seekers. 'Chris always said you should make a difference,' says Ben. 'Do something worthwhile in your life, help people.'

The following afternoon, I ring Jutta, Chris's partner, because Kay has sent me her number as well. Jutta first met Chris in 1990 when her company's office was in the same building as Women in Prison, and they shared a photocopier. She has a wry sense of humour and talks of her late partner with a deep sense of admiration and loyalty.

'Chris wasn't interested in speaking about the past,' says Jutta. 'She was interested in the present and what to do in the future. When I met her, that criminal part of her life was done.' But she does remember that one day there was loud laughter coming out of an office, and when she went in, the women were discussing who had made the most money out of crime. Jenny Hicks, convicted for the Post Office Swindle of 1976, said it was her, 'but someone else said she hadn't taken account of inflation. It was hilarious.'

'What was Chris like?' I ask. 'How would you describe her?'

'She was utterly fearless,' says Jutta, at once. 'That's what struck you; she was utterly fearless in all her work. She gave no apologies; there was no mitigation. And she had fun! There is a sinister view of women committing crime and it wasn't like that. It was a career choice. Chris didn't want the roles that were on offer.'

Jutta remembers when, one day, after Chris had stopped working at WIP because of illness, a TV company asked for an interview. 'It was about an important case, and she couldn't get to them because she was too ill, so they sent a transmission van. I helped her downstairs and outside, to where the sound engineer and interviewer were waiting. I could see them thinking, as we hobbled along, "Oh let's help this little old lady". Then Chris sat down and started to speak, you should have seen their faces! Wow, a radical! She always started with a political statement. There were no questions – there was no such thing as an interview with Chris. She spoke about the case and they sat fascinated. She was a little typhoon!'

Yet, while Chris Tchaikovsky has always been respected in the world of penal reform, it is only recently that she has become known to a wider audience. In 2019, actor and writer Harriet Madeley wrote a drama based on Chris's life, which became *The Other Tchaikovsky*, a Prison Radio Association production for BBC Radio 4. It was billed as 'the untold story of a self-confessed outlaw and villain, activist, fraudster, lesbian club owner and visionary'.

Fragments of Chris's story were recounted by some of the people who knew her, including a former partner, Patti, and her career was used as a way to explore the situation of women in the criminal justice system, both in the past and now. The programme didn't shy away from Chris's criminal life, and she was portrayed as a successful villain, but there were very few details about her crimes and only a passing mention of the 1973 fraud trial.

'The middle period of Chris's life was the hardest to find information on,' Harriet admits. 'I was amazed at how little had been written, and there was no press coverage on the fraud trial at all! Chris was so complex. Everyone remembered her physically, she made a major impression, but I couldn't ever really pin her down.'

The Other Tchaikovsky didn't mention that Chris had a son, but Ben is philosophical. 'People need protecting,' he says. 'That's what my mum was trying to do, protect me by keeping me out of the essay. And the key thing to Chris was to protect people, too, both my mum and others.'

When Chris described her essay as 'a load of tosh', perhaps this was a form of protection as well. So what would she have thought about my attempt to unravel her career?

'Chris would have loved to be in your book,' Ben laughs. 'She would have bitten your hand off! She would have taken you to Café Rouge for steak and a bottle of very expensive wine!'

He has recently been re-reading letters that Chris sent to his mother from prison. 'I'm imagining what her life was like inside, and what it was like for Mum, on her own with me and with her partner in prison. Anyone can see that Chris loved the criminal life, it was exciting. But she did feel guilty about the crime.'

Ben thinks Women In Prison was a form of reparation; a way of making amends as well as 'doing what needed to be done for women'. And while he's found himself airbrushed out of reports on Chris's life, 'I feel it's important that my children know as much as they can about their grandmother. All of this really just makes me want to be a better dad.'

When I finish speaking with Ben, I open my copy of 'Looking For Trouble' again. There, in the acknowledgements, is a line I hadn't noticed before. Chris thanks three colleagues, and then she thanks 'Jenny and Ben Clements for staying the course'.

Of all the women I've found so far, Chris Tchaikovsky is the only one who probably wouldn't want the title 'Queen of the Underworld'. She would have objected to it, I think, as salacious and patronising – although she did work hard to join the criminal sorority and to establish herself as a leader among male villains. 'It's not a title she would have given herself,' agrees Jutta, 'but she would have liked being put in line with her predecessors.'

Now that I'm coming up to more modern times, I'm wondering how to find women who *would* call themselves 'Queen of the Underworld'. Where are the contemporary female crooks? And would anyone be willing to speak to me?

21

JOAN HANNINGTON
DIAMOND THIEF

One winter's morning, with the mud still frosty on the ground, I take my Staffie, Jojo, for a walk in a north London park. We've been coming here for the past few months and when Jojo sees a familiar figure, and hopes she might get a treat, she runs.

The figure is a woman in her early sixties. She has long, bleached-blonde hair and wears a raspberry pink mackintosh. I don't know her name, but she has a miniature Jack Russell and we've chatted a few times about our dogs and swapped bits and pieces from our lives. I know she used to run an antiques business, and that she has a son. I know how her Christmas went, and about an old disaster at the hairdresser's. She's blunt and funny and appears to know everyone in the park, and she also seems like someone you wouldn't necessarily want to mess with.

I wave as Jojo rushes across the grass, and then I hear a scream. 'Fuck!' says the woman, clutching her knees, 'I've got arthritis.' I run up to apologise and put Jojo back on the lead. It must be agony, I say, I'm really sorry. The woman quickly recovers and doesn't seem too angry, so we start talking about arthritis, which I've got in my knees as well. I probably spend too much time sitting down, I say, because I'm a writer.

'I'm a writer too,' says the woman. 'I'm a published author.'

'Are you?' I thought she was a retired antiques dealer. She's never mentioned being a writer before, but then neither have I. 'What do you write?' I ask.

'Crime.' The woman puts her hands in her pockets.

'Oh,' I say, a bit taken aback. 'What sort of crime?'

'True crime.'

'True crime about what?'

'About me.'

'You?' I stare at the woman in the pink mackintosh. 'You were a criminal?'

She draws herself up to her full height. 'I was an international jewel thief.'

'You were what?' I can't believe my luck; all this time I've been walking my dog around a park with an international jewel thief? 'What did you do?' I ask. 'What's your name?'

The woman takes her hands out of her pockets and crosses her arms, 'Joan Hannington.'

'Joan Hannington,' I repeat. I haven't heard of her, but I explain that I'm writing a book about the history of female crooks called *Queens of the Underworld* – would she be interviewed?

'No,' she says, at once.

'Oh.' I'm disappointed. Perhaps I've been too direct.

'Because I've got my own book,' says Joan, 'you understand.'

'What's it called?'

'*I Am What I Am.*'

'Maybe,' I suggest, 'if you did an interview, it could help with your book?'

'I don't think so,' says Joan. 'My book's been optioned by Gwyneth Paltrow.'

'It has? They're making a Hollywood film of your book?'

Joan nods, 'Madonna wanted it, but I said no. Madonna can't act, and she couldn't do the right accent to save her life.'

But Joan says she hasn't liked the scripts so far. She's being made out to be a sexy blonde without much intelligence and the men have been given much bigger roles than they deserve. 'And,' she says, 'they weren't interested in what made me a criminal.'

'I am,' I say. 'I'm interested in what made you a criminal.'

But Joan still won't be interviewed. She says she's been exploited in the past.

We chat a little longer and then she walks me back through the park. I tell her about my book again and all the women I've been writing about.

'Did you know the burglar, Zoe Progl?' I ask. 'What about Shirley Pitts?'

'Queen of the Shoplifters, yeah,' says Joan. 'Only, no disrespect, but she was a shoplifter. I was a jewel thief.'

'Have you heard of Emily Lawrence?' I ask. 'She was a jewel thief in Victorian times.'

Joan looks interested, 'Was she now?'

The minute I get home, I google Joan Hannington. Her book *I Am What I Am* was published in 2002 and is subtitled 'The True Story of Britain's Most Notorious Jewel Thief'.

Joan Hannington 'has more balls than your average blonde', according to the blurb. 'She is that rare thing: a tough woman whose no-bullshit attitude and irrepressible spirit have earned her respect in a man's world.'

I look at the book on my computer screen. Joan is easy to recognise from the cover photograph, even though it's twenty years old, with luminous yellow hair and bright red lipstick. She stares down at the reader, flanked by two anonymous men, and she appears to be holding a weapon – perhaps a cosh – in her hands. This is the Godmother, 'one of the most notorious figures in London's criminal underworld'. I feel embarrassed now that I didn't know who she was.

A few weeks later, I'm sitting in a small, darkened room at the British Film Archives, about to watch a documentary called *Hard Bastards*, which Joan told me about in the park. The presenter is Kate Kray, once married to Ronnie Kray and the author of several books on crime. The programme begins outside a shop in Hatton Garden as Joan explains how she became a crook.

One day in 1978, while working at a jeweller's, she was told to get four trays of loose diamonds from the safe and take them upstairs. Her employer had recently been taken away in handcuffs for 'cooking the books', the shop was closed, and the staff were checking the stock. Joan was hungry and had no money for lunch, and suddenly she saw a golden opportunity. As she walked up the stairs, she grabbed a handful of diamonds off each tray, put them in her mouth, and swallowed 'a load of them'. Incredibly, no one noticed anything was missing, and while there was CCTV at the front of the shop, there were no cameras by the safe.

Joan went to a chemist after work, bought a bottle of cod liver oil and returned home to 'let nature take its course'. Then, she soaked the diamonds in a bowl of gin for a couple of hours until they were 'as sparkly as when they were in the shop's safe'. She buried the gems by the wall of Wormwood Scrubs Prison, near where she'd grown up, and didn't attempt to sell any for three months.

She went to a dealer in Shepherd's Bush. He initially pretended the diamonds weren't real, but eventually offered £10,000. Joan later realised the gems were worth £800,000, so, like Zoe Progl and Chris Tchaikovsky before her, she would have to learn to deal with male crooks who tried to take advantage. The largest diamond, she explains, was an impressive 8 carats.

'Was it hard to swallow?' asks Kate Kray.

'No harder than an eight-inch dick, no,' replies Joan. She's dressed all in black for this TV interview, in a long leather coat and cap, with a big silver chain around her neck. Joan Hannington is being portrayed as suitably hard for *Hard Bastards*. Detective Constable George Gauntlet describes her as 'very skilful' and the 'number one' lady criminal, but the programme seems more interested in visiting places where she was assaulted, rather than providing information on her crimes. When Kate Kray asks if she's rich, Joan declines to say. 'I had choices,' she explains. 'Some people would say I took the wrong ones, I chose to be a thief.'

◆

She was born Joan O'Leary in 1957, the youngest of seven children. Her father, Richard, was from Blackrock in Cork and had worked as a trainer and boxing promoter in Dublin, while her mother, Mary, was from Limerick. They came to England in the late 1930s or early 1940s, and Joan spent her childhood in a prefab with a tin roof in North Acton, west London.

In her autobiography, she describes growing up under the terrifying reign of a violent, abusive father, who smashed his children's kneecaps with a cricket bat and nearly drowned Joan in the bath when she was 3. At school she was bullied and called an 'Irish slag'. Irish people were 'treated like shit' in the 1970s, she writes. 'The fact there was trouble in Northern Ireland … didn't help the Irish living in this country.'

Anti-Irish racism had existed in England for centuries. In Victorian times, Irish immigrants were subjected to discrimination and physical attacks, barred from jobs and pubs. The stereotype of the Irish, and particularly Catholic working-class Irish, as feckless, aggressive and alcoholic gathered pace in the 1950s and early 1960s, when racist shop signs warned 'No Irish, No coloureds'. Such signs were 'everywhere', writes Professor Mary J. Hickman, and in some areas of London and Birmingham there were more 'No Irish' signs than anything else.

Discrimination, physical abuse and restriction of movement increased in times of IRA activity, such as the 1970s, when Joan Hannington was at school. 'In London it felt like everybody hated the Irish,' she writes, 'even the London Irish, like me, were disliked.'

Racist attitudes led to police harassment and discrimination within the courts. When two women were convicted of theft in Rugby, their own solicitor explained that 'the Irish have an unhappy knack of presenting problems to the English, and this is another instance of it'.

Joan felt degraded at school because of her Irish background and the fact she had free dinners. She wanted to 'get a good education, leave school and get a good job, etc., etc.' But school was just like home – she was picked on, excluded and humiliated.

When Joan was 13, she met Raymond Pavey, a handsome man with shoulder-length hair, a double-breasted suede patchwork coat and RAY tattooed on his neck with a snake underneath. He was just finishing a five-year sentence for armed robbery and living in the nearby Wormwood Scrubs Prison hostel.

Soon after they met, Joan ran away from home in an attempt to escape her father. The police found her at a friend's house, put her in a cell and then a male doctor subjected her to a VD test in front of two male police officers. She was sent to a children's home in west London where she witnessed an attendant sexually assault another girl. Joan jumped out of a window and ran but was caught and made a ward of court under the care of Ealing Social Services.

In 1974, at the age of 17, she married Raymond Pavey. They moved to Hastings and transformed their ground-floor council flat into the 'typical successful villain's home of the early seventies', with flock wallpaper, velvet curtains and crystal chandeliers. But Joan resented being expected to socialise with the other criminals' wives, 'and go to their silly Tupperware parties that were full of sex-starved women'. Her husband, meanwhile, was either absent or sat around doing nothing. Like 1960s burglar Zoe Progl, Joan began to think, 'I don't like this marriage game; it ain't all it's cracked up to be.'

The couple had a daughter, Debbie, and Joan worked as a night orderly in a psychiatric hospital. But then Ray met another woman, and she found herself alone with a 3-year-old child, looking for work and a place to live. When Ray was arrested and put on remand 'for a bit of work', a group of men broke in and tortured her.

In desperation, Joan asked Social Services to look after her daughter until she had a safe place to stay. They found a wealthy foster family and Joan was told it was just for a few weeks. Then, a few days before she was due to visit her daughter, she stole an Austin 1100, intending to drive to Brighton to pick up some belongings then return to Hastings where she would sleep in the car. Joan was arrested outside Brighton, given a two-year probation order and told that if she didn't sign away her parental rights, her daughter would be handed over to her own parents. Horrified at the idea, she headbutted the social worker. Joan lost her parental rights – and threw herself into becoming a jewel thief.

Like other queens of the underworld, dressing up and disguise were central to her new persona, and she became a twenty-first-century version of Emily Lawrence, Sophie Lyons and Blonde Alice Smith, the 'Diamond Dolly' of the 1920s. Joan often posed as an American tourist, in expensive wigs and fur coats. 'I loved playing those parts … transforming myself in front of the mirror. Then I'd pick up my fur coat, drape it over my shoulder, and I'd take to the stage.'

She also employed methods similar to those used by Annie Grant when she stole a pearl necklace from Christie's auction house in 1905. First, Joan visited a Bond Street shop, picked up a £50,000 ring and asked what grade the diamond was and how much it weighed. Once the assistant had helpfully written down the details, Joan had a fake version made.

A couple of days later, she booked a room at the Savoy Hotel or the Dorchester and rang the jewellers to say she'd be returning to see the ring. She arrived by a chauffeur-driven car, dressed as if she had a starring role in *Dallas*, and the male assistants fell over themselves trying to help. Joan pretended to try on the ring she wanted, then quickly swapped it for the fake. She gave a loud sneeze, shielded her face, swished her tongue around to make saliva and swallowed it down. Once the fake ring had been put in the window, Joan asked the assistant if he wanted to come to her room at the Dorchester for drinks, then she left, 'as cool and sexy as you like'. From her perspective, she had the power. 'You can think and you can fantasise all you like, but you're the one who's gonna get fucked in the end … so you just keep dreaming, my friend.'

Once home, Joan punched the air in triumph. 'God, it was always such a good feeling, such a rush to the brain.' She described crime in the same way as Zoe Progl – it was 'better than sex'. Joan took off her disguise, rolled a joint, poured a gin and tonic and relaxed in the bath. Her triumph was twofold: she'd just got away with a £50,000 ring, and she had proved herself as a woman. 'Women were considered stupid,' she writes, 'or we were supposed to stay home and make babies or cook nice dinners. Well, not Joan Hannington. I'd tried that before, and the system fucked me. Now I was fucking the lot of them.' Crime was a way to get her own back on society, represented by teachers, police, doctors and social services, as well as the violent men in her life who'd tried to control her.

◆

Joan Hannington wasn't the only female jewel thief intent on screwing the system. Three years before her Hatton Garden theft, an American crook had arrived in London and she too was hellbent on revenge. In September 1975, Doris Payne touched down at Heathrow Airport, ready to begin a four-day onslaught on the jewellers of London, Paris and Rome. The 45-year-old African American was already a highly successful crook; she'd been stealing diamonds for two decades.

Doris booked into Claridge's, the same hotel favoured by Sophie Lyons during her crook's tour of London in the 1880s. Then Doris headed round the corner to Garrard & Co., jewellers to the royal family, where she plucked a pair of diamond and emerald earrings from an open cabinet.

A few days later, after a whirlwind European tour, she flew back to the States, with 'one million dollars' worth of Africa on me'. Doris Payne was a crusader. Stealing diamonds was an act of retribution against a racist world. The gems had been plucked from African mines and the proceeds used to fund war, now an African American was taking them back.

Doris had been born in West Virginia in 1930 and, like Joan Hannington, her childhood was dominated by a violent father. She grew up in a time of segregation, when 'Jim Crow' laws ruled every aspect of daily life, in schools, department stores, buses, hotels, swimming pools and cemeteries. One day, a young Doris went to a local store owned by Mr Benjamin, a white man, and proudly told him her mother was planning to buy her a watch.

Mr Benjamin was initially friendly, but when a white male customer came in, he snatched away the watches and ordered Doris out of the store. Doris Payne had been demeaned, but she also realised that she'd almost walked out of the store without Mr Benjamin noticing she was still wearing one of the watches. She had discovered a miraculous ability to 'make people forget' she was wearing their jewellery, and now she was 'ready for war against him and all of his brothers'.

In 1956, Doris carried out her first big heist in Cleveland, and soon she was stealing thousands of dollars' worth of diamonds. Her trip to London was just one of many European jaunts, taken as 'a monied woman of class', and her last arrest was as recent as 2017.

Joan Hannington, meanwhile, turned to another form of crime. In the late 1970s, she fell in love with Donald 'Benny' Hannington, 'the best fence, the best thief, the best jeweller'. He owned several antique shops, as well as warehouses with £2 million worth of goods. Benny was a professional criminal, 'self-educated, prison-educated, from the nick and the street', while Joan was 'the dogsbody, the apprentice, the joey, the runner – but I was learning'.

In 1980, they committed their first robbery together, stealing an antique piece of furniture worth £30,000 from a house in Ealing, and soon they had become Robbery Incorporated. During the day, Joan went out kiting with stolen cheques, which could now be written for up to £50 without a banker's card. At night she accompanied Benny – for nine years, eight hours a day, 364 days a year, 'and sometimes on a Christmas Day, just for the fun of it'.

She also continued swallowing diamonds, with Benny resetting stolen stones in new gold bands and displaying them in his shop window. He taught her the chewing gum method, which Annie Grant had used in the West End in the early 1900s and Zoe Progl in the 1950s.

Joan rented a limo, dressed up in a mink coat and Cartier diamonds, and hired a man to act as her 'sugar daddy'. Together, they went to a jeweller's, where Joan had already identified the ring she wanted and had it copied. When the assistant wasn't looking, she stuck the genuine ring into a piece of gum under the counter. Her sugar daddy then put down a deposit with a stolen American Express card. The couple left and ten minutes later she sent someone else in to get the ring. 'It was foolproof,' she writes. 'I did it for about ten years.' But one day, she was arrested while kiting in M&S and spent nearly a year on remand in Holloway Prison.

In 1982, Joan and Benny got married, and two weeks later she was back in jail. Like the leader of the Happy Firm, she was realistic. 'When I committed crimes, when I was using stolen credit cards to lead a lavish lifestyle, I didn't give a fuck. I knew if I got caught and went to jail, I'd accept it without tears or regrets.'

On her release, Joan resumed her career and the couple joined the criminal 'millionaire league'. She walked around 'looking like a Christmas tree', with jewels on every finger like Alice Diamond, head-to-toe in gold, wearing designer clothes and fur coats. But while she frequently changed her image for work purposes, she also 'kept a certain image for herself', preferring to wear silver Doc Martens covered in glued-on gold sovereigns. Like Chris Tchaikovsky the 1970s fraudster, she was beginning to lead a double life.

The couple invested their profits in gems and gold watches, as well as Chippendale furniture and paintings by Joshua Reynolds and Matisse. They hid the rest of the cash in shoeboxes under the bed, and Joan's job was to iron the money when Benny brought it home – sorting £20,000 into denominations and then ironing each note to get the creases out. At one point, the couple had about £7.5 million in cash, diamonds and antiques, and 'other things that I choose not to mention'. But like so many queens of the underworld, Joan began to get bored. 'We had shops and cars and everything we wanted,' she writes, 'but I was cracking up ... I had nothing to occupy this brain of mine. I just had to be *doing* something.' The more diamonds she stole, 'the more hungry I got. They were like drugs to me. I had to have them.'

When her son Ben was born, Joan Hannington changed her mind about crime. She didn't want to bring him up 'to believe it was right to go down the road I went down'. She started to feel she was 'losing herself', being Joan Hannington at home and then out all day dressed up as a rich American. Her husband had also become controlling. 'Twenty-four hours a day for twelve years I was on parade. I wasn't a wife ... I was a fucking trophy.' Benny decided on the colour of her hair and the shade of her lipstick, told her what to wear and what to say, and sent her to a diet doctor to lose weight.

Benny died in November 1990, while trying to set fire to a building in west London as part of an insurance scam, and not long afterwards, Joan gave up her criminal career. She also had an operation 'to have half my stomach removed'. She was told she had duodenal ulcers caused by stress, 'but maybe it was years of swallowing diamonds, I don't know'.

Joan ends her autobiography defiantly. She has 'no conscience about how I lived my life, none whatsoever. God is my judge, not anyone down here. I don't regret anything I've ever done ... if I can live the next forty years in relative peace I'll just disappear into obscurity.'

But with film rights bought by Gwyneth Paltrow, that seems unlikely, and when the option agreement was announced in 2004 it drew lots of press interest. The *Sunday World* described Joan as 'the most famous female gangster in 1980s London', and 'a sexy and suave cat burglar'. Joan's response was, 'I'm not a gangster, darling – I'm an artist, a retired artist.' *The Scotsman* portrayed her as 'Raffles in a Wonderbra and killer heels' but paid little attention to what had pushed her into a life of crime, or the actual methods she'd used.

Joan kept control of her own story, but *I Am What I Am*, like all criminal autobiographies, has significant gaps. There is a general lack of details and dates – and as she wasn't ever convicted of swallowing diamonds, there is no press coverage either. Why did she write the book? Is she glad that she did? And what happened to all the money?

It's been several weeks since I've seen Joan Hannington, although I've been constantly looking out for her in the park. Then one morning she comes striding in, wearing an ankle-length brown leather coat with wide lapels, and a yellow handbag slung across one shoulder. I wave and immediately put Jojo on the lead.

Joan is cheerful this morning, she's just about to sign another option for film rights and this time she's very happy with the writers and director. I beg her for an interview, but she explains she can't. Her life story is being made into a film for Netflix and her contract prevents her from being involved in anything else. I explain I've already written about the day she first told me she'd been an international jewel thief, and I've read her autobiography and watched *Hard Bastards*.

'Is that OK?' I ask, slightly nervous now that I've read her autobiography and know what she's capable of when provoked.

'I'll agree, on one condition,' says Joan.

'Oh.' I'm even more worried now. 'What is it?'

'You give me a copy of your book.'

'Of course I will,' I say in relief. 'Of course I will.'

Joan thrusts her hand out. 'Shake on it.'

So I do, and she has a firm grip, just as I thought she would.

We walk to the gates of the park and Joan Hannington stops. 'What's the title of your book again?'

'*Queens of the Underworld*.'

Joan laughs. 'Thank God it's not Gangsters' Molls.'

22

GANGSTERS' MOLLS

By the end of the twentieth century, the title 'Queen of the Underworld' was rarely used, even by the press, but the image of the gangster's moll lived on. The term traces back to Moll Cutpurse's day, when 'moll' was slang for prostitute, and by Victorian times it referred to 'female companions of low thieves, at bed, board, and business'.

The 1920s saw the rise of the 'gun moll' figure in the United States, a 'thief's sweetie or wife who carries the gun', according to one glossary of crime. The term became a way to belittle successful criminal women. Hoister Shirley Pitts was supposedly a 'gunman's moll', and burglar Zoe Progl a 'gangster's moll'.

Today, the title still carries a suggestion of prostitution – of a woman who is sexually immoral and dangerous – and when Linda Calvey was arrested for murder in November 1990, she appeared to epitomise the stereotype. She was 'platinum blonde, harsh-faced and sharp-tongued', according to the *Sunday People*, and she had an 'insatiable appetite for men'. But rather than just being a 'thief's sweetie', Linda Calvey had already pursued a ten-year career as an armed robber.

During the 1980s, she'd organised and carried out numerous armed robberies in London, hiring men as drivers, lookouts and armourers, and earning a reputed £1 million. She was, according to Kate Kray, 'queen of the sawn-off shotgun'. Like shop breaker Elsie Carey and smash-and-grab raider Lilian Goldstein, Linda operated in a 'male' branch of crime, and, like Joan Hannington and Doris Payne, she was driven by 'a burning hatred for authority'.

Linda was born in 1948 and grew up in Stepney in the East End, which she described as 'home of the underclass, the seething, broiling hunting ground of the city's criminal establishment'. Her parents were honest, hard-working people and her home life was safe and loving, but Linda 'wanted excitement like a moth to a flame'. When she was 12, a shiny red Rolls-Royce pulled up alongside her father's car and inside sat an 'impossibly alluring' woman swathed in a fur coat. It was Linda's first glimpse into another world and, like Zoe Progl and Shirley Pitts before her, she 'wanted what they had, but how on earth was I going to get it?'

At 19 she fell in love with Mickey Calvey, a bank robber who'd just served eight years. The couple moved in together, and as Mickey sat around the kitchen table with his associates planning further robberies, Linda listened closely. She didn't ask questions when he came home with bags of cash and expensive jewellery. 'I wasn't daft, I knew where the money came from, but it was all insured and no one ever got hurt, so what was the harm in it?'

Mickey's gang used sawn-off shotguns and took members of the public hostage, but this didn't appear to worry Linda. If you wanted to live in style, she argued, then the criminal life was the only viable option.

Armed robbery was on the rise in Britain in the late 1970s and throughout the 1980s, with raids on security vans delivering wages in cash, as well as banks, post offices, off licences and sometimes pubs. Post offices were particularly vulnerable and could be lucrative targets – in Sunderland, armed robbers came away with the equivalent of £2 million in cash.

The authorities had been struggling to combat armed robbery for decades, and a succession of new security devices had been introduced in the 1950s. 'Thief proof' cases and 'anti-bandit' bags set off alarms if they were grabbed, soaked the cash inside with dye or released coloured vapour. A cosh known as the 'criminal detector' could spray purple dye from a distance of up to 25yds. By the 1960s, staff transporting wages carried police truncheons and Post Office vans were using bulletproof glass and panic buttons. But, as one Pathé news film explained, 'Cashiers and their so-called guards are no match for the ruthless efficiency of the modern highwayman.'

More new inventions followed – a steel-lined waistcoat padlocked around the waist, and a steel-lined bowler hat to protect cashiers and guards from violent attacks. An ingenious briefcase called the 'Arrestor' had 12ft-long metal bars which shot out of the sides if a thief tried to steal it, while a handheld device fired an 'anti-getaway net' made of nylon.

Banks and businesses started to use private security companies and armoured vehicles to move large sums of cash, with 'top-secret alarm devices' and two-way radios. By the end of the 1980s, a nationwide MORI poll found armed robbery was seen as the second most serious crime in the country.

Female armed robbers remained rare, although, in January 1986, a 'beautiful Black 20-year-old bank robber' stole £5,500 in cash from a Barclays in South Lambeth. She wore 'fashion clothes', according to the police, and brandished a shotgun.

In December 1978, Linda's husband Mickey Calvey was shot dead by police during a supermarket robbery, after reportedly threatening to shoot an officer. But according to Linda, there were no bullets in his gun, and she questioned why he'd been shot in the back. It was then that her hatred for the police and authorities began. Society owed her the right to make a good living, and her success as a robber was 'born of a total determination to seize back what was rightfully mine'. As she stood in the mortuary to identify her dead husband, she vowed, 'I will take up your role, babe. I will provide for our children and give them the finest in life. I will take what's owing to us.'

According to Linda, her vow inspired the hit 1980s ITV series *Widows*, written by Lynda La Plante, in which three widows and a friend carry out a million pound security van heist. The central character, Dolly Rawlins, is a born leader – smart, calculating and ruthless, with a 'hidden, almost masculine strength'. Dolly's all-female gang prove themselves more than a match for the male crooks, who believe robbery is a man's game, and male police, who are corrupt, vicious and stupid. Despite its popularity as the highest-rating TV series of the early 1980s, *Widows* was described as 'immoral' by several male reviewers. The problem was not just that a group of women were committing a crime; it was the fact they got away with it.

After Mickey's death, Linda became the lover of gangster Ron Cook, but he soon became violent and controlling. 'I was told who I could speak to, where I should stand. I was a possession to be treated as he wished.' When he was sentenced to sixteen years for attempted armed robbery, Linda started a relationship with another criminal, Brian Thorogood, and began her own career as an armed robber.

When Brian announced that he was going to 'get his balaclava and cosh out to do a job', she said she wanted to come too. 'Something in me clicked, and I just knew that, given half a chance, I could make a go of being a thief.'

Brian wouldn't let her carry a weapon or be actively involved, but she scouted out potential targets, worked out escape routes and where to park getaway cars, timed security vans and noted the guards' routines. Linda took a methodical approach, arranging for three separate getaway cars, and planning robberies in the belief that the police could ambush them at any stage.

She became the gang's driver, and when her first raid on a bank security vehicle went to plan, she was triumphant. 'I'd done it! I'd actually gone out on a raid with the fellas and, oh my God, I'd loved it.' She didn't want to be like other wives, 'sex servants to their husbands'; instead, 'I was a player and I had respect and I didn't have to answer to anyone. I wasn't just a girlfriend – I was one of them.'

Linda began organising robberies herself, recruiting a team a few days, or even a few hours, beforehand 'to avoid any breaches of security'. Once she'd chosen the gang members, she baked a cake and biscuits, prepared a plate of sandwiches and invited them round for tea. As the men studied maps and she timed their moves, 'I felt a bit like a schoolmistress with a class of foolish schoolboys.' She also made use of the men for domestic chores like shaking out rugs and cleaning windows. 'If they couldn't obey me when I wanted something done round the house,' she explained, 'then they wouldn't obey in the heat of a robbery and that could prove disastrous.'

Linda described her robberies as theatrical productions, full of drama and with close attention to detail. Once a raid was completed, she counted the cash and took expenses to cover overheads. The rest was divided equally among the gang, who each gave her 10 per cent back. As they left her house, 'they would each get a kiss and a "Well done, boys"'.

It all seemed like 'harmless fun' to Linda; it was a case of 'us against the law'. The gang stole from wealthy banks and businesses 'and though we didn't freely pass it round, we considered ourselves as working class, and therefore entitled to squander rich people's money'.

In 1983, Linda joined Brian Thorogood on a robbery in a 'quiet corner of London', and this time she was armed. 'She carried a gun,' explained Brian, 'and, let me tell you, it was not for show.' Linda had become 'the number one on the team ... she was the boss. We worked for her. She planned it all.' The gang escaped with 'vast amounts of money', and Linda bought a three-bedroomed mock Tudor home in an east London suburb, and hired an au pair and a gardener.

The gang expanded. Soon Linda's garage was full of props, including 'Road Closed' signs, a utility board hut and a temporary bus stop. 'The really fun part of all this,' she wrote, 'for me, as a woman, was the use of disguises.' Like most underworld queens, she delighted in changing her appearance, and she also disguised the men in the gang with false moustaches and temporary tattoos and scars. 'Perhaps,' she wrote, 'I am a frustrated actress.' One day, she hid a gun inside an artificial 'bump' that was used in the theatre to make a woman look pregnant, and successfully robbed a Securicor van on her own.

Linda still believed that 'no one was hurt by us taking what wasn't ours', but when she was arrested and thrown to the floor by a police officer holding a shotgun, all that changed. She felt 'utterly violated, and completely helpless', and finally realised 'the sheer terror I'd inflicted upon people during all the robberies we'd committed'.

In July 1986, she stood trial for conspiracy to rob, and her defence lawyer used the usual argument – she'd been forced to become an armed robber against her will. But the judge didn't believe she was 'a small cog in this operation. You were in fact, the whole machine', and she was sentenced to seven years, of which she served three.

Around a year after her release, her former partner Ron Cook was shot dead in the family home in Plaistow, while on day-release from prison. Linda insisted she was a traumatised bystander, but she was charged with planning a contract killing and hiring a hitman, Danny Reece. The court was told that Danny fired the first shot but 'lost his bottle', so Linda had grabbed the sawn-off shotgun herself. She was sentenced to life, in what she describes as a devastating miscarriage of justice. She later married (and then divorced) Danny Reece, while both were in prison. According to the prosecution, Linda was a 'woman attractive to, and attracted by, armed robbers', while to the press, she was the 'Black Widow', a housewife turned executioner whose lovers ended up dead or in jail.

Her trial and conviction came against the backdrop of yet another 'shock rise' in female violence. Women were moving into 'independent criminal operator status in their own right', noted one criminologist, as if this was a new development, while sociologists attributed the problem to 'greater emancipation'. But as had happened in the 1970s, the actual figures told another story, and the reason the 'gender gap' in crime had narrowed was because male offending rates had gone down.

Yet fears about violent women continued. Teenage girls were out at night drinking 'alcopops like Hooch' and dreaming of being Lara Croft from *Tomb Raider*, the computer game that became a feature film with Angelina Jolie, a casual killer in hotpants.

The late 1990s also saw the emergence of a new female stereotype – the 'ladette'. She was 'boisterous, bolshy, boozy', explained *Vice*, and 'a product of women's increased equality'. Once again, the emancipation of women was posing a serious threat to social order.

Linda Calvey was released from prison in 2009, and ten years later she published her autobiography, *Black Widow*. The book was widely covered by the tabloid press, but the focus was the gangster men she 'rubbed shoulders' with and the 'evil' women she met inside. In July 2019, Linda appeared on ITV's *This Morning*, but there were no questions about her life as an armed robber, and when she attempted to explain why she'd written the book, the presenters, who'd looked at her with open distaste all the way through, cut her off.

Linda Calvey was a 'notorious gangster's moll', explained the *Mail*, who lured and devoured men like a spider. Like the underworld queens before her, Linda's career as an actual criminal took second place – she was not an independent operator but a sexual predator and an appendage to men.

By the early twenty-first century, armed robberies had fallen dramatically. In 1992 there were nearly 850 recorded cases of bank robbery in Britain, by 2011 it was down to sixty-six. The decrease was attributed to increased security, and the fact that crime was moving online. Financial institutions and their customers would now be targeted remotely. 'Modern villains are earning millions without even getting off their sofas,' complained gangster Freddy Foreman. 'The armed robber has been wiped out … You can't walk into an online bank with a shooter, can you?'

But there was another way to rob wealthy bankers, as one twenty-first-century female crook discovered – and that was by operating from the inside, as a trusted employee.

JOYTI DE-LAUREY
QUEEN OF CASH

It's the summer of 2020 and I'm back where I began, heading towards Shoe Lane, the ancient alley in the City of London, on the trail of a female crook. Only this time it's not Moll Cutpurse, the seventeenth-century outlaw, but Joyti De-Laurey, Britain's 'gravest ever female fraudster'.

The world has changed since I first came here eighteen months ago, looking for the site of Mary Frith's Fleet Street brokerage. At the end of March, a nationwide lockdown was imposed in response to the COVID-19 pandemic, and right now the UK has the highest death rate in the world.

The lockdown has largely been lifted in the capital, but for a sunny afternoon in late July the usually busy pavements are empty. The few pedestrians wear masks, eyes anxious as they hurry past, because no one knows what will happen next. This is the first time I've been into the City for four months. Shops have their shutters closed, signs urge social distancing, buses are only a quarter full.

I'm walking east from Aldwych along the Strand, the street where the Queen of the Forty Thieves, Mary Carr, once worked as a flower seller in Victorian times. I pass a deserted Chancery Lane, near where Ann Duck lived on Little White's Alley in the early eighteenth century, and soon I'm on Fleet Street, where Mary Frith ran her brokery, with the spire of St Bride's in the distance.

Her insurance office lay near the corner of Shoe Lane, almost facing Salisbury Court, and today the site is dominated by Peterborough Court. It's a six-storey building, adorned with neoclassical columns and a huge clock that juts out from the third floor, surrounded with gold. Until recently, this was the European headquarters of Goldman Sachs, and it was here that Joyti De-Laurey committed one of the biggest frauds in UK history, stealing £4.3 million from her bosses' bank accounts.

Unlike Mary Frith, Joyti wasn't an underworld leader, but her case did shine a light into another shadowy world, that of investment bankers. Her trial provided the British public with a rare glimpse inside Goldman Sachs, where super-rich 'vultures' had fortunes so huge they didn't even notice when £1 million was missing. 'She betrayed her employers in a way that has shaken the banking world,' explained an ITV news reporter, standing outside Peterborough Court on the day of Joyti's conviction in April 2004.

Viewers were told that the 35-year-old 'smooth-talking' personal assistant 'had a taste for the good life' and had stolen millions to fund her 'craving' for designer clothes and holidays. She envied her employers' lifestyle, explained Detective Constable Malcolm Driscoll, and when one of her employers described her as the 'cash queen', she became the Queen of Cash – or, alternatively, the Queen of Con.

Joyti De-Laurey came from a relatively privileged background. She was born Joyti Schahhou in Hampstead, north London, in 1968. Her mother was a GP in Camden Town, and her father was an accountant. The press provided very little information on her early life, but repeatedly noted that she was Asian – 'a child of Indian parents', who'd moved to England in the 1960s.

Joyti attended a private school – South Hampstead High School – and her childhood was depicted as happy and comfortable. In 1996, she married Tony De-Laurey, who described himself as 'an old-fashioned bloke', and they lived in the Surrey suburb of North Cheam.

Joyti worked in administrative jobs in a series of car showrooms. Then the couple had a son, and set up their own sandwich bar business. When this collapsed and they were left in debt, she signed up with a temping agency and in 1998 she was sent to work at Goldman Sachs. As a temporary secretarial assistant, Joyti was paid £7.50 an hour, but was soon offered a permanent job as a partner's executive assistant. News reports varied as to how much she earned, and they also varied when it came to how much she stole, when she stole it, and what she spent it on.

According to Joyti, it wasn't long before she was 'innocently initiated' into the world of fraud. She alleged that it was 'normal' for secretaries at Goldman Sachs to forge their employers' signatures. If a bill needed to be paid and the boss wasn't around, then the secretary signed in their name. Joyti undertook various transactions on behalf of her employers, including immigration papers, portfolio trades, house purchases and mortgage papers.

She initially worked for Jennifer Moses, a managing director, and was sometimes 'loaned' to Jennifer's husband, Ron Beller. Joyti was on call day and night. She settled the couple's household bills, as well as their personal travel and family holidays, and organised their children's parties.

Staff worked long shifts at Goldman Sachs, often thirteen-hour days, and one former employee described 'the most incredibly driven atmosphere. You become addicted to the adrenaline, to the arrogance and to belonging.' An ex-executive director condemned the work environment as toxic and destructive; the job was 'just about making money'.

A little over a year after starting at Goldman Sachs, Joyti began forging cheques. She wanted to 'find out if I could simply get away with taking money'. She wrote a cheque to herself for £24,200, left the Goldman Sachs offices, went outside into Fleet Street, and deposited the cheque in the Woolwich. 'I went straight back to my desk,' she recalled, 'having bought a sandwich, and acted like nothing had happened. But inside, the adrenaline rush was just phenomenal.'

Joyti didn't touch her account for nearly two months; just like Joan Hannington after her diamond theft from Hatton Garden, she was waiting to see what would happen. When she realised the theft had gone unnoticed, she went to Waterstones and spent £400 on books. Six months later, she wrote another cheque, this time for £48,000. 'It became a bit addictive,' she admitted. 'It was so easy. I got a huge buzz from knowing they had no idea what I was doing.' Taking money from investment bankers made her feel that 'their aura of superiority masked a reality of almost stupidity. I did not steal the money because I needed it, but because I could.'

When Jennifer Moses and her husband left Goldman Sachs, they asked Joyti to join them. But she'd 'had a good run', having now stolen £1.4 million, and it was time to part company. She began working as a PA to another managing director, Scott Mead. He was an American investment banker who'd recently led a £100 billion Vodafone takeover of Mannesmann, the German conglomerate. He featured on the *Sunday Times Rich List* and was said to be worth £120 million. Scott was 'a City star', explained the *Mail*, and 'while he wheeled and dealed', Joyti De-Laurey eventually took £3.3 million from his personal bank account.

She spent the stolen money on property, buying between six and eleven houses in the UK, as well as a fleet of luxury cars. She gave money to friends and family, and according to one report, donated £880,000 to charities. She also spent £300,000 on Cartier jewellery, and splashed out on designer clothes, five-star holidays and flying lessons for her husband, Tony.

According to Joyti, her mother and husband assumed that her newly acquired wealth meant she was 'doing so brilliantly at work that I was being greatly rewarded'. Some of the stolen cash, however, went into accounts or property in their names. As Joyti became bolder, she took bigger sums. She saw herself as 'a fraudster with finesse' and set a personal theft target of US$7 million.

In January 2001, she stole £2.25 million 'in one hit'. By now, she was sending transfer requests by fax, moving money directly from her boss's account into a new account, held in her maiden name, in the Bank of Cyprus. She intended to move to Cyprus with her family and had already bought a seafront villa, ordered a speedboat and put a deposit on an Aston Martin Vanquish.

But in June 2001, Joyti De-Laurey had a scare when her boss's personal money manager arrived unannounced from New York to check the portfolio accounts. No errors were found, and the money manager 'sent me a bouquet of roses' as appreciation for her hard work. The following March, however, Joyti resigned and gave two months' notice. When she made a transfer of £300,000 at the end of April, it would be her last. Scott Mead had decided to make a donation to Harvard, his former college, and when he checked his accounts, he finally realised that money was missing.

At 7.30 a.m. on 2 May 2002, Joyti De-Laurey arrived at her office at Peterborough Court on Fleet Street, where she was confronted by the head of security and questioned for several hours. That evening, police arrived at the family home in Surrey with a search warrant. They found her diary, a series of letters to God in which she begged for 'one more helping of what's mine', and £150,000 worth of Cartier jewellery.

Initially, the police appeared to believe that her husband was behind the scheme. 'The City of London police refused for months to believe that I, as a woman, could have masterminded this amazing theft,' she explained. Instead, detectives were sure it was a 'cartel'.

Joyti confessed, but when the trial began in the spring of 2004, she pleaded not guilty. Her defence argued that she'd believed her employers were fully aware she was taking money. They knew she forged their signatures and it was payment for the additional services she provided. It was 'a reward for being me', and the amounts were 'little more than pocket money' to her bosses. But her employers denied ever having allowed Joyti to sign their signatures. The trial became even more sensational when she claimed she'd taken the £3.3 million from Scott Mead as 'hush money', for covering up his affair with a lawyer at a rival City firm. Scott denied that 'my personal life had anything to do whatsoever with this criminality' and described Joyti De-Laurey as a 'cash queen'.

Like countless female criminals before her, the press portrayed Joyti as naturally duplicitous and incapable of resisting wealth. Her disposition to pilfer was as uncontrollable as an Edwardian lady in a West End bazaar, or a 1920s shopper browsing in a department store. She'd given into 'irresistible temptation', according to her defence, and was 'spellbound' by the displays of wealth among the directors of Goldman Sachs. Joyti was 'intoxicated by the staggering wealth around her', agreed the *Mail*, and 'greedy for material possessions'.

This inability to resist jewels also had racist overtones. Joyti's husband, Tony, told the court he hadn't ever asked where his wife's expensive jewellery had come from. 'He was not bothered because she is an Indian woman,' explained the prosecutor. 'Indian women like jewellery, he said.'

The Indian *Telegraph* took exception to this and queried her background, 'Joyti certainly looks Asian but it is not entirely clear how "Indian" she is. At first, some suspected Joyti was Bengali.'

A spokesperson for Goldman Sachs told the paper they were unable to help. 'We believe she is half-Indian but really I don't know.'

Tony De-Laurey insisted he'd been duped into 'the greedy scheme' and never dreamed their lifestyle was funded through fraud. Joyti 'sneered at her husband' in court, according to the *Mirror*, and branded him financially inept, but 'as he was led away, he kissed her on the cheek'. The paper portrayed Tony as an innocent pawn, taken advantage of by a ruthless, jewellery-loving Indian woman. When he later remarried, the *Mail* pointed out that his new wife was 'slim, blonde, pale-skinned and softly spoken – everything his ex is not'.

In June 2004, Joyti was found guilty of twenty charges of dishonesty and sentenced to seven years in prison. 'She thought she was worth a fortune,' explained an ITV reporter, 'so she simply took it.' Lying was 'woven into the very fabric of her being', according to the judge. She'd lied to colleagues that she had cervical cancer, and during the trial she'd taken a further £16,000 from her mother's building society account. Her mother received a six-month suspended sentence, and her husband eighteen months, both for money laundering.

The case seemed to split public opinion. Joyti described being cheered and clapped on the Tube on the way to Southwark Crown Court. 'Passengers who recognised me from the news would say things like, "Good on you!" and "Serves them right".' A police officer had called her 'a Robin Hood', and she received 'over 700 letters of support' after her conviction. But while some people congratulated her for 'sticking it to the super-rich', journalist and campaigner Julie Bindel noted that 'others were only too keen to put her down – mainly by attacking her appearance'.

As with every other underworld queen, it was what a female crook *looked* like that was most important. The *Mail* described her as 'plump but well-groomed', TV presenter Jonathan Ross asked if she had 'spent all the money on doughnuts', while a panellist on *Have I Got News For You* asked why she hadn't spent the money on liposuction.

Julie Bindel argued that Joyti seemed to have received a rough deal compared with men charged with similar offences. The average sentence for fraud-related crimes of more than £1 million was 3.3 years – Joyti had received more than twice as long. 'I do believe the crime seems almost too audacious for a woman,' she explained, 'and I made two senior male business partners of one of the world's largest merchant banks look like total pricks.' She admitted she deserved some punishment, but added, 'They could afford to lose that money … I am being punished because I dared to take from people like them. That's not the way it's meant to be.'

In the year that Joyti was convicted, only 14 per cent of detected frauds were committed by women, and high-level female fraud remained rare. Yet back in the 1970s, American criminologist Freda Adler had warned that as women entered more areas of the labour force, taking positions in business and finance, they would have far more opportunity to commit crime. From the very few studies that exist, women don't appear to have taken advantage of this – although they are still less likely to be in senior roles. The first woman to become CEO of a major UK bank, Alison Rose, was only appointed at the end of 2019.

Women convicted for high-level white-collar fraud are usually depicted as greedy and overcome with desire. In 1959, Edna Thatcher was sentenced to eight years for forgery and fraud involving around £11,000, equivalent to just over £250,000 today. The press explained she'd turned to crime because her husband was 'unable to satisfy her desire to be surrounded by beautiful things'. The secretary cashier, known to police as 'Edna the Pen', had spent the money 'living high' and on furniture for her luxury flat in Maida Vale, with a television set in each of the seven rooms, a grand piano and a sunken bath. Edna had seven previous convictions, in a career that had already lasted thirty years, forging her boss's signature on cheques and opening bank accounts under a false name. 'She was suffering from a disease,' explained the *Mirror*, 'greed.' Edna was later convicted at the age of 73, for defrauding the Forestry Commission.

It didn't take long before Joyti De-Laurey's crime became the subject of a BBC docudrama, *The Secretary Who Stole £4m*, starring Meera Syal and billed as 'the true story of a wife and mother'. The drama was interspersed with clips from her in-laws, describing her as self-important and power hungry. She was ambitious and manipulative and, unlike her husband, fascinated by wealth.

The BBC drama sparked an animated thread on Mumsnet. 'If you had nicked all that money,' asked one member, 'what would you have bought?' But the replies focused not on a fantasy shopping list, but the financiers of Goldman Sachs. Could people really have so much money 'swimming around' that they hadn't missed 'the odd million here and there'? Goldman Sachs was 'a very strange place'. Perhaps Joyti 'just thought she deserved some of the big bucks too!' Others described the City as sexist, racist and 'class ridden', arguing that it was a victimless crime, and no one suffered 'except perhaps in the ego'.

Joyti's theft from Goldman Sachs has now become part of fraud history. It forms a case study in the Chartered Institute of Management Accountants' *Fraud Risk Management: A Guide to Good Practice*. She also features in *The Successful Frauditor's Casebook*, which implies she was motivated by 'straightforward greed', expresses scepticism about the innocence of 'those closest' to Joyti, and questions whether she's a 'reformed fraudster'.

Joyti was released from prison in 2007, halfway through her seven-year sentence, and moved into a flat 'bought with the proceeds of her crime … during her incredible spending spree', according to the press. She worked for the Royal London Society, a charity for prisoners and ex-offenders, and then became a consultant at Prison Consultants, a private company which offers the services of 'Prison Life Coaches' for people facing prison terms. Joyti also gives talks on issues of compliance in the financial world, explaining how easy it is to steal via bank transfer.

Today, she declines to comment any further on the Goldman Sachs thefts, but at a talk during a counter-fraud conference at the University of Portsmouth in 2014, she appeared confident and relaxed. 'Twelve years on,' she began, 'I'm still somewhat infamous for being the woman who stole the most in the world but got caught.'

The audience appeared captivated by her criminal career. A woman asked if it was true that the City of London Police had uncovered twelve wardrobes of designer clothes and that Joyti had a penchant for designer jewellery and handbags. 'I think that's probably quite true,' she replied. 'I had some money that needed spending.' A man wanted to know the total amount she stole, and on hearing the final sum he was impressed, 'You're wonderful, you really are.'

Joyti didn't express any regret during her talk, although she emphasised that her son had suffered terribly, and that no crime was worth going to prison for. Instead, she laid the blame on the culture of Goldman Sachs, a lack of proper checks and balances, and modern technology which makes it 'easier to take things that aren't yours'.

Joyti disputed the idea that men are more likely to commit fraud, 'In fact, I believe women are more calculating and possibly more devious. We use the power of flirtation and manipulation more easily than men, and we are possibly the more dangerous of the sexes.'

This was certainly how Joyti was portrayed in the press, although it's not clear how flirtation helped in terms of transferring money from a bank account by fax. But according to Joyti, the corporate world is 'only just getting round to the idea that women can be thieves'. Four hundred years after Moll Cutpurse, women are still seen as naturally law abiding, risk averse and less smart than men.

One audience member wanted to know what happened to the millions Joyti stole. Did she lose everything?

'No,' she replied. 'I didn't actually.' The judge decided that if the victims hadn't missed the money, 'he wasn't going to pay for the state to find it'.

It's still not known how much of the £4.3 million was recovered. 'The details remain shrouded in mystery,' writes fraud expert Peter Tickner, although civil actions had already begun before the court case, and by the time of the trial, lawyers had traced about £1.1 million. Jennifer Moses and her husband largely got their money back, he writes, but 'no one knows how much of Scott's £3.3 million was recovered'.

Goldman Sachs is no longer based in Peterborough Court on Fleet Street, and today the building looks deserted. The golden front doors are locked, the windows are dusty and a pile of rubbish has collected outside. The impressive clock that juts out from the third floor has stopped; it's showing the wrong time.

The company's new headquarters, Plumtree Court, lies just up the road on Shoe Lane, where seventeenth-century pickpockets once hid in wait for unsuspecting gentlemen and then took their loot straight to Mary Frith's brokery. There is not a soul about in the alley this afternoon, and the booth where I tried to talk to a security guard eighteen months ago has been abandoned.

Plumtree Court is not hard to miss, however, as it takes up several blocks, although there's no sign announcing who its occupants are. It's ten storeys high, built at a cost of £1 billion and has the largest trading floor in London. The building curves right along Shoe Lane, following the bend in the alley, and I walk along, peering up, but the walls are so shiny it's hard to see in, just a glimpse of unoccupied desks. I think of Ann Duck and the eighteenth-century Black Boy Alley Ladies, who committed at least two assaults in or near this lane. Ann's first appearance at the Old Bailey came after she'd seized hold of a man in Eagle and Child Alley and stolen his moneybag with 35s. The alley itself no longer exists, it lies somewhere beneath the new headquarters of Goldman Sachs.

I return to the front of the building and look down at the entrance, below street level and where a security guard stands, wearing a smart blue suit and a white facemask. 'Cool,' I hear a young, suited man say, as he hurries up to a door with a colleague. 'Let's do it.'

I think of Mary Frith, who took advantage of her position in the Jacobean underworld to make a profit from street theft, highway robbery and burglary. Four centuries later, Joyti De-Laurey took advantage of her insider position to steal millions from investment bankers. Neither woman displayed remorse. Instead, they took responsibility for their crimes and were often admired – and in Joyti's case, there was little sympathy for her victims.

I stand still for a moment, scribbling in my notebook, and when I look down, I'm certain the security guard is watching me. Eventually, I head back along Shoe Lane, and just as I reach the abandoned City of London security booth, I hear footsteps behind. When I turn around, the Goldman Sachs guard has left his post and is walking quickly in my direction.

'Everything OK?' he asks.

I stop, as if caught doing something I shouldn't. 'Yes,' I say. 'Thank you.'

'I saw you walking around,' says the man, 'taking notes.'

'Ah,' I say, wondering if there's any law that prevents me from loitering outside Goldman Sachs. I decide to try and distract him. 'I've been researching a woman called Moll Cutpurse. Have you heard of her?'

'No,' says the security guard. 'Moll who?'

'Moll Cutpurse. Her real name was Mary Frith. She was a famous criminal, and she had a business, just down there on Fleet Street. It's right where the old Goldman Sachs headquarters used to be.' I tell him about Mary Frith's brokery, where pickpockets and highwaymen brought in stolen watches and jewellery, and where those who'd been robbed came looking for their property, which she sold back for a finder's fee.

'Hmm,' says the security guard. 'That's pretty clever.'

He seems to be interested, so I tell him I'm writing a book about female criminals and that many of them operated in this area. 'It's funny,' I say, 'because I started right here on Shoe Lane looking for Moll Cutpurse, and now I'm ending with Joyti De-Laurey, who stole £4.3 million from Goldman Sachs.'

The security guard doesn't react. I've finally said what I was doing outside the new headquarters, but he doesn't acknowledge this at all. It's tricky talking to someone who's wearing a facemask. I can't read his expression – is he smiling or not?

'What was her name again?' he asks.

'Joyti De-Laurey,' I say. 'She stole £4.3 million.' I turn and point back at the shiny new building, 'From Goldman Sachs.'

Again, the security guard doesn't react. 'I meant the woman with the business on Fleet Street.'

'Oh,' I say, 'Moll Cutpurse.'

He takes a scrap of paper from out of his pocket, and writes down her name, 'That's something for me to research on my way back from work this evening,' he says, putting the paper back in his pocket.

'There are other women around here, too,' I tell him. 'If you go right up Shoe Lane, you come to where Ann Duck once worked, she was in the Black Boy Alley Gang. She was put on trial nineteen times, before she was finally convicted.'

'Ann Duck?' asks the security guard. 'I've never heard of her either!' Then he laughs, 'Where did you find these women?'

'They're all over the place,' I tell him, 'once you start looking.'

And it's true, because every age, from at least the 1600s to the present, has had its share of notorious female crooks. They are tucked away in footnotes, passed over in a sentence or two, referred to dismissively in books about male crooks. Their tales have been partly told in trial transcripts and prison records, they appear in sensational newspaper reports written by journalists who embellished and lied. But they are there – the women do exist. Moll Cutpurse wasn't the only 'Queen-Regent of Misrule', but one of the first in a long line of women who chose to pursue a criminal life – and thoroughly enjoyed it.

24

LADY JUSTICE

On the corner of Newgate Street, just a five-minute walk from Shoe Lane, stands one of London's most iconic statues. She's balanced on a dome at the top of the Old Bailey courthouse, some 200ft above the ground, a glorious golden figure with outstretched arms. In one hand she holds a sword, representing authority and punishment, and in the other, the scales of justice, with which to weigh the evidence. Lady Justice, as she's known, is 12ft tall, but she looks very small from the pavement and it's only in photographs that I can see her expression is grim.

The Old Bailey is a fortress-like structure, built on the site of the old Newgate Prison where Mary Frith was once held in the seventeenth century. Its roots as a courthouse go back to the sixteenth century, and it's been the Central Criminal Court of England and Wales since 1834. It is here that some of the most significant female criminals in British history have been put on trial.

Ann Duck was sentenced to death at the Old Bailey in 1744, after assaulting a man near Chick Lane and stealing fourpence. Emily Lawrence was convicted for stealing a diamond locket in 1860 and had to be removed 'shrieking' from the court. Mary Carr, the first Queen of the Forty Thieves, faced charges of kidnapping, while her successors,

Alice Diamond and Maggie Hughes, stood trial for the Johanna Street riot of 1925. Lilian Goldstein, the Bobbed Haired Bandit, sobbed in the dock and convinced the judge she was an innocent woman, while in 1947 burglar Zoe Progl was found guilty of using forged cheques and sent to borstal.

But none of the queens of the underworld were particularly perturbed by their appearance at England's Central Criminal Court. 'The farce was over,' wrote Chris Tchaikovsky, after her conviction for fraud in 1973. 'The little-wigged players had done their bit and the bigger-wigged had done his. I waved goodbye to my friends in the gallery.'

The Old Bailey has passed judgement on female crooks for centuries, yet these women's trials have been forgotten and the courthouse remains best known for its criminal men – thieftaker Jonathan Wild, pearl thief Joseph Grizzard, murderer Dr Crippen, underworld boss Billy Hill, smash-and-grab raider Ruby Spark, gangsters Ronnie and Reggie Kray.

The men have been celebrated in books and guided tours, while the stories of female crooks have been lost. Why? Because the queens of the underworld didn't just break the law. They were everything women were *not* supposed to be. They were active not passive, strong instead of weak, courageous rather than afraid. They were anti-establishment figures, tough and independent, taking risks and defying authority, displaying daring, initiative and nerve.

The underworld queens weren't victims, they had agency and, like Shirley Pitts, they wanted more. They went into men's places – taverns and coffee shops, theatres, streets and pubs – and they did what men did – riding horses, driving getaway cars, setting up businesses, skippering a smuggler's boat. Whether they meant to or not, female criminals redefined what it meant to be a woman.

The queens in this book may have been exceptional, but they tell us about the lives of ordinary women. What our options were, what we were deemed capable of, where we were allowed to go and what we were allowed to wear. Their stories reveal four centuries of fear and hatred of women, because every negative myth, every stereotypical assumption about the 'real' nature of women has been projected onto female criminals. On the one hand, we were an inferior species – too weak, vain and stupid to commit crime. But when we did, then we were immoral monsters – cunning, scheming, deceitful and greedy.

The queens of the underworld committed a wide range of crimes. They were pickpockets, street robbers, jewel thieves and hoisters, motor bandits, shop breakers, smugglers, burglars, fraudsters and armed robbers. But however varied their criminal activities, they were always slotted into one of two roles – 'masculine' women committing 'male' crimes and emulating men, or fascinating temptresses committing 'female' crimes, often against men.

Yet the queens refused to be categorised, and even if they wore men's clothes and did men's things, they defined themselves as women.

There was no one type of underworld queen. They came from different backgrounds and were the products of different times. Their motivations varied. Most committed crime through need, some through anger or a desire for revenge. But there are strong similarities between their lives, and how and why they made a career out of crime. Many were born into poverty and into families with criminal records and a network of associates and were first persuaded to steal as young children. All described themselves – or were described – as rebels from an early age, deliberately rejecting the feminine role. They didn't want to be meek and mild or do what girls were meant to do. Moll Cutpurse was a 'tomrig', who wouldn't hem handkerchiefs, Ann Duck was 'impatient of Restraint', Shirley Pitts was 'always with the boys', Chris Tchaikovsky refused to 'do what was required'.

The queens were often arrested as teenagers, usually for minor thefts such as stealing chocolate or a jumper. Then they joined a criminal gang, stumbled across an 'underworld' den, café or bar, or fell in love with a criminal man. Most tried legitimate work, in low-paid jobs where they were mistreated and demeaned, as maids, flower sellers, laundry women, factory hands and hospital cleaners. But once they had a prison record 'honest' work was hard to find, and they couldn't shake off the stigma of being a 'bad' woman.

The queens often wondered what they could have been, given the right opportunities and encouragement, but their options were limited.

And, anyway, they liked the thrill and adrenaline of crime. They discovered they were good at it. They were successful, and nearly all described the 'buzz'. Crime gave them authority when women were supposed to defer to the authority of men, and it gave them power when female power was seen as dangerous.

Crime was a way for the queens to prove themselves, and to be taken seriously by male crooks who attempted to cheat, beat and control them. Male crooks believed women's place was as decoys or trophy wives, but the queens saw crime as their job, it was an art form, and they took pride in it.

And, just as importantly, they had fun. They called their gangs the Happy Hoisters and the Happy Firm; they enjoyed plotting, planning, and outwitting police. Breaking the law was exciting – and getting away with it was even better. For Zoe Progl and Joan Hannington, crime was 'better than sex'.

A major part of the fun was disguise. Crime was the ultimate masquerade, and the queens were highly skilled performers. Mary Frith became Moll Cutpurse, with her breeches, lute and pipe; Emily Lawrence became a veiled Victorian lady alighting from a carriage; Joan Hannington regarded jewellery stores as stage sets for *Dallas*. The queens were actresses, making use of the roles available to women and then subverting them for the purpose of crime. Some used the disguise of prostitute, others dressed as men.

Appearance was crucial to the pursuit of crime, and it played a central role when the queens were arrested and put on trial. A female crook was always judged by what she looked like. Was she pretty but not too 'alluring'? Had she taken care of her appearance but in a non-'provocative' way? Was she a 6ft Amazon like Alice Diamond or an Eton-cropped rebel like Lady Jack?

The queens were judged along lines of class. Judges frequently found it 'painful' to see a privileged woman in the dock, but had no problem condemning working class women as 'inured to crime and plunder'. The queens were condemned for their sexuality, and discriminated against because they were 'swarthy', 'coloured', Black, Asian or Irish. If a queen had children, then she was also judged as a mother. A male criminal wasn't castigated for heaping suffering on his poor children or giving birth to a new generation of criminals. But a 'lack of maternal affection' had always been proof of a female born criminal, and if a woman admitted her failings and promised to reform, then she was usually treated more sympathetically.

Noreen Harbord insisted that crime was 'no way of life for a woman and mother'; Zoe Progl said much the same. Criminal and mother were mutually exclusive. A woman couldn't be one without rejecting the other. The queens rarely did manage to combine crime with bringing up children, yet many were motivated by the fact that they *were* mothers. They stole to look after their babies, to feed and clothe their children and support the family. They escaped from borstal and prison to be with their children or declared war on the world because they had lost their child.

Some queens pleaded innocence, arguing they'd been led astray by the men they loved, used unwittingly and persuaded against their will. But on the whole, they accepted full responsibility and admitted their guilt. 'If you can't do the time,' declared Chris Tchaikovsky, 'don't do the crime.' And the queens did do their time.

They were all institutionalised, in workhouses and Houses of Mercy, industrial schools, reformatories, borstals and prisons. For 400 years, the forces of law and order attempted to domesticate female criminals, sending them to be trained as servants, and then hoping they'd become obedient wives and mothers. The queens all experienced punishment, confined in leg irons and straitjackets, locked in dark cells, sentenced to transportation and death.

But they refused to be repentant – and when they did apologise, it was rarely convincing. Mary Frith was 'heartely sory' for her dissolute life, and so was Zoe Progl, but having apologised, they went straight back to thieving. Ann Duck 'appear'd but little Penitent', even when facing her own execution, while some refused to apologise at all. 'I have never suffered from qualms of conscience,' wrote American Queen of Crooks, Chicago May. 'I have had no regrets – except when I was caught. I am not really sorry I was a criminal.' Eighty years later, Joan Hannington used similar words, 'I have no conscience about how I lived my life, none whatsoever … I don't regret anything I've ever done.'

The queens of the underworld weren't just law breakers, they taunted police and laughed in the face of arrest, challenged and insulted judges. They refused to stay silent, not even in the hallowed courtroom. Helen Sheen mocked a magistrate as a 'tallow faced fool', Lady Jack threatened a detective sergeant, 'We will get you!' and Queenie Day threw her handbag across the courtroom. When a judge ordered Maggie Hughes to be 'taken down', she once called out, 'You didn't say that when making love to me last night!'

No wonder the press portrayed the queens as subversive figures, twisting facts, inventing motivations and fabricating quotes in their eagerness to sell papers. 'I guess when the newspapers don't know any-thing,' said American Bobbed Haired Bandit, Celia Cooney, 'they just make things up.'

The press has always had a strange relationship with criminal women, and editors and journalists have gone to great lengths to exaggerate their danger. They have given them titles – 'Worst Woman in London', 'Worst Woman in England', 'Terror of Soho', the 'Black Widow'. But they have also belittled them. A daring prison escapee became 'Zippy Zoe', a ruthless, violent gang leader became 'Baby-Faced Maggie'.

Journalists have repeatedly searched for a sexual angle when it comes to criminal women, as have criminologists and detectives, interpreting their actions as motivated by sexual desire and their behaviour as a result of sexual deviancy. The true female born criminal was a 'lustful' savage, according to Cesare Lombroso, and her aim was self-satisfaction.

Press coverage of female crooks has reflected the pervading fears of the time, whether street crime or property theft, motorcars or guns. But mostly it has been fears about women, 'the New Woman', the modern woman, the Women's Liberation Movement, and the women who want to 'ape' men. Female crooks have served as frightening symbols of what might happen if women and men became equal.

Yet women have never committed nearly as much crime as men, and their acts have very rarely been violent. The vast majority of those in prison today have been found guilty of petty offences, just as in

Victorian times, and nearly a third of all female convictions in 2019 were for not having a TV licence. Men and boys still commit 92 per cent of robberies, and account for 95 per cent of the prison population. But every couple of decades, there has been a moral panic that women are becoming more violent, and these fears have been projected onto female crooks.

But however unfairly they have been judged, the queens of the underworld shouldn't be glorified. Their crimes weren't victimless, even though some liked to think they were. People had their pockets picked, their wages and chequebooks stolen, homes and businesses broken into and ransacked. The queens were not crusading feminists – some recruited, exploited or prostituted young girls. They could be racist and they could be violent. People were slashed in the face with knives, glass bottles, tin openers and hatpins, beaten, drugged, threatened with sawn-off shotguns, and at least one was murdered. But while the queens shouldn't be glorified, they also shouldn't be ignored – they need to be taken seriously and re-examined.

Finding out the truth about female crooks, however, is tricky. Most of their stories have been written by men, from the three anonymous authors of Mary Frith's seventeenth-century 'diary', to the tabloid jour-nalists who wrote Noreen Harbord's 'confession' and 'sexed up' Zoe Progl's autobiography. Emily Lawrence's career was fictionalised by a prison governor, Lilian Goldstein exists through the words of male detectives and her former boyfriend.

Some of the queens have written their own stories, especially in modern times, but they have a tendency to embellish, to change names, protect identities and settle scores. They tell us what crimes they com-mitted, but they don't usually say why. 'Autobiographies of crooks are all plot and no theme,' writes Nuala O'Faolain. 'Crooks do things; they don't reflect on them.' Reading a queen's story, even in her own words, often leaves as many questions as answers.

I leave the corner of Newgate Street, bid goodbye to Lady Justice with her sword and scales of justice, and head back to Fleet Street to get a bus home. I think about how, when I first started looking for female crooks, I didn't know where I would find them, and sometimes I wasn't even sure that I would. But now I seem to come across new clues all the time. Who was 'Foxy', for example, who ran a mob of post-war thieves from her headquarters in a Soho cellar club? Or 'Pauline', the brains of a gang of male criminals in the 1930s? Or the 'Jelly-babe', who blew up safes with gelignite gangs in the 1950s?

New material about underworld queens is becoming available online all the time but, as usual, not all of it is true. I recently found a photo of Queenie Day in the *Mirror*, smiling and waving from the window of her flat opposite Holloway Prison, shortly before she was jailed as the Terror of Soho. Two days earlier, the *Mirror* had also published a photo of Elsie Florence Carey on its front page, but her niece Linda Sansum doesn't believe it is her at all.

Some of the queens are now being rediscovered, and their stories will be told on stage and screen. But the fictional character of the female criminal remains unusual, appearing mainly in psychological thrillers. Women are liars and psychopaths, but we are not professional crooks. Yet there are plenty of real-life professionals to draw on.

The ones in this book operated largely in London, but every city has its own tradition of underworld queens. And these are just the ones who got caught – who left behind a record of their arrest, trials and punishment – so what about the really successful female crooks? What about all of the queens of the underworld who got away?

SOURCES

The main sources available on each queen are listed below, with a brief selection of newspaper articles. Records can be found at the National Archives (TNA), but some are only available through Freedom of Information Requests; at the London Metropolitan Archives (LMA), City of London; and in the HM Prison Holloway Collection, CLA/003, some of which are restricted access. Many records appear under aliases too numerous to list.

Other sources include birth and death certificates, census records, wills, electoral rolls, marriage certificates, the 1939 register, baptism records, deed poll and probate records.

Brian McDonald's *Alice Diamond and the Forty Elephants: The Female Gang that Terrorised London* (Milo Books, 2015) is an invaluable resource on the Forty Thieves, the Forty Elephants and their contemporaries, and provided information for several chapters in this book.

USEFUL WEBSITES

Ancestry: www.ancestry.co.uk – Licences of Parole for Female Convicts, 1853–71, 1883–87; Criminal Registers, 1791–1892
The British Newspaper Archive: www.britishnewspaperarchive.co.uk
British Pathé: www.britishpathe.com

Capital Punishment UK: www.capitalpunishmentuk.org

The Dictionary of Victorian London: www.victorianlondon.org

The Digital Panopticon: www.digitalpanopticon.org

Find My Past: www.findmypast.co.uk – England & Wales, Crime, Prisons & Punishment, 1770–1935

Newgate Calendar: www.exclassics.com/newgate/ngintro.htm

The Proceedings of the Old Bailey, 1674–1913: www.oldbaileyonline.org

The Victorian Web: www.victorianweb.org

CHAPTER 1 – MARY FRITH: JACOBEAN PICKPOCKET AND FENCE

Ackroyd, Peter, *Queer City: Gay London from the Romans to the Present Day* (Chatto & Windus, 2017).

Andrews, Charles, 'Moll Cutpurse, Thief and Receiver' in *Lives of Twelve Bad Women*, edited by Arthur Vincent (T. Fisher Unwin, 1897).

Bennett, Judith M. and McSheffrey, Shannon, 'Early, Erotic and Alien: Women Dressed as Men in Late Medieval London', *History Workshop Journal*, Vol. 77 (2014).

Brandon, David, *Stand and Deliver! A History of Highway Robbery* (The History Press, 2001).

Bucholz, Robert and Key, Newton, *Early Modern England 1485–1714: A Narrative History* (Wiley-Blackwell, 2009).

Drouet, Pascale, 'Appropriating a Famous Female Offender: Mary Frith (1584?–1659), alias Moll Cutpurse' in *Female Transgression in Early Modern Britain*, edited by Richard Hillman and Pauline Ruberry-Blanc (Routledge, 2016).

Exploring the Character of Moll Cutpurse, Royal Shakespeare Company, www.youtube.com/watch?v=ZWVHRSxw8ds

Forsyth, Hazel, *London's Lost Jewels: The Cheapside Hoard* (Philip Wilson Publishers, 2013).

Frith, Mary, *The Life and Death of Mrs. Mary Frith Commonly Called Mal Cutpurse* (London, 1662).

Griffiths, Paul, 'Frith, Mary', *Oxford Dictionary of National Biography* (Oxford University Press, 2015).

Howard, Jean H., 'Cross-Dressing, the Theatre, and Gender Struggle in Early Modern England', *Shakespeare Quarterly*, Vol. 39, No. 4 (Winter, 1988).

The Lesbian Historical Motif Podcast, Episode 26d, 'Moll Cutpurse', September 2018, thelesbiantalkshow.podbean.com/e/episode-26d-moll-cutpurse

Rees, Sian, *Moll: The Life and Times of Moll Flanders* (Chatto & Windus, 2011).

Rietz, John, 'Criminal Ms-representation: 'Moll Flanders and Female Criminal Biography', *Studies in the Novel*, Vol. 23, No. 2 (The Johns Hopkins University Press, 1991) www.jstor.org/stable/29532777?seq=1

Todd, Janet and Elizabeth Spearing, *Counterfeit Ladies: The Life and Death of Mary Frith, The Case of Mary Carleton* (William Pickering, 1994).

Ungerer, Gustav, 'Mary Frith, Alias Moll Cutpurse, in Life and Literature', *Shakespeare Studies , Vol. 28* (Associated University Presses, 2000).

Whibley, Charles, *A Book of Scoundrels* (London, 1897).

CHAPTER 2 – ANN DUCK: EIGHTEENTH-CENTURY STREET ROBBER AND CHAPTER 3 – A CONSCIOUS MISTRESS OF CRIME

Ann Duck's trials and confession can be found in *The Proceedings of the Old Bailey*, 1674–1913.

Rictor Norton provides a wealth of information in *The Georgian Underworld* (rictornorton.co.uk/guoo.htm) and *Georgian Life & Literature* (www.rictornorton.uk) and grubstreet.rictornorton.co.uk

Bulkeley, J. and J. Cummins, *A Voyage to the South Seas, in the Years 1740–1741* (R. Walker, 1745).

Brand, Emily, *The Fall of the House of Byron* (John Murray, 2020).

A Catalogue of Jilts, Cracks, Prostitutes, Night-walkers, Whores, She-friends, Kind Women, and Others of the Linnen-lifting Tribe, who are to be seen every Night in the Cloysters in Smithfield, from the hours of Eight to Eleven, during the time of the FAIR, viz. (London, 1691).

Chater, Kathleen, 'Duck, Ann', *Oxford Dictionary of National Biography* (Oxford University Press, 2010).

Chater, Kathleen, *Untold Histories: Black People in England and Wales During the Period of the British Slave Trade, c.1660–1807* (Manchester University Press, 2011).

Hitchcock, Tim, *London Lives* (Cambridge University Press, 2015).

Ipswich Journal, 17 August 1743.

Kaufmann, Miranda, *Black Tudors: The Untold Story* (Oneworld Publications, 2018).

Linebaugh, Peter, *The London Hanged: Crime and Civil Society in the Eighteenth Century* (Verso, 2003).

Locating London's Past, www.locatinglondon.org

London Evening Post, 18–20 October 1744.

London Lives 1690 to 1800: Crime, Poverty and Social Policy in the Metropolis, www.londonlives.org/

Sharpe, James A., *Crime in Early Modern England 1550–1750* (Routledge, 1998).

The Stamford Mercury, 8 November 1744.

Ward, Richard, 'Print Culture, Moral Panic, and the Administration of the Law: The London Crime Wave of 1744', *Crime, History & Societies*, Vol. 16, No. 1 (2012), JSTOR, www.jstor.org/stable/42708849

White, Jerry, *London in the Eighteenth Century: A Great and Monstrous Thing* (Bodley Head, 2012).

CHAPTER 4 – LADIES GO A-THIEVING

Records relating to Phoebe Price and Sarah Rockley can be found at TNA, HO 10/2, and discovery.nationalarchives.gov.uk/details/r/

C3083364; convictrecords.com.au/ships/mary-anne/1815; www.jen-willetts.com/convict_ship_mary_anne_1816.htm

Abelson, Elaine S., *When Ladies Go A-Thieving: Middle-Class Shoplifters in the Victorian Department Store* (Oxford University Press, 1998).

Burnette, Joyce, 'Women Workers in the British Industrial Revolution' (Wabash College) eh.net/encyclopedia/women-workers-in-the-british-industrial-revolution

Butler, Alice, *Stealing Desire*, www.freud.org.uk/2019/01/29/stealing-desire

Cameron, Ann Michaela, 'The Factory Above the Gaol: Australia's First Female Factory' in *Female Factory Online* (2018), femalefactory-online.org/about/history/the-factory-above-the-gaol

Camhi, Leslie, 'Stealing Femininity: Department Store Kleptomania as Sexual Disorder' in *Differences: A Journal of Feminist Cultural Studies*, Vol. 5, No. 1 (Duke University Press, 1993).

Cressy, David, 'Rough Roads for Travellers and Gypsies', *History Today*, Vol. 70, Issue 3 (March 2020).

'Extraordinary Instance of Female Depravity', *Chester Chronicle*, 16 September 1814.

Head, Richard, *The Canting Academy or The Devils Cabinet Opened* (London, 1673).

Holmes, David Cooper, *Who was Ann Gregg?* (P3 Publications, 2019).

Storey, Neil R., *The Victorian Criminal* (Shire Library, 2011).

Tickell, Shelley, *Shoplifting in Eighteenth-Century London* (The Boydell Press, 2018).

Whitlock, Tammy, 'Gender, Medicine and Consumer Culture in Victorian England: Creating the Kleptomaniac', *Albion: A Quarterly Journal Concerned with British Studies*, Vol. 31, No. 3 (Autumn, 1999), www.jstor.org/stable/4052958?seq=1

Wilkes, Sue, 'A (Working) Woman's Place', *History Today* Vol. 67, Issue 6 (May 2017), www.historytoday.com/working-woman%E2%80%99s-place

Williams, Lucy and Barry Godfrey, *Criminal Women 1850–1920* (Pen & Sword, 2018).

Vickery, Amanda, *Voices from the Old Bailey* (BBC Radio 4, 2014).

CHAPTER 5 – EMILY LAWRENCE: VICTORIAN JEWEL THIEF

Emily Lawrence's prison and criminal records can be found on
  Ancestry and Find My Past, and her 1860 trial in *The Proceedings of
  the Old Bailey.* Annie Grant's records can be found on Find My Past.

'Daring theft at Christie's', *Daily Mirror*, 30 June 1905.
'The Great Jewel Robbery', *Illustrated London News*, 16 June 1860.
Griffiths, Arthur, *Mysteries of Police and Crime, a General Survey of
  Wrongdoing and its Pursuit, Vol. 1* (Cassell and Company, London,
  1899).
Griffiths, Arthur, *A Prison Princess: A Romance of Millbank
  Penitentiary* (London, 1893).
'Impudent Jewellery Robbery and Capture of the Thieves', *Brighton
  Guardian*, 3 August 1864.
Lyons, Sophie, *Queen of the Underworld* (Combustion Books, 2013),
  originally published as *Why Crime Does Not Pay* (J.S. Ogilvie
  Publishing, 1913).
'The Necklace Theft at Christie's', *Morning Post*, 26 July 1905.
Summerscale, Kate, *The Suspicions of Mr. Whicher or The Murder at
  Road Hill House* (Bloomsbury, 2009).

CHAPTER 6 – MARY CARR: QUEEN OF THE FORTY THIEVES

Records relating to Mary Carr can be found on Ancestry, and her 1896
  trial in *The Proceedings of the Old Bailey.* Papers relating to Minnie
  Duggan and Helen Sheen can be found at TNA, HO 140/186,
  HO 140/242, HO 140/234, HO 140/250, HO 140/266, and MEPO
  6/20. Records for Chicago May are on Find My Past.

Aston, Elaine and Ian Clarke, 'The Dangerous Woman of Melvillean Melodrama', *New Theatre Quarterly*, Vol. 12, Issue 45 (Cambridge University Press, 1996).

'Beware of Pickpockets – and Others', *The Tatler*, 15 April 1908.

Binny, John, 'Thieves and Swindlers' in *London Labour and the London Poor*, Vol. IV (Henry Mayhew, 1865).

'The Flower-Sellers of the Street', *Pall Mall Gazette*, 5 June 1885.

'The "Lady", the Safe, and the Funeral', *Globe*, 7 May 1906.

Mumm, Susan, '"Not Worse than Other Girls": The Convent-Based Rehabilitation of Fallen Women in Victorian Britain', *Journal of Social History*, Vol. 29, No. 3 (Oxford University Press, Spring 1996) www.jstor.org/stable/3788944?seq=1

Nokes, Harriet, *Twenty-Three Years in a House of Mercy* (Rivingtons, 1886).

O'Faolain, Nuala, *The Story of Chicago May* (Michael Joseph, 2005).

'Old Tallow-Face!', *South London Chronicle*, 25 May 1906.

'Polly's Prison Home', *Fort Wayne Sentinel*, 1 June 1896.

'The Queen of the Forty Thieves', *Western Times*, 26 March 1896.

Rubenhold, Hallie, *The Five: The Untold Lives of the Women Killed by Jack the Ripper* (Doubleday, 2019).

Sharpe, May Churchill, *Chicago May: Her Story* (Macaulay Company, 1928).

'Shop Thieves', *Dundee Courier*, 23 September 1905.

'The Strange Story of Child Stealing', *Lloyd's Weekly Newspaper*, 8 March 1896.

CHAPTER 7 – ALICE DIAMOND AND MAGGIE HUGHES: THE FORTY ELEPHANTS

Records on Alice Diamond and Maggie Hughes can be found at TNA, MEPO 6, HO 140/3971, HO 140/477, PCOM 6/28, HO 140/361, HO 140/367, HO 140/379, HO 140/421, and HO 140/397.

Benedetta, Mary, *The Street Markets of London* (John Miles, 1936).

'Outwitting the Wily Shoplifter', *Dundee Evening Telegraph*, 15 July 1927.

Parr, Eric, *Grafters All: A Guide to the Art of Robbery* (Max Reinhardt, 1964).

'Queen of the Forty Thieves and her Gang Broken Up', *Illustrated Police News*, 25 March 1926.

'Two Shoplifter Queens', *The People*, 21 March 1926.

CHAPTER 8 – LADY JACK: SHOP BREAKER

Records on Elsie Carey can be found at the TNA, HO 140/464, and at the LMA, CLA/003/PR/02/019, CLA/003/PR/02/021, and CLA/003/PR/02/023 (all restricted access).

Ashton-Wolfe, Harry, *The Underworld* (Hurst & Blackett, 1926).

Collis, Rose, *Colonel Barker's Monstrous Regiment: A Tale of Female Husbandry* (Virago, 2002).

'Gang Queen Calls Up Home', *Daily Mirror*, 25 October 1937.

'"GOOD LUCK BERT" Says Blonde Bandit TO BOYFRIEND IN DOCK', *Mirror* (Perth), 26 March 1938.

'Head of a Gang of Thieves', *Illustrated Police News*, 13 September 1934.

Houlbrook, Matt, 'Commodifying the Self Within: Ghosts, Libels, and the Crook Life Story in Inter-War Britain', *The Journal of Modern History*, Vol. 85, No. 2 (June 2013).

Houlbrook, Matt, *The Trickster Prince*, tricksterprince.wordpress.com/

'Lady Jack goes to Gaol', *Uxbridge Gazette*, 29 October 1937.

Lucas, Netley, *Crook Janes: A Study of the Woman Criminal the World Over* (Stanley Paul, 1926).

Lucas, Netley, *London and its Criminals* (Williams & Norgate, 1926).

Masson, Sophie, *Harry Ashton-Wolfe: True-Crime Writer of 'The Golden Age'* (2016) firebirdfeathers.com/2016/09/12/harry-ashton-wolfe-true-crime-writer-of-the-golden-age/

Norton, Rictor, 'Cross-Dressing', *Gay History & Literature*, rictornor-ton.co.uk/though17.htm

'We Will Get You', *The Illustrated Police News*, 30 January 1936.

'A Woman Who Murdered a Child Became My Friend!', *Sunday Pictorial*, 16 April 1939.

CHAPTER 9 – QUEENIE DAY: THE TERROR OF SOHO

Records relating to Queenie Day can be found at the TNA, HO 140/481, HO 140/469, MEPO 6/42, CRIM 1/1170 and CRIM 1/1144, and at the LMA, CLA/003/PR/02/013 (open access) and CLA/003/PR/02/023 (restricted access).

'Charge of Housebreaking', *Ealing Gazette*, 21 September 1918.

'Coloured Women Lash Out', *Thanet Advertiser*, 6 August 1937.

'Girl Housebreaker', *West Middlesex Gazette*, 17 June 1922.

Higginbotham, Peter, 'Approved Schools', *Children's Homes*, www.childrenshomes.org.uk/AS/

'Missed the Train', *Thanet Advertiser*, 10 August 1937.

'Sent to Borstal Institution for Three Years', *Ealing Gazette*, 17 June 1922.

Slater, Stefan, 'Containment: Managing Street Prostitution in London, 1918–1959', *Journal of British Studies*, Vol. 49, No. 2 (Cambridge University Press, April 2010) www.jstor.org/stable/23265205

Slater, Stefan, 'Prostitutes and Popular History: Notes on the "Underworld", 1918–1939', *Crime, History & Societies*, doi.org/10.4000/chs.689

'Woman's Rage in Police Court', *Birmingham Gazette*, 26 October 1928.

'"Worst Woman" Joins Friend in Gaol', *Daily Mirror*, 14 January 1938.

CHAPTER 11 – LILIAN GOLDSTEIN: SMASH-AND-GRAB RAIDER

Papers relating to Lilian Goldstein's 1940 trial can be found at the TNA, CRIM 1/1215 and MEPO 3/659. Elizabeth Murray's record can be found in MEPO 6.

Arnold, Catharine, *Underworld London: Crime and Punishment in the Capital City* (Simon & Schuster, 2012).

Brown, Alyson, 'The interwar 'motor bandit' – and what it tells us about the fear of new technology', *The Conversation*, theconversation.com/the-interwar-motor-bandit-and-what-it-tells-us-about-the-fear-of-new-technology-80988

Brown, Alyson, 'The Bobbed-Haired Bandit and the Smash-and-Grab Raider' in *Fair and Unfair Trials in the British Isles, 1800–1940: Microhistories of Justice and Injustice*, edited by Anne-Marie Kilday and David Nash (Bloomsbury, 2020).

Brown, Alyson, 'Britain's Bonnie and Clyde', *History Extra* (December 2017).

Campbell, Duncan, 'Whatever Happened to Gangsters' Molls?', *The Oldie* (October 2019).

Clarsen, Georgine, '"The Woman Who Does": A Melbourne Motor Garage Proprietor' in *Sapphic Modernities: Sexuality, Women and National Culture*, edited by Laura L. Doan and Jane Garrity (AIAA, 2007).

'I Confess: I Was the Bobbed Bandit!', *Sunday Pictorial*, 25 February 1940.

Dodson, Gerald, *Consider Your Verdict: The Memoirs of Sir Gerald Dodson Recorder of London, 1937–1959* (Hutchinson, 1967).

Mattson, Andrew and Stephen Duncombe, *The Bobbed Haired Bandit: A True Story of Crime and Celebrity in 1920s New York* (NYU Press, 2006).

'A Perfect Beast', *Illustrated Police News*, 22 July 1920.

'Romance of Blonde Alice', *Belfast Telegraph*, 24 November 1923.

Sharpe, Frederick Dew, *Sharpe of the Flying Squad* (John Long, 1938).

'Smash and Grab?', *The People*, 30 July 1961.

CHAPTER 12 - THE FORTY ELEPHANTS BAR

'Crime: Government to Tackle Problem of Shoplifting', *British Pathé* (1938), www.britishpathe.com/

Green, Nicola, 'Great Scotland Yard: Bob Haired Bandit', *Nicola Green*, www.nicolagreen.com/great-scotland-yard

CHAPTER 13 - NOREEN HARBORD: QUEEN OF THE CONTRABAND COAST

Noreen Harbord's criminal record can be found at the TNA, HO 140/543.

Bray, Roger and Vladimir Raitz, *Flight to the Sun* (Cengage Learning, 2001).

'Cars in Books', *MotorSport Magazine* (May 1973), www.motorsport-magazine.com/archive/article/may-1973/57/cars-books-may-1973

De Ruvigny's Roll of Honour 1914–1918.

'Former Debutante Confesses: I was the Queen of the Smugglers', *The People*, 20 April 1952.

'Getting Married', *The Bystander*, 25 September 1935.

Gosling, Lucinda, *Debutantes and the London Season* (Shire Publications, 2013).

'Mrs. Harbord: "International Boy Friends"', *Daily Mirror*, 14 December 1950.

Pollak, Otto, *The Criminality of Women* (University of Pennsylvania Press, 1950).

Sillitoe, Alan, *Life Without Armour: An Autobiography* (Robson Books, 2004).

'Watch Queen Jailed', *Daily Herald*, 15 December 1950.

'The Women Who Go To Jail', *Britannia and Eve*, 1 February 1953.

CHAPTER 14 - ZOE PROGL: NO. 1 WOMAN BURGLAR AND CHAPTER 15 - THE GREAT ESCAPE

Zoe Progl's prison records can be found at the LMA, CLA/003/ PR/02/037 and CLA/003/AD/01/002 (both restricted access), and at the TNA, CRIM 9/93.

Borstal Allocation Book, 194?–195?, LMA, CLA/003/HB/02/001 (restricted access).
'Escaper Zoe Wins Back Ring', *Daily Mirror*, 3 January 1962.
'I Found Zoe in Bed', *Daily Mirror*, 10 September 1960.
Kirby, Dick, *London Gangs at War* (Pen & Sword Books, 2017).
Progl, Zoe, *Woman of the Underworld* (Arthur Barker, 1964).
'Watch at Ports for Blonde Zippy Zoe', *Liverpool Echo*, 25 July 1960.
'Welfare of Illegitimate Children', *Hansard*, February 1967, Vol. 280.

CHAPTER 16 - SHIRLEY PITTS: QUEEN OF THE SHOPLIFTERS AND CHAPTER 17 - THE CRIMINAL MASQUERADE

'Blonde on Run Caught in Flat', *Daily Herald*, 17 August 1954.
Campbell, Duncan, 'At Funerals Old-School Gangsters Still Say it with Flowers', *The Guardian*, 9 October 2012.
Campbell, Duncan, 'The Luck of the Drawers', *The Guardian*, March 1995.
'Can Baby Reform This Girl?' *The People*, 5 September 1954.
Centre for Retail Research, www.retailresearch.org/
Design Against Crime, www.designagainstcrime.com/
Farry, Kim and Katherine Jackson, *My Money Tree: The Life of Kim Farry, the 'Million Pound Shoplifter'* (Self-Published, 2019).
Gamman, Lorraine, *Gone Shopping: The Story of Shirley Pitts – Queen of Thieves* (Bloomsbury, 2013).

Kray, Reg and Ron Kray, with Fred Dinenage, *Our Story: London's Most Notorious Gangsters, in their Own Words* (Pan, 2015).

'The Theft Trail of the Happy Hoisters', *Daily Mirror*, 22 February 1958.

Wisbey, Marilyn, *Gangster's Moll* (Little Brown & Company, 2001).

CHAPTER 18 - LIBERATION OF THE FEMALE CRIMINAL

Adler, Freda, *Sisters in Crime: The Rise of the New Female Criminal* (McGraw Hill, 1975).

Borrell, Clive and Brian Cashinella, *Crime in Britain Today* (Routledge & Kegan Paul, 1975).

'Gun-Girl Siege Drama', *Daily Mirror*, 12 June 1965.

Klein, Dorie, 'The Etiology of Female Crime: A Review of the Literature', *Issues in Criminology*, Vol. 8, No. 2 (Autumn 1973).

Smart, Carol, *Women, Crime and Criminology: A Feminist Critique* (Routledge & Kegan Paul, 1977).

'Vanity of the Gun-Siege Girl', *Daily Mirror*, 20 July 1965.

CHAPTER 19 - CHRIS TCHAIKOVSKY: QUEEN OF CHARISMA AND CHAPTER 20 - LOOKING FOR TROUBLE

Records relating to Chris Tchaikovsky's 1973 trial can be found at the TNA, J 268 and J336.

Bardsley, Barney, *Flowers in Hell: An Investigation into Women and Crime* (Pandora, 1987).

Benn, Melissa, 'Women in Prison … Breaking the Silence', *Spare Rib* (December 1983).

Carlen, Pat, 'Criminal Women: Myths, Metaphors and Misogyny', *Criminal Women : Some Autobiographical Accounts*, edited by Pat Carlen (Polity Press, 1985).

Carlen, Pat, *Women in Prison: The Early Years*, www.womeninprison. org.uk/media/downloads/wip-early-years-pat-carlen-1.pdf

Eaton, Mary, 'Chris Tchaikovsky, Director of Women in Prison, talks to Mary Eaton', *Criminal Justice Matters*, Vol. 38, Issue 1 (Winter 1999), doi.org/10.1080/09627259908552807

Gilbey, Ryan, 'Kink, Drink and Liberty: A Queer History of King's Cross in the '80s', *The Guardian*, 2017.

Hicks, Jenny, 'In a Criminal Business', *Criminal Women : Some Autobiographical Accounts*, edited by Pat Carlen (Polity Press, 1985).

'The Other Tchaikovsky', *Prison Radio* prison.radio/ the-other-tchaikovsky-on-bbc-radio-4/

'Our Story', *Women in Prison*, www.womeninprison.org.uk/about/our-story

Roberts, Yvonne, 'Chris Tchaikovsky Obituary', *The Guardian*, 24 May 2002.

Tchaikovsky, Chris, 'Looking for Trouble', *Criminal Women : Some Autobiographical Accounts*, edited by Pat Carlen (Polity Press, 1985).

CHAPTER 21 - JOAN HANNINGTON: DIAMOND THIEF

Caden, Sarah, 'I Am What I Am, Babe, a Diamond Geezer', *Sunday Independent* (Dublin), 4 July 2004.

Hannington, Joan, *I Am What I Am: The True Story of Britain's Most Notorious Jewel Thief* (Headline, 2002).

Hard Bastards (Meridian, 2002), British Film Institute, BFI identifier: 644033.

Hickman, J. Mary, 'Reconstructing Deconstructing "Race": British Political Discourses about the Irish in Britain', *Ethnic and Racial Studies*, Vol. 21, No. 2 (March 1998).

Murphy, Sean, 'Fleecer', *Sunday World* (Dublin), 18 April 2004.

CHAPTER 22 – GANGSTERS' MOLLS

Calvey, Linda, *The Black Widow* (Mirror Books, 2019).

Clancy, Ray, 'Black Widow Who Executed her Lover is Jailed for Life', *The Times*, 13 November 1991.

'Has the Curse of the Black Widow Struck Again?', *Daily Mail*, 6 September 2015.

Kray, Kate and Chester Stern, *The Black Widow: The Life and Crimes of Linda Calvey* (Headline, 2002).

La Plante, Lynda, *Widows* (Zaffre, 2018).

Thompson, Barney, 'Hatton Garden Gang a Throwback to Britain's Criminal Past', *Financial Times*, 15 January 2016.

CHAPTER 23 – JOYTI DE-LAUREY: QUEEN OF CASH

Blindel, Julie, 'The High Price of Robbing the Rich', *The Guardian*, 17 September 2005.

Croall, Hazel, 'Men's Business? Some Gender Questions About White Collar Crime', *Criminal Justice Matters*, Vol. 53, Issue 1 (Autumn 2003), www.crimeandjustice.org.uk/publications/cjm/article/mens-business-some-gender-questions-about-white-collar-crime

Fraud Risk Management: A Guide to Good Practice (Chartered Institute of Management Accountants, 2008).

Giles, Steve (ed.), *Managing Fraud Risk: A Practical Guide for Directors and Managers* (John Wiley & Sons, 2012).

Roy, Amit, 'Indian "Weakness" Link in Fraud – Secretary Siphons £4,404,678 from Goldman Sachs Bosses', *Telegraph India*, 24 April 2004.

'Secretary Stole £4.4 million', *Daily Mail*, 21 April 2004.

'Seven Years for Secretary Who Stole £4.5 million from Bosses', *The Telegraph*, 14 June 2004.

Smith, Greg, 'Why I Am Leaving Goldman Sachs', *The New York Times*, 14 March 2012.

Sorkin, Ross Andrew, 'Ex-Secretary Guilty of Embezzling $7 Million', *New York Times*, 21 April 2004.

'Tales of Temptation: White Collar Crime Does Not Pay', Q&A with Joyti Schahhou-Waswani and Steve Dagworthy, LSUSE Penal Reform Society, beaveronline.atavist.com/tales-of-temptation-white-collar-crime-does-not-pay

Tickner, Peter, *The Successful Frauditor's Casebook* (John Wiley & Sons, 2012).

Waswani, Joyti, 'The "Picasso" of Con Artists', Counter Fraud & Forensic Accounting Conference (2014), Portsmouth Business School, upstream.port.ac.uk/web/showvid.php?id=9b509126-d0c4-427b-8d99-b81d07b92166&_ga=2.199996654.1157210393.1593508633-895255814.1593508632

CHAPTER 24 - LADY JUSTICE

Beard, Mary, *Women & Power* (Profile, 2017).

Speel, Bob, 'Justice Statue, Old Bailey', www.speel.me.uk/sculptlondon/oldbaileyjustice.htm

Ministry of Justice, 'Women and the Criminal Justice System 2019', (26 November 2020), www.gov.uk/government/statistics/women-and-the-criminal-justice-system-2019

SELECT BIBLIOGRAPHY

Bingham, Adrian and Martin Conboy, *Tabloid Century: The Popular Press in Britain, 1896 to the Present* (Peter Lang Ltd, 2015).

Capstick, John, *Given in Evidence* (John Long, 1960).

Carlen, Pat, *Criminal Women* (Polity Press, 1985).

Cox, Pamela, *Bad Girls in Britain: Gender, Justice and Welfare, 1900–1950* (Palgrave Macmillan, 2013).

Darby, Nell, 'The Female of the Species' (2018), www.criminalhistorian.com/the-female-of-the-species/

Davies, Caitlin, *Bad Girls: A History of Rebels and Renegades* (John Murray, 2019).

Donaldson, William, *Brewer's Rogues, Villains, Eccentrics* (Cassell, 2002).

Emsley, Clive, *Crime and Society in England 1750–1900* (Routledge, 2018).

Emsley, Clive, *The Great British Bobby: A History of British Policing from 1829 to the Present* (Quercus Publishing, 2010).

Felstead, Sydney, *The Underworld of London* (1923).

Flanders, Judith, 'The Creation of the Police and the Rise of Detective Fiction', *British Library* (2014), www.bl.uk/romantics-and-victorians/articles/the-creation-of-the-police-and-the-rise-of-detective-fiction#

Foreman, Freddie, *The Godfather of British Crime* (John Blake, 2018).

Fraser, Frankie, *Mad Frank and Friends* (Little, Brown and Company, 1998).

Fryer, Peter, *Staying Power: The History of Black People in Britain* (Pluto Press, 2018).

Gosling, John, *The Ghost Squad* (Odhams, 1959).

Gosling, John, 'Women of the Underworld', *Sunday Mirror*, 18 February 1962.

Hill, Billy, *Boss of Britain's Underworld* (Billy Hill Family Limited, 2008).

Holloway, Gerry, *Women and Work in Britain Since 1840* (Routledge, 2005).

Horler, Sydney, *London's Underworld: The Record of a Month's Sojourn in the Crime Centres of the Metropolis* (Hutchinson, 1934).

Horn, Pamela, *Behind the Counter: Shop Lives from Market Stall to Supermarket* (Sutton Publishing, 2006).

Jenkins, Simon, *A Short History of London: The Creation of a World Capital* (Viking, 2019).

Kirby, Dick, 'The Real Sweeney', *The Express*, 8 October 2009.

Knight, Charles, *Knight's Cyclopædia of London* (London, 1851).

Lacey, Nicola, *Women, Crime and Character in Twentieth Century Law and Literature: In Search of the Modern Moll Flanders* (LSE Law, Society and Economy Working Papers, 20/2017).

Laite, Julia, 'Paying the Price Again: Prostitution Policy in Historical Perspective', *History & Policy*, www.historyandpolicy.org/policy-papers/papers/paying-the-price-again-prostitution-policy-in-historical-perspective

Lombroso, Cesare, and Guglielmo Ferrero, *Criminal Woman: The Prostitute and the Normal Woman* (Duke University Press, 2004).

Mayhew, Henry, *London Labour and the London Poor* (1865).

Mayhew, Henry and Others, *The London Underworld in the Victorian Period* (Dover Publications, 2019).

Mayhew, Henry and John Binny, *The Criminal Prisons of London and Scenes of London Life* (1862).

Meier, William M., 'Going on the Hoist: Women, Work, and Shoplifting in London, c. 1890–1940', *Journal of British Studies*, Vol. 50, No. 2 (April 2011), www.jstor.org/stable/23265318?seq=1

Murphy, Robert, *Smash and Grab: Gangsters in the London Underworld 1920–60* (Faber & Faber, 1993).

Morton, James, *East End Gangland* (Sphere, 2001).

Morton, James, *Gangland: The Early Years*, (Time Warner, 2003).

Morton, James, *Gangland: London's Underworld* (Little Brown, 1992).

Olusoga, David, *Black and British: A Forgotten History* (Pan, 2017).

Thomas, William I., *The Unadjusted Girl* (Little, Brown, and Company, 1923).

Thomson, Basil, *The Story of Scotland Yard* (Grayson & Grayson, 1935).

Thornbury, Walter, *Old and New London: Vol. 2* (Cassell, Peter & Galpin, 1878).

Vincent, Arthur, *Lives of Twelve Bad Women* (1897).

White, Barbara, 'Bracey, Joan', *Oxford Dictionary of National Biography* (2004), www.oxforddnb.com/

Williams, Lucy, *Wayward Women: Female Offending in Victorian England* (Pen & Sword Books, 2016).

Zedner, Lucia, 'Women, Crime, and Penal Responses: A Historical Account', *Crime and Justice*, Vol. 14 (1991), www.jstor.org/stable/1147464

ACKNOWLEDGEMENTS

It's been a real challenge trying to trace some of the queens of the under-world, and I'm very grateful to their relatives for trusting me with their stories, providing documents from their own family history research, and allowing me to use their personal photographs in the book.

Thank you to Susan Leggett at Bob O'Hara Public Record Searches for repeatedly going above and beyond the call of duty and pulling me out of all sorts of rabbit holes. So many dates, places, people and events are still to be established, I'd be grateful if anyone could add new information.

Thank you to the Society of Authors for a much-needed research grant, and to the Royal Literary Fund for supporting writers with gain-ful employment. I couldn't have done this book without either.

Thank you to Brian McDonald for being so generous with his knowledge; Rictor Norton for his interest and help; Alyson Brown for sharing her article on the Bobbed Haired Bandit; Emily Brand for providing documentation on John Duck; Carole Steers for transcrib-ing Emily Lawrence's prison letters; the staff at the National Archives who responded to numerous Freedom of Information requests; Charlie Turpie, Head of Public Services at the London Metropolitan Archives; Stewart McLaughlin at the Wandsworth Prison Museum; and Keith Green, Judy Spalding and James Anderson.

Thank you to Laura Perehinec at The History Press for her constant support and encouragement, my agent Robert Kirby, and Nigel, for listening to tales of underworld queens over and over and over again …

OTHER TITLES BY CAITLIN DAVIES

FICTION:

Jamestown Blues
Black Mulberries
Friends Like Us
The Ghost of Lily Painter
Family Likeness
Daisy Belle: Swimming Champion
of the World

NON-FICTION:

The Return of El Negro
Place of Reeds
Taking the Waters
Camden Lock & the Market
Downstream: A History and
Celebration of Swimming the
River Thames
Bad Girls: The Rebels of
Holloway Prison

INDEX